HAMLYN BOOK OF
Decorating

HAMLYN BOOK OF
Decorating

Publishing Director Laura Bamford
Creative Director Keith Martin
Executive Art Editor Mark
Winwood
Designer Ginny Zeal
Executive Editor Julian Brown
Managing Editor Kate Yeates
Editor Jane Royston
Picture Researcher Jo Carlill
Production Controller Bonnie
Ashby
Illustrator Jane Hughes

This edition published in 1998 for
The Book People Ltd, Hall Wood
Avenue, Haydock, St Helens
WA11 9UL
by Hamlyn, an imprint of Reed
Consumer Books Limited, Michelin
House, 81 Fulham Road, London
SW3 6RB

Copyright © 1998 Reed Consumer
Books Limited

ISBN 1 856 13422 9

A catalogue record for this book is
available from the British Library

Produced by Toppan
Printed in Singapore

Contents

Introduction

This splendid loft has been turned into a comfortable seating area in which mirrors help to enhance the height and the sofa has been covered with throws and cushions which are comparatively inexpensive and easy to make. The bare floorboards and simple banisters complement the beams and ladder.

Decorating the home has, in recent years, taken on the fun and excitement of choosing or making one's own clothes. Materials and equipment have become much more user-friendly and decorating techniques – particularly decorative paint techniques and other special effects – are much more widely understood. Wallpapers are easier to paste and to remove, paints are specially formulated to provide a particular look or finish, and tools are designed to make all tasks simpler and quicker for the home decorator.

On the whole, modern home owners also have greater confidence in their ability to assess, design and make decisions about their homes. They are not only well able to master the practical techniques of decorating and making soft furnishings, but they also have an eagerness and willingness to think through the whole design process, including the all-important use of space and colour scheming. Decorating is, rightly, seen as an adventure and approached with enthusiasm and a spirit of discovery.

For these reasons, decorating can no longer be considered in isolation from the subject of design, and the aim of this book is to combine basic guidelines on planning what you want in terms of practicality, comfort and style with information on simple techniques for achieving those aims. Good design should consider the whole environment – not just the walls and floors, or the curtains and cushions – so there is also a section on lighting the home, which is essential to the final look and feeling of any room. This is a subject that still tends to be shrouded in mystique but, once understood, is not difficult to put to wonderful effect.

paint well, do not spread it well and drop hairs as they go. The same rule applies to materials: cheap paints often do not spread as well as more expensive ones, while cheap fabric may lose its crispness in the first wash and spoil the look of the grand curtains you have made. Remember, therefore, that it is always worth spending a little more at the outset – it will pay dividends later.

The intention of this book is to contribute to the successful creation of your own individual interior environment. Its important message is that planning and decorating are to be undertaken with enthusiasm, enjoyment and the confidence that all will turn out as you wish. Decorating does require time and effort, but the results will be infinitely worthwhile.

Above An elegant wooden-framed sofa with its pretty little legs and painted decoration sits well in the corner of a Georgian interior and benefits from light from the windows. *Right* A bare wood table just under the window acts as a display shelf for a varied collection of ethnic objects.

There is nothing magical about good design. Anybody can achieve it, although – as with any other skill – it takes practice to develop and train the eye, the mind and the memory. This process involves making notes, experimenting on paper, playing with colour, looking at what other people have done, and adapting good ideas to your own taste and circumstances. This is equally true of the practical skills of home decorating, and the more experience you gain the more professional you will become. However, even a beginner can produce a workmanlike result by reading the instructions at the start, following them carefully and taking time and patience to get the small details right.

It is always important to use the right tools, and to buy the best you can afford. For example, cheap paintbrushes often make painting much more difficult because they do not hold the

Planning for the
Perfect Effect

Planning

Decorating is the spice of interior planning, and it is always tempting to rush out to the shops and buy up curtains and wallcoverings straight away. However, it is important that you assess the arrangement and intended use of your rooms and spaces, as well as the cost of decorating, before deciding on your actual materials and techniques. Look at your lifestyle: do you entertain a great deal, do you have children, and do you work at home? Think, too, about the overall style: would you like the décor to be bright and pretty, workmanlike or formal; or perhaps to conform to a particular historical style?

Take time to carry out some research. Other people's homes can be a source of ideas and, while you would obviously not wish to copy these slavishly, you can take from them what you like and adjust different aspects to suit your own decorating scheme.

Homestyle magazine articles are full of practical ideas, and often list useful addresses for stockists and suppliers. Room sets in large stores can also be a good starting point, and houses open to the public will provide plenty of inspiration, particularly if you are interested in decorating your home in a period style. A feeling for colour and texture combinations, and for the effects of different types of paint, paper and fabric used in juxtaposition needs practice, but the learning process is fascinating.

Planning and surveying

Make notes throughout the planning and decorating process. A good-quality notebook will be invaluable for jotting down ideas, addresses of suppliers, prices and photographs, as well as details about your home such as measurements of rooms and features within them. Such a book will help you to organize your thoughts, and will be extremely useful if and when you come to redecorate in later years.

The savings made on a 'partial' loose cover, as used on this small sofa, can release enough cash from the budget to pay for a luxury item such as this ornate mirror, reflecting the elegant lamps with their parchment shades. A complete cover can be bought later, when funds allow for this.

Budgeting for the whole scheme

Do budget for the entire scheme before you embark on buying anything at all so that, once you know how much you have to spend, you can allot sums of money to specific items. You can also juggle the available funds: for instance, if you would like something very expensive in one area, you may be able to reduce the costs in another. You could buy an expensive carpet, say, by putting off buying a new sofa for a year; or you could add the exotic effect of a sumptuous fabric that you have set your heart on by using it just for cushion covers, so that you need only buy a short length. Equally, if you love the craftsmanship and colours of an oriental rug, you could possibly find the money that you need to buy one by putting up with unlined curtains in the short term.

However, try not to become too enthusiastic about one particular carpet or wallcovering before you have made some general decisions on colour schemes and textures for your home. The wrong choice about something so central to the whole scheme could upset all your careful budgeting and may also mean that you have to redesign from scratch around the new object. Don't start with too many fixed ideas. Decide what material, colour and quality you would like on each

Above The transparent quality of these display shelves dividing the stairs from the main room, gives a much greater sense of space than if the stairs were conventionally boxed in.
Bottom right This little wall niche is just large enough to provide an effective and charming display case for a carefully selected collection of fine china and ornaments. The slim, round-edged shelves perfectly suit the small proportions of the space.

surface, and then work to get as near as you can to this within your budget. Even if you have set your heart on something very expensive, there is such an enormous choice nowadays that you will almost certainly be able to find a cheaper alternative.

Measuring

Accurate measuring is an important part of the planning and budgeting process. Carry a tape measure with you wherever you go, along with your notebook and a pencil to write down measurements. Measure every surface that you intend to decorate, every area in which you wish to put a piece of furniture and every item that you are considering in the shops.

Know your materials

Check the state of the walls and floors before buying your materials. Some types of paint require almost perfect walls if they are to look their best, which may mean expensive and time-consuming preparation; others are thick enough to cover blemishes – leaving attractive brushmarks as part

of the effect – and will be cheaper and quicker to apply. The state of the walls may also restrict your use of paint effects: for instance, a sophisticated marbling effect requires smooth plaster walls, while a technique such as stippling or sponging will distract the viewer's eye from cracks or lumps. Wallpaper is another good option for uneven wall surfaces.

Quality is also a consideration with wallpapers. Some are easier to hang than others: for instance, very cheap papers are likely to tear easily, making them difficult to apply. High-quality, hand-printed wallpapers often need trimming, which is difficult to do and really needs professional skills; this makes them even more expensive, and if you go for this option you will need to make allowances in your budget.

If you would like to use tiling on your bathroom or kitchen walls and/or floor, you may find that a few hand-made tiles will look better than a whole wall of machine-made, cheap ones. Remember that they will last a lifetime, and that it may be worth saving in some other part of your scheme to afford the tiles you really love.

Bare floorboards can be attractive, particularly when embellished with colourful kilims or hand-knotted rugs, but old boards may need draught-proofing, sanding and sealing. Sanding is an economical option, provided that the boards have not previously been sawn and cut about to make way for central-heating pipes. In this case, new wood-strip or wood-block floors may be a better solution; these are inexpensive and not difficult to lay.

Where carpets are concerned, remember that different rooms

demand different qualities. There is no need to buy the most hardwearing carpet for a bedroom where traffic is light, for instance, but a pale-coloured, poorer-quality carpet in the living room may soon look shabby. If you would like the same carpet colour throughout, you will be able to buy it in different qualities for each space.

Flexible thinking

You are likely to start off with a few pieces of furniture that you do not wish to throw away. The house itself will also have features which may not fit in with your chosen style.

It is possible, of course, to ignore the style of the house and to impose a modernist, minimalist, high-tech or historical style on any interior, and this can often be done with great success. However, if you have a feeling for the architecture in your home, you may find it worth compromising your chosen style in order to make the most of aspects such as interesting ceiling mouldings. You don't have to be a slave to the style suggested by the house, but you can still appreciate and enjoy the best parts of it.

Space, balance and contrast

This room has generous proportions and a stunning window. The height has been used with ingenuity, providing a small library at the top of the wall, where the natural light from the window is reinforced by spotlights in the ceiling. A pale floor and sofa cover, white walls and woodwork accentuate this further.

A leap of the imagination is needed when envisaging what you are going to do in a room – even more so if you are dealing with the whole house. You will want your home to have a co-ordinated appearance, so think about ways in which you can link colour schemes and areas of flooring.

Making the most of space

Look for vistas that you can exploit: for example, from the hallway through to the living room, or from upstairs looking down. If you have an archway, you can lead the viewer's eye from one space through the arch into another by careful use of colour, or you can turn the arch itself into a feature by painting it white, or in a contrasting colour to the rest of the room.

If you want the transition between spaces to be quite subtle, it is best to use different tones of the same colour. However, it can often be very exhilarating to use bright, contrasting colours, provided that you choose them with care to excite – rather than to confuse – the eye.

Manipulating space

Creative decorating can make the most of good proportions and conceal the unfortunate – such as squat rooms with low ceilings, or narrow rooms which feel uncomfortably restricted. Tall ceilings allow opportunities for different treatments of dado and/or picture rails; by dividing the wall into two or even three sections with different colours or patterns, you can effectively diminish the sense of height. Painting the ceiling in a darker colour will reduce the apparent height of a room, while a low ceiling will seem higher if you paint it white.

Narrow rooms often cause problems, particularly in houses which have been converted into flats. Not only are the proportions awkward, but the windows are often in inconvenient places and may even have been cut in half by the insertion of a new wall.

However, the use of pale colours, small patterns and mirrors can often help rooms to appear more spacious.

The dimensions of a small window will seem more generous if you frame it with curtains (draw these well back in the daytime so as not to obscure any part of the window itself); you could even use a *trompe l'oeil* paint technique to create another 'window' next to the real one.

Finding the right balance

Creating an harmonious balance of colour, pattern and texture is important. A restrained scheme of neutral colours may be exactly what you are looking for, but it will still need some splashes of colour to relieve the otherwise inevitable blandness.

Balance in colour

Warm, strong colours are exciting, while cool, pale colours are restful. The colours that you choose will depend on your temperament, on your lifestyle and on the effect that you are trying to achieve but, whether you decide to go for the bold or the subtle, you will almost certainly need some neutral colour to hold the whole scheme together.

Architects traditionally use white as the colour for all woodwork, window frames, doors and skirtings. This almost always looks good, particularly in period eighteenth- and nineteenth-century houses where it can be used to pick out any interesting features

such as arches and mouldings. Whatever colour you choose, sticking to it throughout will give cohesion to the overall scheme.

Balance in pattern

Too much pattern in a busy area – such as a work room or a kitchen – can detract from the room's efficiency and become tiring on the eye. Work or kitchen equipment already provides plenty of visual distraction, so in these rooms a plain background is often best. Deep colours can highlight objects dramatically and give collections of china or kitchen equipment a sculptural look.

Pattern in a living room or bedroom can be an integral part of the general scheme, providing interest and a distraction from large, plain surfaces. A patterned wallpaper can provide a focus for the eye if its design is large and striking, but small, all-over patterns are better for providing a backdrop for paintings, or in small rooms. A stencilled border or frieze can provide the 'join' between two colours of wall at dado height, and you could also use this to outline doors and windows. A line of patterned tiles in the bathroom will provide interest where plain tiles have been used on the walls, and this usually gives a more decisive look than patterned tiles dotted about among plain ones.

Another way to introduce pattern is through your soft furnishings – curtain, upholstery and cushion fabrics – and with carpets and rugs.

Balance in texture

Achieving a balance of the textures in a room is as important as balancing its colour and pattern. Texture affects a room to a surprising extent. Shiny surfaces are physically and emotionally cold, but they do reflect light, objects and colours and can make a room seem larger. In contrast, rough, warm textures absorb light and will give a denser quality to a particular colour. You will need both of these elements in order to produce a comfortable balance in a room.

Looking for contrast

The general rule in decorating is to choose a main colour and to complement it with a secondary one. This makes for tasteful results that are excellent for many historical styles. You can also create a successful scheme using different shades of the same colour, but you will need to give them all at least a splash of contrasting colour or they will look dull. It is also possible to create exciting interiors with bright, contrasting colours, particularly when looking through a doorway into another room or area.

Above The gentle differentiation between the smooth, sunny yellow walls of the dining room and the panelled white and blue of the kitchen blend well, while providing a separate character for each room. *Below left* The long, white shelves of this kitchen dresser make a marvellous backcloth for the collection of bold blue and white plates and the row of exotic ersatz flowers beneath.

Assessing your home

The strong, traditional architectural style of this farmhouse has been respected and maintained by its owners, who have furnished it with sturdy wooden tables, generous and comfortable chintz-upholstered seating, a large log basket, a collection of china ornaments on the shelf above the fireplace and wood-framed paintings and prints.

One of the hardest aspects of decorating is to look at your own home objectively, but this is the time to do it. Take your notebook around the house and list all the salient features – both good and bad – as well as noting which room is really most suitable for whom and for what purpose.

Architectural styles

If you live in an interesting building, use the architecture for all it is worth. Look for anything which provides an opportunity to create vistas and views, where you can lead the viewer's eye with one colour and then surprise it with another at the end, such as through doorways and archways, along corridors and up a staircase. Take note of any features that you can exploit for added interest, such as alcoves or an L-shaped room.

If a space is architecturally interesting enough to merit a style suited to the period in which it was built, then make the most of it. Eighteenth- and nineteenth-century homes often look their best when treated in this way. On the other hand, most homes of the twentieth-century – particularly modern blocks of flats and homes with square rooms that are devoid of alcoves or fireplaces – will adapt to almost any modern style, from Art Deco to minimalist or high tech.

Taking size into account

Dealing with a very small, modern house creates its own problems. The house may have conventional proportions and plans, but too much furniture and a fussy style may result in the inconvenient and crowded atmosphere of a dolls' house. Simplicity will work here, whereas grandeur will not.

A converted warehouse or barn offers precisely the opposite problem. In this case, you may have an utterly simple, modern interior or something exceedingly grand, but, either way, you must think big. Substantial pieces of furniture, wall-to-ceiling bookcases, big patterns on the walls (perhaps in the form of paintings), and spaces leading into one another – not through doors but through the arrangement of furniture and your choice of colour – are all good options.

Practical considerations

How you choose to decorate will, inevitably, depend on the make-up of your household. If you entertain a great deal, for instance, you can dress up your home in the grand manner. However, if you are out at work in an office all day and your interests lie mainly out of doors, you could opt for a spare, minimalist interior, whereas a house full of children requires cheerful, informal and easily cleaned décor.

If you have a young family, you will also need plenty of storage and space to play, and sturdy furniture to withstand the inevitable knocks. There will obviously be little point in laying pale carpets and hanging expensive, unwashable wallpaper. Painted walls offer lots of possibilities for a home with children. You could paint scenes from one of their favourite books. Apply a protective coat of matt varnish over the top in areas that are vulnerable to sticky fingers. Glazing techniques need no extra varnish.

Dual-purpose rooms

In most modern homes, at least one room in the house has to do the work of two. Often the kitchen and dining room have to share one space, for example, or perhaps the spare bedroom has to double up as a work room. Whatever your situation, the decoration of any room must be compatible with the activity that will take place there, and this usually means a somewhat more simplified décor than you might otherwise choose.

If a kitchen and dining area are divided by a kitchen worktop, you could perhaps decide to emphasize the different areas further by using plain paint and tiles in the kitchen and a patterned wallpaper in the dining area, although the whole effect will, in fact, appear much more co-ordinated if you use compatible colours and run the same floor surface right through both areas. In a spare bedroom, the work space should be as workmanlike as possible so that the detritus of the materials does not dominate the bedroom side. You can use wallpaper or paint finishes that will reflect the studiousness of one part of the room while still lending a relaxed feeling to the other.

Awkward spaces

The space under the stairs is all too often neglected, largely because it generally becomes the final resting place for all the flotsam and jetsam of the home. However, incorporating this space into the general decoration can lift the look of your home, as well as providing useful additional space.

The landing is another area in the home which often gets left out, but this is where your thinking in terms of views and vistas from one room to another is very important.

Top left This tiny room is just adequate for a young person's bedroom and large enough to house low seating with cushions and a table to work at. There is even a balcony bed. *Above* Plenty of natural light is brought into this modern conversion through the glass roof, whose supports are mirrored by the elegant, metal stair rail and the door handles.

Looking for potential

Even the most basic of spaces and the smallest of bedsits have hidden potential, once you start looking for it. In addition, if you draw attention to the good features – such as well-proportioned windows, a generous staircase or original mouldings – people will be less likely to notice uneven walls or a low ceiling.

An attractive kitchen has been created round an unlikely corner of a wall under a sloping window, with more light coming in through a window in the roof. The kitchen is very simple, but sculpturally designed, and its style and colours blend well with the living room without competing with it, so both areas together create a satisfying whole.

Interesting features to highlight

Write down in your notebook the features which could add to the room's attractiveness. When it comes to decorating, you can highlight these by shining a spotlight on to the particular area in question.

Windows

Tall windows are a real asset in any room, and you can emphasize them with drapes, headings and tie-backs. If the original shutters remain, be sure to include these in your scheme. French windows leading out on to a garden are also a lovely feature, and you can bring the garden into the room by using pale, sunny paint or wallpaper colours and crisp cotton curtains.

Doors

A fine door is definitely something to feature. Panelled doors are usually well made with good proportions, and you can decorate them in various subtle ways: for instance, using different tones of the same colour or even with contrasting colours for the panels.

Archways

You can make the most of an elegant arch by painting it in a noticeable colour, and also by ensuring that the view through it – from both directions – is enticing. Exploit contrasting colour schemes and subtle lighting, not just to highlight the curve of the arch and any corbels or other pieces of carving or woodwork, but those in the room beyond as well.

Plasterwork

Ceiling roses and moulded covings are always worth highlighting. White is an obvious choice for these and will look elegant, but you might like to pick out the features in another colour, particularly if there are damaged areas that you would like to conceal. Bear in mind, however, that plasterwork generally looks best in pale colours – bold colours are likely to hide the subtleties of the design, and to divide the room up rather than uniting it.

Above There is plenty of height in this room to accommodate children's bunk beds, with enough room for each child to sit up and read. Bright fabrics and wallpaper contribute to the cheerful atmosphere. *Right* Tailor-made shelves are invaluable in a tiny sink area to make the most of a small corner.

Skirtings

Some period homes – particularly those with high ceilings – have very tall skirting boards with interesting moulding at the top. If you pick these out in pure white, they can lend a stately feel to the whole room.

Alcoves

An alcove can be very attractive if you give it a character of its own, perhaps with a different paint colour or by papering it in contrast to the rest of the room. An obvious place for shelves, an alcove can also have great charm when simply hung with a mirror, a painting or some small pictures.

The hallway and staircase

If you have a generous-sized hallway, you could treat it as an extra reception room or even as a picture gallery. It will benefit from well-made and interesting furniture, seating for visitors and a table large enough to hold a vase of colourful flowers. Perhaps most important of all is good lighting to provide a welcoming first view of your home for any visitor.

If you are lucky enough to have an attractive staircase, make the most of this feature. You could, for instance, varnish, polish or paint an elegantly curved banister and wooden uprights so that they stand out as features in their own right.

Features to disguise

At the same time as noting down features in your home that you can emphasize, make a list of any that you wish to conceal, such as ceilings that are too high or too low, rooms that are too narrow, or an electricity meter or a gas boiler in an unsightly position.

Uneven walls

Disguising ugly features is as much of a skill as highlighting fine ones, and the options that seem easiest may not actually be the best. For instance, the woodchip paper that is often used to cover rough walls can have its place, but it does not respond well to decorative paint techniques or to other wall-coverings. A better option could be to even out the surface with professional-grade lining paper before painting.

Narrow passages

You can make a narrow corridor appear larger by using pale but cheerful colours and subtle lighting. A number of mirrors will also help by seeming to enlarge and dignify the whole space.

Low ceilings

A room with a low ceiling will look taller if you paint the walls slightly darker. White is probably the best colour for a very low ceiling, but a very pale orangey-yellow can help by bringing a sunny feeling into the room.

Modern doors

The flat, unpanelled doors so often fitted in modern homes can be very uninteresting and bland, but you could paint them in a bright colour. Another possibility is to create 'panels' by adding and then painting stick-on strips (widely available in kit form).

Ill-proportioned archways

A squat, square arch can sometimes be the result of knocking two rooms into one. Play down an arch by making the view through it more interesting than the arch itself.

Colour

Putting colour on the walls is the easiest, quickest and usually the cheapest way of transforming the dullest of rooms. Colour is the magic ingredient of decorating. It can brighten up a sober room and lighten one that has little natural light of its own, and a pale, sunny yellow can make even the darkest basement room seem less bleak. Deep reds add dignity, and are often used in formal dining rooms; with its luxurious effect, rich red is also among the colours most used in Persian carpets.

Colour provides contrast, and is often effective when used for detailing. Just one or two cushions covered with a bright fabric can greatly enliven a room, while a brightly painted dado rail or stencilled frieze can make all the difference

to an otherwise pale-coloured scheme. Contrasts can also be used on a larger scale. One bright colour carried over a whole wall may sound rather alarming but, once toned down by other items such as furniture and pictures, this is often not as startling as you might suppose and it can have an immensely cheering effect.

Another role played by colour is that it can be very effective in concealing discrepancies such as uneven walls, particularly when a subtle decorative technique – such as stippling or sponging – is used so that the eye is far too busy taking in the effect to notice what is underneath.

Exploring colour, pattern and texture

Try to avoid rushing into colour decisions too quickly. It really is worthwhile consciously noting which colours affect you in what way, what you have liked in other contexts, and which colours you like together. Take time to look at them in both daylight and artificial light, as these different conditions can alter a colour's original appearance quite dramatically.

Although these colours are bright and used in an unusual combination, they work well together to produce an attractive and very user-friendly kitchen. The clear purple is offset by just enough deep red and brilliant yellow not to be overbearing and complemented by blue and white tiles. A white ceiling and natural wood edges to the work surfaces hold the effect nicely together.

Colour characteristics

Colour offers endless variations and subtleties for the home decorator, and you can use it to make the best of a room's proportions. Bold colours nearly always result in a room looking smaller; this is often a disadvantage although, if you are after a cosy effect, you will welcome this characteristic. The 'cold' colours – such as pale blues and greens – make a room feel cool and airy, while the 'warm' colours – including yellows and reds – make it feel welcoming and warm; yellows and oranges will also help to brighten a sunless room. Neutral colours can be peaceful, but they do need 'lifting' with a fillip of extra colour to save them from dullness.

Remember that colour changes under different conditions: for example, an object that looks magically rich and exotic under a spotlight in the evening can look tawdry and dull in the white light of day. The amount that you use will also affect a colour's final appearance, so that a particular shade painted over a large area will look different from the same paint applied in just a small area, and may appear unrecognizable from the example on the colour chart. The same colour may also produce a completely different result depending on the type of paint you choose. Gloss paint reflects light, whereas a water-based, matt paint such as distemper (often used in colourwashes and decorative techniques) absorbs it. A colour will also change depending on the colour or colours against which it sits.

For all these reasons, it is important to experiment with test pots of paint before going ahead. You could use these to paint either directly on to the wall, or on to a board that you can then move around and try out in different situations.

Colour and pattern

Plain colours and patterns go well together, provided that there is a common colour to link them. The main colour of a pattern is very often picked up as the paint colour in a room, but you can achieve a subtle effect by selecting an inconspicuous colour in the pattern and using that as your main paint colour. This often brings a new dimension to a pattern, highlighting the subsidiary colour and giving further opportunities for using it in accessories and furnishings.

If you do not want the room to be too 'busy', the best plan is to use pattern on two – or, at the most, three – surfaces, and to leave the rest plain.

Above The bright rose-red of these tent-like bed curtains and the yellow walls look especially cheerful in a room that faces north and receives little sun.
Below Medieval motifs on this splendid upholstered chair complement the hand-knotted Persian carpet. Both give life and contrast to the smooth floorboards and white upholstery of the upright chairs.

You could then match the pattern with the curtains and other fabrics in the room, or choose some patterned and some plain fabrics to match the walls.

Different patterns, like different paint colours, have their own characteristics. Strong patterns appear to come forward and will make the room seem smaller, while small, overall patterns will blend into the rest of the room. Also like paint, bold patterns and rich, strong colours will seem even bolder and stronger when seen on a large expanse of wall.

Combining different patterns in one scheme can be very effective, but this needs some discipline in the planning stages; there should also always be something to link the different patterns. In most schemes, it is best to use exactly the same colourway for each pattern, and you will achieve an even more co-ordinated look if you choose the same design, but in different proportions. For example, a pattern of fruits and flowers in miniature on a bedroom wall can look very stylish when used together with the same – but larger – pattern for the bedspread and curtains.

Colour and texture

The texture of objects – particularly of textiles – can affect their colour to quite a marked degree, and the same colour will look completely different on a dull surface and on a shiny one.

If you use a particular colour of eggshell paint on a wall, for instance, it will appear lighter than the same colour in a textured upholstery fabric. Different types of paint will also produce completely different results, so that a decorative technique using distemper will suit a simple, rather cottagey scheme, while the same technique carried out with oil paints will seem more sparkly and sophisticated. If you use a gloss paint for window frames, doors and skirtings, these features will stand out not just because of the colour that you choose, but because the shiny finish gives them a different quality to other surfaces. Carrying this through to objects, shiny textures, such as mirrors or polished tables, will reflect light and make the room seem larger, whereas matt textures such as pile carpets and tweed upholstery will give a more solid, less sprightly feeling.

Wallcoverings and textiles have their individual characteristics, too. Vinyl wallcoverings do not 'take' colours as well as paper ones, and their textured sheen makes colours less vibrant and typically rather downbeat. In the case of textiles, wool gives colours a rich sheen, as can be seen in hand-knotted carpets and wool upholstery fabrics; cotton takes colours well, with cotton prints and weaves having a fresh and pretty look; while man-made fibres are usually somewhat less brilliant in colour.

Complementary colour schemes

Right The attractive colouring of this scheme relies on a purple-pink wall with harmonizing warm wood (not far away from it on the colour wheel) and subtle touches of silver and bright colours in the objects and plants.

If you have an understanding of how colours relate to one another, and of how they work together, you will find it much easier to devise a satisfying scheme and to achieve the best results. A look at the colour wheel is a good first step.

Colours that go well together

The three primary colours are red, yellow and blue, and all other colours originate from these. If you mix two primary colours, you will create a secondary colour: for example, when the primary colours blue and red are mixed together, they produce a secondary colour, purple. If you mix a primary colour with a secondary colour, you will create a more subtle tertiary colour: for example, red (primary) and purple (secondary) will produce reddish-purple (tertiary). You can mix colours in endlessly different proportions to produce any effect, but bear in mind that mixing too many colours will simply result in a muddy tone.

Vivid, pure colours – particularly the warm reds, oranges and yellows – are dominant. You can use these strong colours to good effect in rooms that receive little natural light or sun, and in the bathroom, hallway and children's bedrooms, where colour can be enjoyed uninhibitedly. Opt for the cool colours – such as blues and greens – when aiming for a relaxed, peaceful interior; these are particularly good in bedrooms. Either group, when used in an interior scheme, needs to be carefully balanced by a neutral colour such as grey or beige.

'Light' colours are produced by adding white to a basic colour and 'dark' colours by adding black, so, for instance, red plus white becomes pink, while red plus black becomes maroon. Light colours reflect light and therefore make a room seem brighter; dark colours absorb light, making it seem much darker.

Colour harmonies

Colour harmonies are created by using three colours positioned at equal distances from one another on the colour wheel, such as red, yellow and blue.

Adjacent colour harmony

This means the use of colours positioned next to one another on the wheel. They can be anywhere on the wheel, but some combinations are more successful than others: for example, yellow harmonizes well with yellow-orange and yellow-green.

Complementary colours

Colours sitting opposite one another on the wheel are known as complementary colours; these go particularly well together.

Monochromatic colour harmony

A completely monochromatic scheme, when only one colour is used but with dark and light variations, always needs to be combined with black or white – as well as some sharply contrasting complementary accents – or it will become boring.

Accepted colour rules

Experience in decorating in the West over many years has produced a set of accepted colour rules. These can be helpful when you are decorating for the first time, because they do work and can prevent expensive mistakes. Once you are more experienced and confident, you can experiment with breaking the rules if you wish, but you will find it useful in the meantime to know what they are.

- Choose a main colour for each room, as this will provide the room with a strong 'character'. (If you wish to have a co-ordinated scheme for the whole house, you can extend this colour into the 'common areas' such as passages and the staircase.) Use this main colour on the walls and possibly also on the floor.
- Choose a secondary colour to complement the main colour. You can use any of the harmonizing colours from the colour wheel or, if you wish, a light or a dark version of it. Use this colour in alcoves, or perhaps on just one wall; in patterns that are predominantly in the main colour, and in accents such as cushions and curtains. If you have not used the main colour on the floor, the secondary colour would be the best choice here.
- Paint the woodwork white or grey. If you do choose some other colour, at least make it the same throughout.
- Decorate basement rooms or rooms with very small windows mainly in warm colours to counteract the lack of light. On the other hand, you can decorate rooms that receive a lot of sunlight in blues, greens or other cool colours.
- Small rooms are best decorated in fairly light colours. These will cause the walls to appear to recede, thus making the room appear larger.

- Decorating large rooms in richer, darker colours will add to the 'presence' of the rooms and also helps to diminish the feeling of space, which can sometimes be overpowering.
- For a balanced scheme, use colours from opposite ends of the spectrum – such as orange and turquoise, yellow and purple, or green and cyclamen – always with a neutral third colour to hold the whole design scheme together.

Getting your eye in

Get into the habit of jotting down colour combinations that you have seen and liked. These need not be anything to do with interiors, but could be a grouping of flowers, for instance. Try out the combinations in your notebook, or put them together on a colour board (see pages 28–9) to test the effect.

Left The colour wheel can help you to establish harmonious and complementary colours. *Below* Blue and green are harmonizing colours on the colour wheel and they can be used to create a charming and interesting subtlety, as shown here in this cottage-like kitchen where the panelling and doors have been painted in similar shades of blue and green.

Contrasting colour schemes

Every period has its own particular favourite colour schemes. In the early days, colours were earthy in tone and varied according to the soil and rock in a particular area. Today, the choice available is vast and using contrasting colours can be a real adventure, with endless opportunities for experimentation and exciting results.

Contrasting colours in this scheme are used in small quantities, creating a harmonious whole rather than a sharp shock to the eye. Red and green are opposite one another on the colour wheel; yellow has been used as a co-ordinating element and the effect is lifted by daylight coming through the roof on to white walls.

The most obvious and striking contrast is, perhaps, that of white and black. This is currently very popular, particularly among architects and others who live in small spaces and have a love of the precise, the minimal and sculptural. White walls and black furniture create a very clean, stark interior which should be complemented with the occasional accent of strong, bright colour. In general, such a bold and positive choice needs a disciplined way of life if it is not to appear too overbearing, although you can soften it by the use of natural wood in features such as cupboard doors and table tops.

Another modernist approach is to use primary colours boldly on walls and floors, expanses of strong colour in large paintings, or bright, plain-coloured curtains or blinds against white walls. Mediterranean walls are painted white to reflect the sun, and typical colours used to contrast with the white are geranium red, ocean blue and sunny yellow. The combination of these colours can conjure up relaxed and happy feelings even in a city apartment. Primary colours are always very appealing to children, so you will be able to use reds, blues and yellows to good effect in a play room. However, the primaries are very dominating so it is usually best to keep walls to areas of single colour, rather than to use too much rioting pattern; they can then form a solid background

against which books, pictures and toys will stand out attractively.

The simple black grid patterns interspersed with vivid sections of primary colour that characterize some work of the twentieth century painter Mondrian demonstrate the impact of blocks of primary colour with white and black. Mondrian's grid paintings are often used as inspiration for modern interiors, and it is useful to study his work to gain an idea of the balance and proportion of solid colour used with black and white.

If you wish to find out more about the effects of contrasting bold colours, you could glance back at other styles and periods that have combined colour in characteristic and effective ways. For example, during the Art Deco period of the 1920s and '30s, colours were influenced by Cubism, the opening up of Egyptian tombs, and Diaghilev's Ballet Russe. Carpets and walls were often white, but were complemented by colours of rich red, deep blue, purple, pink and chrome yellow. In today's interiors, these colours can be used on walls and ceilings, and as a way of attracting the eye from one space through a doorway into another area. The contrast of purple leading through into an orangey yellow, for instance, can be spectacular.

Houses built in the eighteenth century respond very well to modern colours; the tall ceilings, elegant proportions and the generous amount of light coming in through tall windows all encourage the use of positive, clear colours. Here, too, the vistas created

by elegant stairwells and views through doorways into other rooms encourage the use of imaginative colour contrasts. Originally, the owners would have mainly used white, stone, cream and chocolate colours – all of which were cheap to buy – although they often favoured deeper blues, greens and brilliant yellows in grander rooms. For an authentic style in a house of this type, choose from reddish and chocolate browns, deep purply blue, pale blue, bright orangey yellow, a variety of greens or a dusky pink, sticking to one colour per room.

Gustavian style – which was prominent in the late eighteenth century – has a character all of its own, and its simple yet decorative look fits in very well with contemporary lifestyles. The basic colours are white, contrasted with soft blues and greys, and walls are painted in plain colours using limewash or dragging techniques. Modern Scandinavian style is, again, ideally suited to modern lifestyles since it is both simple and bold. This look revels in bright colours offset by white, and by natural or white-painted wood. Red and yellow are also popular colours, and the use of checks and stripes gives a fresh appearance.

Japanese style, with its simple yet positive look, uses black in contrast to red and white. 1950s' style used quite different colours, often combining orange or olive green and white. It was usual to paint just one wall in a colour and to leave the others white. Another popular combination of the 1950s was bright green and indigo.

Building a colour board

A colour board is a board on which to pin pieces of fabric, trimmings, paint samples, and carpet and other types of flooring, until you achieve an harmonious collection of colours and textures to fit in with the scheme you have in mind. If you are interested in decorative paint techniques, pin on small samples along with the other items. This fascinating exercise helps to focus the mind and should enable you to find a pleasing solution.

When building a colour board, try to get samples of the actual fabrics, wall-coverings and floorings you are thinking of using. Move them around, trying different combinations and juxta-positions until you get a harmonious result. This will make it easier to produce a co-ordinated yet intriguing result like this warm, red room.

Practical decisions

Practical decisions should be the first ones that you make, and will assist you in deciding what sort of decorations you need on all surfaces and furniture. It is important to think about the practicalities before you decide on aesthetic qualities, because otherwise they may not stand the test of time; you may also end up choosing items priced beyond your budget.

The main question to ask yourself is: what is the room for? If you are dealing with the kitchen or bathroom, the surfaces you choose should be practical, easy to clean, waterproof and non-slip. In a child's room, the surfaces must, again, be easy to clean but also bright and pretty, smooth for building bricks and warm to the touch for playing on. In the living room you will want comfort, elegance, and colours and textures that suit your personality and the social life you wish to lead. In the bedroom, essentials include warm flooring, relaxing décor and perhaps matching curtains, bed-covers and so on.

Aesthetic decisions

These decisions come next, and will help you to decide on colours, patterns and texture within the practical limits you have already set. Decide on the colours you think you would like to use. Do you want paint or paper on the walls? Do you want large patterns, small, all-over patterns, floral patterns or a decorative paint finish, or just plain colour or ceramic tiles? Think at the same time about colours for floors and textiles. Decide where you would like smoothness and where you would prefer texture: for example, do you want a polished or sanded wooden floor, vinyl or ceramic tiles, or perhaps carpet or a natural floorcovering such as sisal matting?

You will be able to decide all this much more easily if you arrange the different possibilities on your board and then eliminate those that do not seem to be working. In other words, the board gives you a chance to test your ideas in miniature, to try colours, patterns and textures together before splashing out on expensive mistakes.

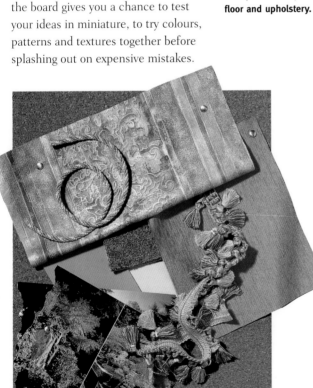

Right **Many different fabric, wallpaper, carpet and paint swatches were pinned up, moved around and removed before this final selection for a bedroom was settled on.** *Below* **The rich colours of an autumn landscape provided the starting point for this living room colour scheme. The irresistable curtain fabric became the central element. Its perfectly blended colours made it easy to pull out and match blues, russets and golds for the walls, woodwork, floor and upholstery.**

Creating the board

For the board itself you can use anything on to which you can pin your samples: hardboard, cardboard, stout card or a cork pinboard will all do. If the board is in bad shape, cover it over first with a piece of canvas or hessian.

Begin by cutting out and pinning on to the board paint samples, photographs, pictures from magazines, pieces of fabric or carpet – in fact, anything that seems to fit in with your ideas and gives the effect that you are trying to achieve. Think about the textures as well as the colours that you want. Move the samples around and exchange some items for others as you find specific materials, paints and papers that give you a feeling of the scheme being 'right'. These may turn out not to be exactly what you originally had in mind, but you may like them better. By putting these in place of your original sketchy ideas, you will gradually build up a picture of how the scheme could look. Actual samples will give you a truer picture of the way in which the elements will combine but, if you cannot get these, try to find similar textures and patterns, as they will make a great difference when you are trying to get the 'feel' of a scheme. Carry the board around and look at it in varying lights. Each item will react differently to light, and you need to

know how these alterations will affect the items in relation to one another.

Don't compromise when you first start the board. There is nothing to stop you choosing the outrageous and way out – at this stage the materials cost nothing, and this is a good way of making sure that you have not missed out on a good idea. Slowly whittle down the items to what you are seriously considering and go back to the practical decisions you made at the beginning, until you have a realistic picture of what your scheme is going to be like.

Turning the board into reality

Once the board is made up of samples that you have chosen for your design theme and you are satisfied with the results, go ahead. If it is made up of photographs, or of bits that you like the look of but need to match up, take the board with you to the store to check that what you are buying is really what you want.

Checklist of items

Make sure that you have included all of the following (as appropriate) for each room:
- Paint samples and/or wallcoverings.
- Flooring (carpets, floorboards, ceramic tiles, vinyl, etc.).
- Upholstery and either curtain or blind fabrics.
- Other soft furnishing fabrics (bedclothes, cushions and trimmings).

Lighting

Well-designed lighting can change a rather dismal 'waiting-room' feeling into a welcoming atmosphere at very little cost. In the outside world, light is endlessly varied with shadows, bright spots and filtered rays, and you also need to introduce variety indoors for efficiency, interest and to spotlight particular objects. In the home, you need three categories of lighting:

- General lighting is the main light that we use to see properly without bumping into furniture, or tripping over steps or any other impediments.
- Task lighting is for working by, and should be directed on to work surfaces or places where good light is needed for activities such as reading or sewing.
- Decorative lighting is not purely functional but is used as an 'added bonus' to look attractive in its own right and/or to highlight objects, pictures, plants or interesting architectural features.

You can achieve these effects by directing light in certain ways, as well as by choosing the right type of light – such as one with a narrow beam or a wide 'wash' – and by filtering it through different shades.

You may wish to select light fittings to fit in with a particular style, or simply for their attractive shape or practicality. Whatever you choose, avoid any lamp that glares into people's eyes, as some will do if they are angled wrongly or are not shaded correctly.

Overview of lighting options

Overhead spotlights have been set into the ceiling of this small U-shaped kitchen to provide both general light and task light over the work surface. They are positioned near to the wall so that the cook will not cast his/her shadow over the work area. These spotlights are pleasant and quite unobtrusive, and no other light is necessary.

How best to use lighting in your own home can seem a mysterious and complicated problem. This can often be because there is so much choice in the shops and so little guidance, even though different light bulbs all do a different job, have different wattages and must be used with the correct fittings. This short overview of the various types of lighting available should help to make your choices easier.

General lighting

General, or background, lighting is the first type to consider because it is important to the practicality and safety of your home as a whole. The most common form of general lighting is the ubiquitous central light bulb hanging from a fitting in the ceiling. This is fairly efficient but gives a very 'dead' light which can be depressing; for this reason you should always use it together with other types of lighting to create a good overall effect.

Better forms of general ceiling lighting include 'eyeball' spots. These are set neatly into the ceiling, usually with several included in one room so that the source of light is not coming from just one direction. Another option is ceiling-mounted spotlights (which may be fitted on a track), although these are more difficult to direct without glaring into people's eyes. Also available for ceiling lighting are low-voltage miniature spots, but these need transformers and should be installed by a professional electrician.

General lighting does not necessarily have to come from the ceiling, however. You will be able to achieve an attractive, overall and efficient light by casting it upwards from wall-mounted fittings so that it reflects back off the walls and the ceiling; this works most

Above **This room makes the very best of the natural light coming in through its many windows. The pale surfaces on floor and walls all help to reflect the light.**
Right **A powerful uplighter shining on to a white ceiling provides good general light for a room of average size and gives it a welcoming atmosphere.**

of interior design. These lamps should be for task lighting, but are often mistakenly chosen purely for the charm of their fittings while being impossible to direct for comfortable reading in bed. Don't forget that children need bedside lights, too.

Other task lights include overhead spots or eyeball lamps (where they can double as general lighting). An angled lamp will be invaluable in a study or office, because you can shine the light on to different aspects of your work as required. Fluorescent strips are excellent for designers and other people working with colour, because of their white light. This should be screened behind some sort of baffle, but fittings these days usually take this into account. Small fluorescent or tungsten tubes hidden under the cupboards above a worktop will provide good working light and give the kitchen a comfortable glow. A standard lamp positioned behind an armchair can provide good light for reading.

Decorative lighting and highlighting

Decorative lighting should add a feeling of well-being and interest to an already efficient lighting scheme. It includes beaded Art Nouveau lamps and Art Deco maidens holding glass globes, as well as paper bags of glowing light.

Decorative lighting also includes low-voltage modern lamps with elegant, minimalist forms. These use tungsten-halogen bulbs, in which built-in transformers are included as

part of the design, and can often be used for general lighting and task lighting as well.

Other decorative lamps may be quite inconspicuous in themselves but they may have the job of highlighting other objects. For example, a floor spotlamp placed behind an architectural plant will bring the glossy leaves into relief in a spectacular way. Spotlamps can be used to highlight

sculptures, paintings or collections, and discreetly hidden fittings can light up the interior of a cabinet to show off its contents. Table lamps with ceramic, glass or metal bases and large shades can be decorative on two counts: as objects in themselves, and for highlighting a collection of small objects ranged beneath them.

efficiently if the ceiling is white. Whatever form of general lighting you install, you will almost certainly create a more pleasant environment if you combine it with lighting intended for specific tasks, and with some form of decorative lighting.

Task lighting

Good lighting, designed specifically for the purpose, is essential for any job involving close work. You will need task lighting in the kitchen, particularly over the worktop or chopping board; at your desk or work table; at your work or hobbies bench, if you have one; and over the table on which the children do their homework.

Finding an attractive yet functional bedside lamp is one of the challenges

Choosing the right lighting

A small, discreet picture light fixed to the wall will highlight a painting without glare, although it will not provide adequate general light; it is purely for decorative purposes. This brass fitting is perfectly designed for its purpose and does not vie for interest with the objects on the wall and table.

Much of the desirable effect of any lighting is achieved not so much by the fitting as by the light source – in other words, by the bulb or tube. Specialist suppliers and large lighting sections in department stores will have a wide range of lighting from which to choose, but don't always go for pretty fittings – look at the way in which the light is directed.

The light source

The fact that the light source is so important makes this a key decision when you are trying to create a particular lighting effect. Some bulbs direct light via a narrow beam, others 'wash' the wall with a wide beam; some bulbs – the standard tungsten variety – give a yellowish light, while others – such as tungsten-halogen low-voltage bulbs and fluorescent tubes – emit a much whiter light.

It is worth experimenting with different light sources to see what effect they will have. For close work such as sewing, drawing, painting and so on, a white light is usually better than a yellow one. White light is also good for uplighters that reflect the light off the walls and ceiling to provide a very good level of general lighting. A yellowish light can give a warm glow for decorative lighting and can be used for general lighting, if you combine it with other forms of lighting to add interest.

Some low-voltage bulbs (mini fluorescents) can now be fitted into basic light fittings and their basic design is improving all the time, but check that the large ones will not poke out of the top of the shade and that they are not too heavy for the lamp in which you intend to use them. Check, too, whether the lamp fitting that you are buying takes a bayonet or screw-fitting bulb, and that the bulb in question is widely available. Supermarkets and household stores do stock a fairly good variety, but the more unusual bulbs may be difficult to find.

Remember that each light fitting will specify a maximum wattage for the bulb to be used. Never put in a bulb exceeding that wattage or you may well damage the lamp.

Making a lighting plan

If you have several individual lights in a room, you will be able to achieve a number of different atmospheres if you can turn off or dim the general lighting separately. A good way of doing this is to install a different wiring circuit for each group of light sources. This can give you a much more flexible lighting system, enabling you to raise the light level when necessary and to lower it to a more intimate level as you wish, or to switch on several lights at once. Being able to raise or lower the light level can be particularly useful in a dining room, where you may want a more intimate atmosphere during meals; in the kitchen, where you may not want a working light on all the time, but need to be able to see what is where; and also in

children's bedrooms, where a little light at low level may help a child to sleep. Computerized lighting controls are available and these can be set to switch lights on automatically as soon as a certain level of voice is heard.

Decide where to position light sockets for easy access and safety. Also give some thought to the switches that you install for your lighting. These can be decorative as well as functional, and many colours are available to give switches decorative appeal or to integrate them into a scheme.

Positioning your lighting

You can get an idea of what the general effect of a particular light in a certain place will be by asking someone to hold a workman's portable light in place and then standing back to see the result. When you come to install the proper light, direct the beam carefully and make sure that it will not glare into people's eyes – especially in the case of a spotlight.

Whether you set the light high or low in a room will make a big difference to the final result. Lights placed at table height in a room are more restful to the eye than those fixed to a wall or to the ceiling, but those positioned higher will provide better general light. Lighting at floor level can be very effective for highlighting interesting woodwork or the glossy foliage of a large plant.

Safety lighting

Safety lighting has two functions: to provide sufficient illumination for people to see adequately, and to be safe to use. Good general lighting fulfils the first, and should illuminate steps, furniture, other obstacles and uneven surfaces without casting shadows which could confuse the eye. This is

important for people whose sight is poor – older people, for instance, often require a higher level of lighting than you might normally consider.

Lighting that is safe to use means no trailing flexes (this is where a lighting plan comes in useful, in which each light fitting has its own socket); you must also follow regulations when installing lighting in 'wet' areas such as the kitchen and bathroom. Seal all fittings in these rooms with glass or plastic covers, leaving no exposed metal which could be affected by steam and condensation. In the bathroom, you must either have a pull-cord switch inside, or a wall switch fitted directly outside the door.

Above Concealed downlighters have been used to illuminate this mirrored, recessed shelving, highlighting and reflecting its fine display of objects. *Below* Uplighters set into the floor of this meticulous bathroom add an eighteenth-century grotto-like quality to a thoroughly modern space and also highlight the glass basin surround.

Directory of light fittings

General light can be provided in many ways, as long as the light is adequate and casts no shadows. Here, a pendant light in the form of a chandelier with several small bulbs has been used to cast light over a landing and staircase. The pale-coloured ceiling will help to reflect the light downwards.

Before buying fittings, always decide first what type of light you need in a particular place – general lighting, task lighting or decorative lighting – and then look for a fitting that you like within this category. In department stores or specialist lighting shops the lights are normally switched on, so you will be able to judge the effect they will have in your home and whether they provide the lighting that you require.

Uplighters which take tungsten-halogen bulbs are usually more powerful than those designed for filament bulbs, and one of these lights can be enough to provide efficient general light for a small living room. Hundreds of uplighter designs are available, from Art Deco to modernist and high tech, so you should be able to find one to complement almost any kind of interior scheme that you choose.

Downlighters

These direct light straight downwards. They generally use reflector bulbs such as PAR 38, ISL reflector bulbs or multi-mirror low-voltage bulbs, all of which incorporate reflectors to direct the light downwards. More sophisticated downlighters also have a reflector as part of the fitting.

Downlighters may be recessed or semi-recessed in the ceiling, and include adjustable eyeball fittings. A group of downlighters can give efficient general light, a row can provide task lighting over a worktop, and one single downlighter positioned over a table will provide effective local light without illuminating the whole room.

Wallwashers

Wallwashers are ceiling-mounted fittings which cast light evenly across and down a wall rather than on to the floor or ceiling. They can contribute to the general lighting by using the wall as a reflector, but will also emphasize the texture of a wall surface or illuminate paintings. They are similar to downlighters but must have additional reflectors to shine the light in one direction only.

Uplighters

These shine light on to the ceiling so that it is reflected back into the room, producing good general lighting and increasing the sense of space. The paler the ceiling, the more light will be reflected. Many different fittings are available, and these may be wall-mounted, suspended from the ceiling on stems, made in the form of standard or table lamps, or designed as floor-standing drums.

1. Wall-mounted spot lamp that can be swivelled to face in different directions; useful as general or task lighting.
2. Decorative, shell-shaped light in brass with a flexible 'stalk'; useful to highlight objects in a cupboard or on rows of shelves.
3. Wall bracket uplighter; if placed high enough, it will reflect light directly off the ceiling.
4. Shelving uplighter; used to light up glass shelving and ornaments on display.
5. A low-voltage spot light with dichroic reflector gives a brighter and more sparkly light than standard bulbs, and it also uses far less electricity.
6. Low-voltage spot lamps on flexible 'stalks' that can be angled in any desired direction.
7. Wall-mounted 'bowl' uplighter; these are unobtrusive and give a gentle, yet effective light, reflected on walls and ceilings.
8. A decorative light made of paper; it may give adequate general light but its main function is to provide a warm and pleasant glow.
9. Pendant lamps with an exotic Eastern influence; because of their deep colours, these lamps are more for decoration than general light.
10. Small, inexpensive angled metal lamp; ideal as a bedside light.

The positioning of wallwashers is important: do not set them too near the centre of the ceiling or people may walk into the path of the beam. A distance of 80–100cm (31–39in) from the wall usually works well.

Angled lamps

These lamps can be attractive in their own right, but they are basically designed as task lights and can be adjusted to suit different tasks as required. There are innumerable types available, including wall-mounted lamps, which are useful by the bedside; clip-on lamps, which you can use on anything from a table to a drawing board; and floor or table lamps.

Specialized lighting

Lighting intended for local illumination can be used to create a huge number of different effects. This category includes traditional picture lights, spotlights used to emphasize particular spaces or objects, and lights which are in themselves simply decorative objects or provide an attractive soft glow to add extra warmth and interest to a room.

Low-voltage lighting

This operates on an electricity supply of only 12 or 24 volts, as opposed to mains voltage of 240 volts in the UK or 100 volts in the USA. The bulbs are a fraction of the size of conventional bulbs, and the fittings are correspondingly small. Optical control from the bulbs' reflectors can be very precise.

A low-voltage lighting system needs separate transformers and there are strict regulations governing their installation, so you will need the advice of a qualified electrician.

Directory of bulbs and tubes

A combination of different light sources has been used in this stylish modern dining room. These include a filament bulb in the pendant lamp, tiny decorative candle bulbs on the walls and a low-voltage dichroic reflector bulb high on the ceiling. The latter is angled to illuminate the impressive oil painting hanging on the inner wall.

The eight types of bulb and tube described here are commonly used in the home, but there are many variations on these. Some bulbs have bayonet caps, others have screw caps, and some caps are smaller than others and are not interchangeable. Various light fittings will only take bulbs of a limited wattage (this will be stated on the fitting); make sure you buy what you need.

Filament bulbs (tungsten bulbs, GLS bulbs)

Still the most common type of bulb, these provide most of the light needed in the home. They are used for general and local illumination, and give out a yellowish light. Available in many different wattages up to 150, filament bulbs may have bayonet or screw caps. Some fittings use miniature or decorative bulbs with small bayonet or screw caps. Clear bulbs emit the brightest light of all, but pearl bulbs are much less harsh.

Architectural strip lights (linear bulbs)

These are filament bulbs in strip rather than bulb form, used in picture lights and in kitchen worktop lights positioned beneath cupboards. Curved and circular strips are also available.

Compact fluorescent bulbs (CFLs)

These are energy-efficient bulbs and have long lives. They are available in a variety of shapes, with bayonet or screw caps, and are suitable for both general and local lighting. They work on the same principle as fluorescent tubes but can be used in conventional light fittings. The bulbs are heavier than the conventional type and often larger, so check that they are suitable for your fittings or shades, or they may poke out of the end.

Fluorescent tubes

These consist of a glass envelope containing a low-pressure mercury vapour through which a diffuse electric arc passes, producing a faint blue light, rich in ultra-violet. This activates a fluorescent powder coating on the inside of the glass tube, causing it to emit visible white light with little shadow. Fluorescent tubes are good for lighting in the kitchen, work room and garage. Modern electronic control equipment ensures that the light comes on rapidly and does not flicker visibly. The tubes are available in a wide range of colours (not standard between manufacturers); 'Warm White' or its equivalent is usually best. Circular tubes are sold for pendant fittings and dining lights.

Tungsten-halogen bulbs (TH bulbs)

These are used in some types of downlighter, uplighter and wallwasher fittings. They are a form of filament bulb, in which the coiled filament is mounted in a narrow tubular envelope of fused silica (quartz) containing a halogen gas. This gas combines with the tungsten, extending the life of the

1. An elaborate chandelier uses candle-shaped bulbs to add a touch of old-fashioned elegance.

2. This glass demi-drum, concealing a tubular bulb, will provide a certain amount of general light with Art Deco overtones.

3. The filament bulbs used in these two uplighters provide a warm, general lighting.

4. Elegant, Victorian-style glass pendant using standard bulbs; useful for a dining room, it may provide just enough glow for general lighting in a hall.

5. This star-shaped glass pendant in blue is designed more for effect than general lighting.

6. Low-voltage spot bulbs, recessed into an alcove, cast light down onto the items displayed on the shelves below.

7. A 'dressing room'-style lighting display adds a novel touch to a stairway.

8. Old and new: a large filament bulb sheds light on the central table while candles line up on the mantelpiece.

9. Table lamps, with 'soft' shades in various colours, offer pools of light for a wide variety of different situations.

10. Classic angled lamps with an engineered look are suitable for desk lamps, bedside lamps or decorative lighting.

bulb to 2000 hours – twice the longevity of an ordinary filament bulb.

Tungsten-halogen bulbs are highly efficient and produce a whiter light than filament bulbs.

Low-voltage tungsten-halogen bulbs (TVLH bulbs)

These are tiny spotlights used for task and emphasis lighting. In operation they are similar to mains-voltage tungsten-halogen bulbs, and they are more efficient and produce a whiter/bluer light than standard filament light bulbs. They are used mainly in modern downlighters and spotlight fittings. As they get very hot, always buy those with clear heat-resisting glass covers over the reflectors.

Internally silvered reflector bulbs (ISL bulbs, mushroom bulbs)

These bulbs are useful in domestic lighting. Most have screw caps so that they can be accurately positioned in spotlight fittings, and all incorporate their own reflectors to direct light downwards. Always ensure that the bulb is the correct size for the fitting.

Parabolic aluminized reflector bulbs (PAR bulbs)

These are similar to ISL bulbs except that they are housed in a robust pressed-glass envelope. PAR 38 are available as 60 watt, 80 watt and 120 watt bulbs, and are suitable for use in downlighters and wallwashers. The 80 watt types are also used in spike lamps for decorative garden lighting. Special PAR spotlamps are available for indoor plants; these consist of a 75 watt reflector lamp with a special internal reflector coating.

Walls

In many ways, decorating the walls in your home could be thought of as an easy task today, because there is such a wealth of materials, patterns, designs and colours from which to choose. When it comes down to it, however, this can make the process much more of a problem because wonderful alternatives keep presenting themselves so that it can be very difficult to make a decision.

There are three rules to remember here. The first is to give yourself time to establish what you really want, and not to rush into choices without thinking them through. The second is to make sure that you work out your practical priorities first, including how far your budget will stretch and who is going to use any particular room, and for what purpose. The third is to decide on a style – whether traditional, ultra-modern or anything in

between – and to stick to it, as this will help to concentrate your mind and to exclude enticing but unsuitable decorations from your final scheme.

Keeping to the second and third of these rules is particularly important. Remaining within your budget can eliminate much wasted yearning for the unaffordable, ensuring that the materials you decide upon are practical; while remaining true to a particular style will whittle the decision-making down to manageable proportions.

Overview of walls

Walls can make an important contribution to colour in a room. Here, a bold orange complements the poppy-red of the window frame, skirting, door and bath panels. White tiles by the bath provide protection for the wall and also necessary relief from the bold colours.

Thinking of the practicalities first, make sure that your chosen paint or wallcovering is easy to apply and suitable for its purpose. Consider, too, your overall intention with the scheme – how colours and any patterns and textures will work, both with one another and with the proportions of the room.

Finding the right materials

As your first priority will be to choose suitable materials for their situation, make a list of the options, take this with you on shopping expeditions and do not be tempted to stray from it. Using the right materials is especially important in the most 'hardworking' parts of the house – children's rooms, the kitchen and the bathroom are often the prime candidates.

In children's rooms, the walls will need to be washable. It may also be a good idea to cover part of one wall with blackboard paint so that the children can legitimately draw on it, and this does make a lovely big surface for creativity. You could cover one wall with children's pictorial wallpaper or with a mural based on a favourite story, but it is wise to keep at least one wall surface for the occupants to 'use'.

If you are planning to decorate your kitchen or bathroom, be sure to buy materials which will not absorb water or be affected by condensation. Special water-resistant paints and papers are now sold specifically for use in these rooms. If the room suffers from condensation, make sure that there is adequate ventilation before you start decorating and that there is a constant source of heating. If you have set your heart on ceramic tiles, there are many practical designs from which to choose (a non-slip type is essential if you intend to use the same tiles on the floor as well). Most suppliers are informative and helpful, and will point out suitable tiles for your purpose; 'seconds' shops can also be a useful and economical source of interesting end-of-range tiles.

Choosing wallcoverings

If you wish to paper large areas of wall but have discovered that your ideal wallcovering is exorbitantly expensive, you might be able to use this expensive paper in a smaller area – such as an alcove – and to supplement it on the remaining wall area with a complementary, cheaper wallpaper or even with a paint effect. At the other end of the scale, bear in mind that the cheapest wallpapers are not always cost-effective. Sometimes they can be difficult to hang because they stretch slightly or tear easily when wet; they may also become damaged very easily once hung, and can be difficult to wash if they become grubby. Vinyl wallcoverings – while undeniably practical – usually look better in kitchens or bathrooms than living rooms.

Many modern wallpapers are based in style on those from the eighteenth or nineteenth centuries, and you can use these if you wish to create a particular period or traditional feel. If you would like an even more authentic look to decorate a house dating from a particular era you could buy 'document' papers, which are made using manufacturing techniques from the

past and these are based on papers discovered during renovations in old houses. Document papers are expensive because they are often made in small quantities or to order, and are often printed by hand. They do, however, have a rather individual and expensive look.

Choosing paints

Plain painting requires clean walls, sturdy supports and good equipment. You will need to decide whether you have time to do all the preparation and painting yourself, or whether to pay someone to come in and do part or all of this for you. If your time is limited, a good option may be to have the preparation done, and then to carry out the painting yourself.

Modern paints – including gloss paints – are mostly water-based. They cover an area well, do not smell particularly strong and dry quickly. This makes basic painting of the home an

easy, quick and practical option. Tackling decorative paint techniques is also highly satisfying. Specialist paints and brushes are now widely available, as is specialist advice – you may well be able to find weekend or evening courses being run in your area if you would like personal tuition. With such help you should be able to tackle most techniques with confidence, even if you are a beginner.

Like wallpapers, there has been a recent upsurge of interest in paints conforming to those of earlier times. A number of ranges are available based on ingredients and pigments used in eighteenth- and nineteenth-century paints, including earth pigments which can be very attractive in a traditional interior. Some of these are thick enough to cover most blemishes.

One advantage of painting walls is that if you don't like the result, you can cheaply and quickly cover it with a new colour. However, experimenting with patches of colour on a wall, as well as testing ideas on your colour board (see pages 28–9) can save time and effort in getting the colour and consistency right before you begin.

Left Stripes can be extremely elegant and these unassuming yellow stripes make a good foil for the floral fabric and a quiet background for the arrangement of paintings.
Below This wallpaper, with its meticulously drawn exotic flora, sparsely arranged on a pale background, is enchanting for a bedroom. It goes well with the floral arrangement and has a refreshing 'unbusy' quality.

Paint

Paint has many wonderful qualities for decorating the home. It can provide any colour you like, quickly and cheaply, and it can change the proportions of a room: for instance, a pale colour will make the walls and ceiling appear to recede, while a darker colour will seem to bring them forward. By using gloss paint you can make any room appear to be larger than it really is, because the shine on the paint will reflect light; matt paint, on the other hand, will make a room seem smaller and much more intimate.

You can use paint to conceal eyesores, such as the confused sprouting of water pipes running up through a bathroom. By painting these with the same colour as the walls, they will almost seem to 'disappear' into the background. If you go to the other extreme and paint such features in a contrasting colour, however, you can turn them into a positive part of the décor and give them quite a sculptural effect.

Exposed beams are often a widely loved architectural feature, but some beams – such as those found in attic rooms – are not particularly attractive. Painting these in the same colour as the walls and ceiling will help to merge them into the general decorating scheme, and will also make the

Main picture Here, deepest blue is illuminated by plenty of natural light; the white throw over the sofa and lively picture gallery of Indian paintings help to break up the colour which makes a good backcloth for them. *Right* Paint has been used in this open plan interior with great inventiveness; the yellow wall has a white edge following the lines of the steps and this makes a good foil for the paintings.

ceiling appear higher. Sloping ceilings in such rooms can be turned into an attractive feature if you bring attention to their eccentric and interesting shapes by painting them with bright colours.

In addition to the many different effects you can create with plain colours, paint can introduce depth and pattern to walls and woodwork, if used for various decorative techniques, including stippling, glazing, dragging and stencilling. With these – and with a little practice – you will be able to achieve results almost indistinguishable from those a professional could produce. The basic equipment required for these techniques is the same as for general painting so, if you take this option, you can create exciting finishes with little extra expense or effort.

Painted murals are another possibility for walls, and one good way of using these is to create a trompe l'oeil window or door in a small, dark room, thus appearing to bring in light and make the space seem larger. Another idea is to include a mural in a child's room, where you can create a scene with characters from a book or video that will give the child hours of pleasure and interest. Freehand drawings can be charming, if you have enough confidence; otherwise, if funds allow, you could seek the services of a local artist.

Overview of paint

As has already been touched on, painting is the quickest way to transform the character of a room. A change of colour can – on its own – bring a room to life, but it is important to choose your paints carefully. Gloss, eggshell and matt paints, for example, will each give very different results.

The eggshell paint on the panels on this imposing bath is easy to clean but less aggressive than gloss. Its effect is softened by the generosity and draping of the deep red window curtains and the general civilising influence of the flowers, pictures and plaster figure holding the shelf.

Using the right paints

Matt and eggshell paints are often considered to be the most suitable finishes for walls (and using one of these standard paints is indeed the quickest way to give a room a new look), while gloss paints are considered 'correct' for doors, window frames and other woodwork. In the past, gloss paints were held to be suitable for areas of the house which needed to be as hygienic as possible, such as the kitchen and bathroom, but today's matt paints are often washable. Other finishes such as vinyl silk, eggshell and vinyl gloss are also much less aggressively glossy than the earlier gloss paints, and are popular for kitchens, bathrooms and hallways because grease and scuff marks can be washed off quite easily. Textured paints have come into their own recently, and will cover minor cracks and other blemishes on a wall despite being only slightly more textured than traditional matt emulsion. It is best not to use textured coatings in a kitchen, however, because the texture can harbour grease and dirt.

When choosing paint shades, always hold the colour chart in an upright position. This will allow light to shine on the samples as it would do on a wall, and will give you a better

impression of what the final colour will be like. Remember that a strong colour on a colour chart will become darker when applied to a large area so, if anything, you should choose a colour slightly paler than you would like the finished effect to be.

Achieving the desired effect

The paint finish that you choose will be important to the result. Matt paint absorbs any light shining on to it, and so it does not produce reflections from the surface. This creates a soft effect which provides a good background for objects and dense colour. Matt is an ideal finish for both formal and informal rooms, where the quality of the colour is all-important.

In contrast, gloss paints reflect light and give a sparkling quality to a room that cannot be ignored. Modern gloss paints seem to have overcome their quality of hospital hygiene, and decorative glazing techniques mean that you can use them in many subtle ways to give a highly effective, sophisticated and vivid paint finish to formal or modern rooms.

In between the matt and gloss paints come the eggshells and vinyl silks, which are ideal in children's rooms, the bathroom, kitchen and any

Above This French-style bedroom, with its wooden bed-stead, floating muslin and tiered chandelier, is the epitome of thoughtful design. The plain walls are decorated with a restrained stencil motif that complements the curtain fabric.
Below right Interesting shapes, such as this range of cooking implements always look best set against solid, bold colours, as this deep green wall demonstrates.

other rooms where you want washable surfaces without the ultra-glossy 'hygienic' surfaces traditionally associated with them.

Colour ranges

Selecting colours for home decorating is, if anything, more difficult now than ever before, because the range of available colours and tones is almost endless and colours can be mixed and added to *ad infinitum*. The various manufacturers provide a staggering selection, particularly in matt, eggshell and vinyl silk paints. Added to this choice is the opportunity offered by paint effects to combine colours and achieve subtle two-tone effects which can give walls a greater depth.

Choosing your colours will be very largely a matter of individual taste. A few bright, primary shades may be suitable for a city apartment or a home of high-tech simplicity but, if you wish to use decorative techniques, a more subtle mixture of colours will work best. These techniques owe their popularity to their ability to soften yet enliven an interior, to provide pattern without insisting on it, and to create a pleasant yet unobtrusive background for the myriad interests and objects which have to fit into the modern home.

White is the best colour for reflecting light, but many people consider this rather cold. If you find pure white a little stark, you could use one of the many 'nearly white' colours, with their

hints of peach, apricot, lilac and so on. With these, take care when using the yellows which often have a greenish, cold tinge.

Paints for older houses

It can be relatively simple to devise a 'correct' or 'genuine' colour scheme for a twentieth-century interior – such as Art Deco – because more documentation and more photographs of the style are available. However, if you wish to use colours compatible to a particular historical style – such as Georgian – this has also now become much easier. After carrying out research, some manufacturers have produced a whole range of colours within their normal paint types, similar to those which would have been used at the time. The Georgian range includes some surprisingly bold colours, and the mid to late nineteenth-century range – reflecting the discovery of chemical pigments – has even brighter ones.

If you would like to be more authentic still, there are paint ranges using earth colours and similar pigments, as well as other ingredients – such as casein or buttermilk, which were often used in some of the early American interiors.

Paints and varnishes

Paint can provide a richly luxurious background for many different styles of interior. Here, the deep rose red complements an eclectic collection of furniture and the colours in the rugs and throws. A glaze has been used which gives added lustre to the walls.

The chart opposite provides information at a quick glance on the uses and properties of the paints and varnishes discussed in this book. Advice is also given on what you can use to dilute these products, their advantages and disadvantages, what types of pigment and coloured paints you can mix with them, and also their levels of toxicity.

Safety first

Remember that some of the ingredients used in paints are toxic, and that most solvents are highly toxic as well as flammable. These toxins can be absorbed into the body by inhalation, by swallowing or through the skin. When using paints, varnishes or solvents, you must therefore make sure that your work room is well ventilated and that there is no naked flame in the vicinity. Do not eat, drink or smoke while working, and always wear gloves, goggles and/or a face mask whenever you are handling materials that could possibly burn your skin or splash into your eyes.

Few lead-based paints are sold nowadays, but calcium plumbate primer is the one exception. This is used for priming galvanized metal and it should always carry a warning on the label. Whatever materials you are using, remember to keep all containers meticulously labelled and well out of the reach of children.

Rules for safe painting

- Wear a face mask – especially when abrading old or brightly coloured paintwork, which may contain lead.
- Do not use paint that claims to contain a fungicide and also has a warning about keeping it away from children and animals.
- Do not use a blowlamp to strip old or brightly coloured paintwork in areas with poor ventilation. Never use paints without adequate ventilation as many give off unpleasant and sometimes dangerous fumes.
- Do not buy and use paints offered cheaply – for example, from a car-boot sale – as they may contain lead. Throw such paints away rather than risk lead poisoning.
- If you wish to throw paint away, do not pour it down the drain because it may pollute the water supply. Instead, make sure that the container is tightly sealed and take it to your local recycling centre.

Using solvents

Solvents can be extremely hazardous if wrongly used. As with paints, never dispose of solvents by pouring them down the drain, and always keep them well away from children – preferably clearly marked and in a locked cupboard. Commonly used solvents include the following: methylated spirit (denatured alcohol), methanol, wood alcohol, methyl violet, turpentine, white spirit and acetone.

Paint/varnish type	Solvent	Advantages	Disadvantages	Mix with	Toxicity
Emulsion matt and vinyl silk water-based use on wood, plaster, paper, brick, stone, concrete, paint	water	quick-drying (1–3 hours); waterproof finish; wide range of colours	dark colours lack depth	universal stainers, powder colours, gouache, artist's acrylics	skin contact * inhalation * swallowing **
Gloss paint, eggshell, oil-based undercoat oil-based use on wood, plaster, paper, brick, stone, concrete, paint	turpentine/white spirit	durable; good depth of colour; wide range of colours	needs undercoat (and primer on absorbent surfaces); slow-drying	universal stainers, artist's oil paints, transparent oil glaze	skin contact ** inhalation *** swallowing *****
Distemper and buttermilk (casein) water-based use on plaster	water	allows passage of moisture	not waterpoof; adheres only to porous surfaces	gouache, powder colours	skin contact * inhalation * swallowing *
Limewash water-based gives chalky matt finish; may be used instead of white distemper	water	disinfectant; insecticidal; allows passage of moisture	caustic when wet; rubs off easily; semi-waterproof only	alkali-resistant powder colours	skin contact ***** inhalation ***** swallowing *****
Spray paints solvent-based convenient for stencilling; may be used as a base coat for gilding	nothing	quick-drying to a smooth, hard finish; adheres to most surfaces; quick to apply	highly toxic; smells unpleasant; spray 'fall-out' can be considerable; may contain hazardous propellants	nothing	skin contact ** inhalation ***** swallowing *****
Artist's oil paint good for colouring transparent oil glaze, varnish and eggshell paint	turpentine/white spirit	wide colour range; dilutes well, and can be mixed with other oil-based paints and glazes; slow-drying, so easy to work with	covering power varies; some colours are expensive so not good for use over large areas	transparent oil glaze, eggshell paint, gloss paint, beeswax furniture polish, and oil- and resin-based varnishes	skin contact ***** inhalation ***** swallowing *****
Powder colours mix at home for colourwashing, etc.	water	make attractive washes; can be mixed dry for accurate colour matching	powder colours vary greatly; some are highly toxic; painted surfaces need protection to prevent colour from rubbing away	emulsion, transparent oil glaze, oil-based and poluyurethane varnishes	skin contact ***** inhalation ***** swallowing *****
Gouache/artist's acrylics tubes of concentrated colour; use for solid colour and washes	water	strong colours; dilute well and make good colour washes; acrylics are waterproof when dry	dry rapidly (in 1 hour), so difficult to work with; not waterproof	emulsion	skin contact ***** inhalation ***** swallowing *****
Transparent oil glaze use with artist's oil paints or universal stainers to make coloured glazes for dragging, stippling, etc.	turpentine/white spirit	cheap and effective; can be worked for up to 30 minutes; dries in 6 hours	yellows if exposed to sunlight; dries soft, so needs protection with varnish coating	artist's oils, oil-based paints, universal stainers, oil-based varnish and polyurethane varnish (polyurethane varnish gives a glossy finish)	skin contact ** inhalation *** swallowing *****
Polyurethane varnish available in matt, semi-gloss and gloss; hard and durable all-purpose varnish	turpentine/white spirit	easy and pleasant to use; easily removed with solvent; waterproof	sometimes yellows and becomes brittle; liable to flake when sanded	oil-based paints, artist's oils, powder colours, transparent oil glaze	skin contact ** inhalation *** swallowing ****
Acrylic varnish quick-drying, water- or petroleum-distillate-based varnish; suitable for all types of decorative varnishing	varies according to composition	water-based acrylic varnish is quick-drying; tough and clear finish; pleasant to use	petroleum-distillate-based varnish is highly toxic (use the water-based version wherever possible)	universal stainers and powder colours	skin contact * inhalation * swallowing *
Universal stainers intense colours in liquid form; can be combined with all types of oil- and water-based paints and glazes	turpentine/white spirit	strong colours; dilute well; good mixing qualities; inexpensive and adaptable	limited range of colours	ready-coloured paints (e.g. emulsion, eggshell)	skin contact ** inhalation *** swallowing *****

Key to toxicity levels

Toxicity levels are symbolized by the number of asterisks, with one asterisk indicating fairly low toxicity and five asterisks indicating a highly toxic product.

Tools and equipment

Collect up all the tools and equipment that you need before you start work to make sure you haven't forgotten anything. Many items, such as brushes, scrapers, rollers and sponges, can be kept permanently, for use on other occasions. Remember that it will pay you to buy the best tools you can afford. They will not just do a better job, but will make the work easier and more pleasant. Make sure that you always clean brushes and other equipment immediately after you have finished using them.

It is always worth investing in good-quality equipment, because this will give better results and be much easier to work with than items of mediocre quality. It will cost a little more, but will last twice as long and the finished effect will be altogether more satisfactory. In addition, careful preparation is as important as good equipment if you want the results to last.

Equipment for preparation

Depending on the extent of the preparation that you need to carry out, you may need some or all of the following items. While this may seem to involve a considerable financial outlay, remember that much of the equipment should last for years, provided that you clean and store it correctly.

Repairing cracks and holes

The basic items for these tasks are a wire brush, filler (sold ready to use or in powder form to mix with water), a filling knife, a board for mixing and a small paintbrush for dampening the crevice or hole.

You will need to sand most repaired and wooden surfaces before painting them: remove the excess dried filler with emery paper or glasspaper wrapped around a cork, rubber block or a wood offcut.

Washing down walls

After carrying out any repairs, or if a wall is dirty and dusty, you must wash it well before painting. For this you will need sugar soap, a large decorator's or car-cleaning sponge and a bucket for water.

Paintbrushes, rollers and pads

You will need a brush at least 125mm (5in) wide for covering large areas of wall quickly, and a 50mm (2in) brush for more precise painting in smaller areas such as around the frames of both doors and windows.

Specialist brushes, such as dusting, stippling and stencilling brushes, are needed for certain paint effects alongside standard decorating brushes. Artist's brushes of various sizes are also useful to have to hand when doing paint effects.

Rollers and pads allow quick and easy coverage of large areas of wall. To achieve an even coating on the roller or pad, pour the paint into a roller tray or pad trough. A roller with a short pile will give the smoothest finish, a medium pile will produce a lightly textured finish and a long pile will leave a heavily textured finish. For general use, foam pads are the cheapest, but lambswool and mohair produce the best results.

Other equipment

Other general items of equipment include the following:

- A paint kettle.
- A bucket and sponge.
- Dust sheets or plastic sheeting.
- Lint-free rags.
- Low-tack masking tape (narrow to protect light switches and sockets; wide for edges of ceilings or walls).
- An old knife to open tins of paint (never use a good screwdriver for this, as you will damage it).
- Lengths of wooden dowel or sticks for mixing paint.
- Clean glass jars for soaking and cleaning brushes.

Safety equipment

Taking proper safety precautions is essential for any decorating job. Wear protective goggles and a face mask for sanding or other tasks where particles could get into your eyes or be inhaled; disposable gloves are also a good idea if you have sensitive skin. For high-level work, use a sturdy, lightweight step-ladder; or, for painting a stairwell, use a non-slip ladder with suction pads on the feet which will stand securely on two different levels. A clip-on shelf will hold your paint pot securely on the ladder.

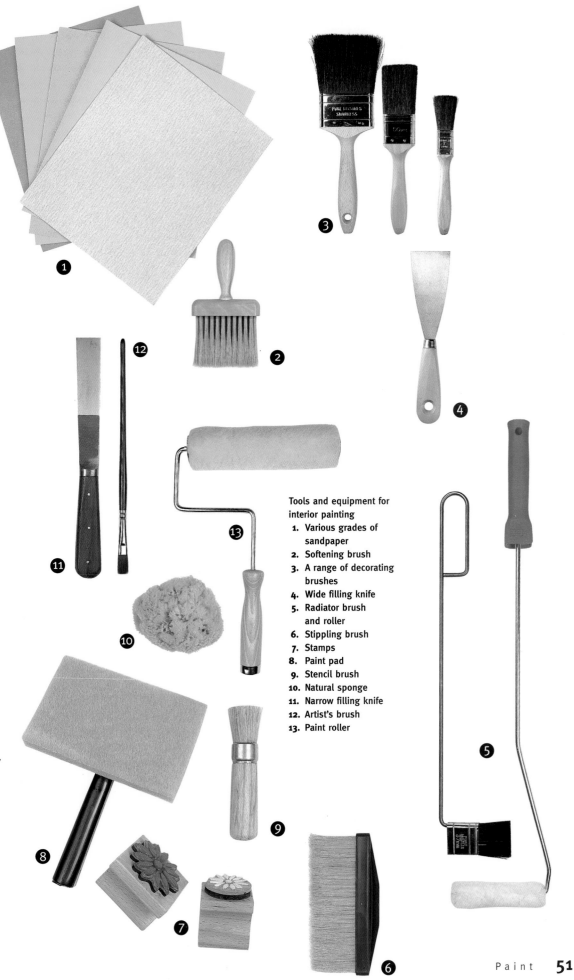

Tools and equipment for interior painting
1. Various grades of sandpaper
2. Softening brush
3. A range of decorating brushes
4. Wide filling knife
5. Radiator brush and roller
6. Stippling brush
7. Stamps
8. Paint pad
9. Stencil brush
10. Natural sponge
11. Narrow filling knife
12. Artist's brush
13. Paint roller

Directory of paints

Matt paint has been used on the walls and woodwork in this charming traditional interior. Special floor paint will last for a year or two, especially if it is given several coats of seal after painting.

When buying paint, don't be guided by price alone. It is better to buy a well-known brand, because unknown, cheap paints – particularly emulsions – often do not cover the wall well enough or last very long. Estimate the quantity that you will need and buy the full amount at one time, as different batches of paint may vary slightly; this is also important if you have the colour mixed in the store. If you are mixing your own colour, try to mix enough for the whole job, but keep a note of the quantities and pigments that you use just in case you need more.

Using a primer

If you are painting over existing paint, and the walls are in good condition, you may simply be able to paint over a top coat. If the walls are bare plaster, paint them with a coat of diluted emulsion to prime the surface (in other words, to seal it and reduce the plaster's absorbency). Alternatively, you can use a water-based primer intended for use on plaster (water- and oil-based primers for wood and metal are also available for window frames and so on).

Top coats

The following are all suitable for use on walls. If you are unsure of what a certain type of paint will look like in a room, try it out on a small area first, or paint a board with the colour and move it around to test the effect.

Vinyl matt emulsion

This water-based paint has a matt type of finish and is suitable for walls and ceilings. It is cheap, easy and quick to use, and is useful for decorative paint effects. You can thicken vinyl matt emulsion with whiting for a textured effect, or thin it to create a colour-wash. However, the finished surface is not easily washed.

Vinyl silk emulsion

Another water-based paint, this is similar to vinyl matt emulsion but is more durable and has a slight sheen. It is good for the kitchen, bathroom and children's rooms, can be used for decorative paint effects and mixes well with stainers, artist's gouache and powder colours (these are available from art stores).

Eggshell

This water- or oil-based paint has a smooth, hardwearing surface and also a slight sheen very like the shell of a bird's egg. It is more attractive and subtle than gloss paint on walls where a hard, washable finish is required – such as the kitchen, bathroom and hallway – and you can also use it on furniture. Water-based eggshell dries more quickly and is more pleasant to use than the oil-based variety.

Gloss

Gloss paints are usually thought of as being oil-based, but water-based paint is now available in a range of semi-gloss, gloss and high-gloss finishes. High gloss reflects light and so it will show up every flaw in a wall surface, which can be an important consideration. All gloss paints are long-lasting, resistant to damage and washable, and they can be used in heavy-duty areas such as the utility room, hallway and work room.

Kitchen/bathroom emulsion

This water-based paint contains fungicide to inhibit the growth of mould, and is designed for use in the 'wet' areas of the house such as the kitchen and bathroom.

Satin-finish (mid-sheen) paint

This is an oil-based paint. It is similar to eggshell, but gives a slightly less attractive finish on walls.

Whitewash and limewash

These inexpensive, old-fashioned matt paints have a powdery finish which cannot be washed. You can mix whitewash with powder pigment to give it colour if you wish. When dry, both paints can be rubbed off with a brush; always remove them completely before applying any other type of paint.

Buttermilk (Casein)

A matt paint made from buttermilk, pigment and fungicide, and available in dark and pale colours, this was much used in early American interiors and is still popular today for its old-fashioned, rustic appearance.

Flat oil paint

Only available through specialist suppliers, you can use this durable and good-looking matt oil paint on its own or thin it as a glaze.

Textured paint

More of a coating than a paint, this water-based finish adds texture to plaster surfaces, and so is generally used on walls and ceilings. It is good for covering poor wall surfaces, but is difficult to clean and to remove.

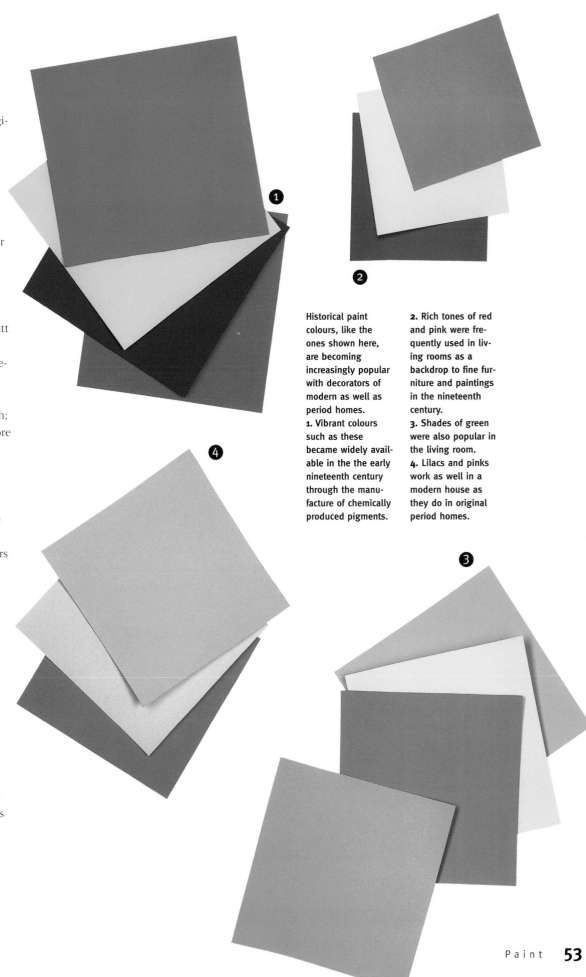

Historical paint colours, like the ones shown here, are becoming increasingly popular with decorators of modern as well as period homes.
1. Vibrant colours such as these became widely available in the the early nineteenth century through the manufacture of chemically produced pigments.

2. Rich tones of red and pink were frequently used in living rooms as a backdrop to fine furniture and paintings in the nineteenth century.
3. Shades of green were also popular in the living room.
4. Lilacs and pinks work as well in a modern house as they do in original period homes.

Basic techniques: Preparation

Prepare the walls thoroughly before starting to paint. Any major repairs such as re-wiring or installing a damp course should be done first, then fill any holes or cracks and sand flat. Finally wash all the surfaces to be painted to remove grease and dust.

It is well worth spending time preparing your walls and filling cracks and holes before you start painting. The finished result will then be much more impressive, and the paint itself will last longer. Ready-to-use filler in tubs or tubes, or powder filler for mixing with water, is suitable for most plaster or wood surfaces.

Initial preparation

Before you begin any work, move as much furniture as you can into another room, or push larger (and heavier) pieces of furniture into the centre of the room. Take down curtains and pictures, roll up and remove carpets (if possible) and rugs, and cover the floor with dust sheets or plastic sheeting, taped down securely at the corners. Preparation is all-important to achieve a good final result. Make sure that you have the right equipment, including ladders, cover the floor with sheeting and be prepared to spend several days working on the job. Any major repairs to the wall, such as damp proofing and re-wiring, should be done before you carry out any decorating. The walls should be made good and any replastering be given time to dry out too.

Washing down old paint

If the existing paint on the walls is sound, you will only need to wash it down. First of all, remove surface dirt with a vacuum cleaner or a long brush, and flick out particles of dust and debris from corners and picture rails with a small knife. When washing, start at the top of the wall and work your way down by degrees, making sure that water does not get into any electric fittings. Allow the wall to dry thoroughly before painting.

Filling chips and crevices

You will be able to fill small, superficial chips in walls with a fine surface filler. Work this into the surface and spread it with a filling knife, then leave it to dry thoroughly before sanding away the excess with glasspaper.

When filling a small hole or crack, first widen the cavity with the side of the filling knife and brush away any debris. Moisten the sides of the cavity using a small paintbrush soaked in water; this will help the filler to adhere. Prepare only as much filler as you need (if you are not using it straight out of the tub) and pack it tightly into the crack by drawing the filling knife across the surface at a right angle.

When dealing with a deep crack, put in a shallow layer of filler, allow this to dry and then apply another layer. Leave the filler slightly proud of the surface and let it dry and harden for a few hours, then rub with glasspaper to achieve a smooth finish.

FILLING A SMALL CRACK

1. Rake out loose material from the crack using the corner of a filling knife.

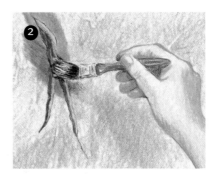

2. Use a small paintbrush to wet the crack with water to help the filler adhere and stop it from drying too quickly.

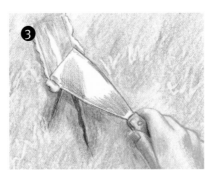

3. Fill the crack with a loaded filling knife.

4. When set, sand flush to the wall surface with medium grade sandpaper.

Cracks in doors and windows

Cracks often appear where door and window frames meet the wall. These are caused by movement of the woodwork through temperature and humidity changes. Clear any loose plaster away from cracks with the point of a small filling knife. Fill the cleared gaps with acrylic sealant, which grips better than cellulose filler.

Basic techniques: Painting a room

Before painting, remove as much furniture as possible from the room. Move any pieces which are to remain well away from the walls and cover with dust sheets. The floor covering should be removed if possible, otherwise carefully covered over.

Before you begin painting, make sure that you have enough paint for the first coat, all the brushes you will need (or rollers or pads, if using) and a rag to mop up smears. Flick the bristles of the brushes to dislodge any dust. Finally, check that the dust sheet or plastic sheeting on the floor is still securely in position.

Painting walls

The tools that you choose for painting will be largely a matter of personal preference – some people swear by brushes, while others opt for the quick and easy coverage of a roller or pad. If you do use a roller, you may also need a brush for small areas, such as between doors and window frames.

Using a brush

A brush 125mm (5in) or larger will enable you to cover the area quickly. Stir the paint thoroughly and pour enough into a paint kettle to cover half the length of the bristles. Coat the brush in a generous layer of paint, then apply it in horizontal bands about 60cm (24in) wide. With matt emulsion, finish off with criss-cross strokes; with a silk or satin emulsion, lay off with light, upward strokes to give an even finish.

Using a roller

A roller is the fastest way of applying emulsion. Paint the edges first with a small brush before using the roller. Pour some paint into the well of the roller tray and dip in the edge of the roller, then run it up and down the slope to get an even layer of paint on the sleeve. Do not overload or jerk the roller, or the paint will spatter. Use a random criss-cross movement, covering every bit of wall and keeping the joins merged.

ORDER FOR PAINTING A ROOM

1. Ceiling; 2. Walls; 3. Window frame; 4. Doors; 5. Ceiling mouldings; 6. Skirtings; 7. Radiators.

Painting a ceiling

Paint systematically from wall to wall, starting at the window end in a corner and working away from the light. You should be able to paint a low ceiling without needing a ladder if you use a roller attached to an extension pole. Paint the ceiling edges first with a small brush to ensure a neat finish.

Using a pad

Dip the pad lightly into the paint and wipe away the excess on the side of the can, or use a special applicator. Smooth the paint on to the wall in random directions, reloading the pad as soon as the paint becomes thin.

General advice on painting walls

- You will need to paint bare plaster walls with a coat of diluted emulsion to prime the surface, but pre-painted surfaces need no primer. Allow the emulsion to dry thoroughly before painting the top coat.
- If the paint does not cover well, don't try to paint on a thicker coat, but wait until the paint is dry and then add another coat.
- Start at the top corner of a wall and work down to the skirting; cut in with a narrower brush around windows and door frames.
- Try to work in a uniform light – don't start in natural light and finish in artificial light or you may find yourself covering the same area twice.
- Always complete the whole of a surface in one session: if you decide to stop halfway through, the edge of the dried paint will show up as a conspicuous line. Close the windows to prevent paint from drying too quickly and causing join lines, and open them again after painting to accelerate the drying time. Silk

ORDER FOR PAINTING A CEILING AND WALLS

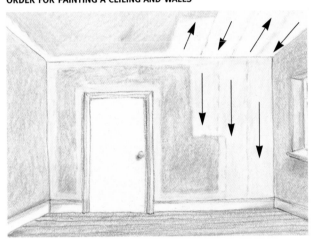

Always start at the window end of the ceiling and paint in strips. For the walls, work from the top down in strips.

and satin finishes dry more quickly than matt. If you find that your paint is drying too fast, then work in narrower bands.

- When using a roller, don't work too fast or paint will splatter all over the place. Allow the roller to shed all of its paint before reloading it.
- You will always get a better finish with two thin coats of paint than with one thick one.

USING A ROLLER

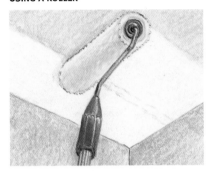

Work a roller in straight lines over a ceiling.

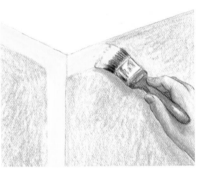

Carefully cut in around edges with a narrow brush before covering the main wall area.

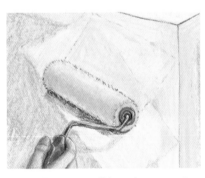

Run a roller over a wall in a criss-cross pattern, merging joins and filling gaps.

Basic techniques: Specific painting tips

Meticulous painting was required here to achieve the precise ziggurat line of the stairs. Masking tape can make this job easier. The white emulsion makes a good contrast to the polished stairs and the strong picture on the wall.

To achieve a really professional finish throughout your home, there are many tricks of the trade that are useful to know. It is also helpful to be forewarned about possible problems and to know how to prevent them. The most common decorating mistakes are caused by poor preparation, inadequate working conditions and bad painting techniques.

Painting the kitchen and bathroom

Anti-condensation emulsion paints containing insulating material can help to minimize condensation in the kitchen and bathroom. If you cannot find a colour that you like, you could overpaint one of these with standard emulsion. Do not use gloss paints in these rooms, as they will exaggerate any condensation that appears.

You may have exposed pipes in the kitchen and/or bathroom. Copper pipes will not need primer if you paint them with a suitable undercoat and then gloss; other surfaces may need priming. Normal gloss paint will withstand temperatures of over 32°C (90°F), although white and pale colours may turn slightly yellow over time; water-based paints tend to crack when heated. Do not paint connections on pipes or they will be difficult to undo at a later stage.

Using ladders

Ladders must be secure and sturdy. A convertible ladder will double as a large stepladder and as a straight ladder placed against a wall. Connections must be firm and the ladder non-slip when extended; check that screws are tight and that no parts have jammed. Make sure that the ladder reaches at least 1m (3ft) above the highest level at which you need to stand, and never stand above the third-highest rung. Face the ladder as you climb and do not lean too far to either side while painting. When working in a larger area, set up a working platform.

A ladder which will stand on two different levels is useful on stairs, provided that it has suction pads on the feet to provide a secure grip.

Painting the stairwell

It may be best to leave the stairwell until last, since it is likely to suffer from damage while you move furniture in and out of other rooms. When you come to paint this area, remove the carpet and fittings, clean the entire staircase, cure any creaks and carry out any repairs, then set up a secure workstation. Working from the top down, paint the landing ceiling, followed by the stairwell walls; leave the stairs (if painting) and banisters until last.

Painting radiators

Paint any radiators once you have finished work on the walls. Always paint them when they are cold, and allow the paint to dry thoroughly before turning on the heating again. You may need to treat old radiators for rust, and to apply primer and undercoat. Use a 25mm (1in) brush for the main painting, and a crevice roller or brush for tricky areas. The following are typical pitfalls to avoid when painting:

- Runs, sags and wrinkles: when the paint is applied too thickly or not brushed out adequately.
- Specks and pimples: if the old surface is not sanded thoroughly, or dust has blown on to the wet paint.
- Blisters: when paint is applied to a damp surface or to old, soft paint.

In any of these cases, leave the paint to harden for a week. Rub it down with glasspaper, clean the surface and apply fresh paint.

Take time to set up a strong, safe workstation when painting stairwells. A firm platform can be made from two sturdy planks bound tightly together and supported on well balanced ladders.

PAINTING RADIATORS

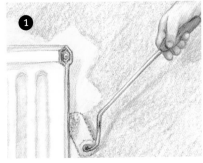

1. A long-handled roller makes painting behind a radiator much easier.

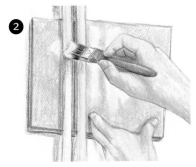

2. When painting pipes, hold a piece of paper or cardboard behind the pipes to receive any paint splatters from the brush.

Directory of paint effects

This paint effect, chosen to give the antique-plaster look of old Italian buildings, gives a pleasantly informal style and has been courageously used throughout the room. The ceiling is left white.

Paint effects have been used to decorate homes for hundreds of years. They have imitated marble and other expensive and attractive stones, as well as wood grains, sun-bleached stucco work and much more. Interesting effects of stippling and ragging have also been employed, not to imitate but simply to give an extra dimension to the colours and finish of walls. These finishes are still popular today – with good reason, since they can be used not only in traditional-style interiors but also to add depth of interest to modern rooms. They are economical and – with a little practice – are easy to achieve.

Using paints and glazes

There are a myriad of paint effects which can be worked on walls, doors and furniture. Here are just a few of the more straightforward techniques which are perfect for decorating large or small areas of wall. Further details such as gilding or stencilling (see pages 66–7), look wonderful on top of an effect like a colourwash or splattering. When using glazes, it is worth remembering that they tend to dry quite quickly, so it can be easier to work with another person, with one person applying the glaze and the other following behind and working the effect.

Dragging

This produces an elegant, softly lined effect which looks very effective on doors and panelling as well as on walls. This glaze effect is an excellent finish for sophisticated town houses and grander country homes. A similar technique, called 'under the brush', is a form of dragging in which the brush is wielded in a series of curves rather than straight up and down; these give a freer, more relaxed look to the wall.

Ragging

Here, an interesting textured pattern is created by bundling up a piece of clean, lint-free fabric (such as hessian or a piece of old net curtain) and pressing it on to a glaze coat on the wall. You can achieve different effects by using two tones of the same colour or by using contrasting colours.

Rag-rolling

Rag-rolling is similar to ragging, but it can be used to create a rather more sophisticated finish. In this technique, the cloth (muslin is ideal for this) is crumpled up into a long sausage shape and rolled, rather than pressed, on to the wall. This method produces an informal, almost striped look but with uneven, rather than straight, edges.

Sponging on

Here, a mottled look is created by using a large, natural sponge to add colour to a neutral background. The final finish can be fairly hard-edged or blurred, depending on the colours used. The sponged-on colour can be glaze or emulsion. This is an easy technique and gives a pretty finish to an informal country-style interior.

Sponging off

Rather than adding more colour with a top coat, in this case the base coat is sponged to break up the paint. This is a quick and cheap way to produce an attractive textured surface which can take the blandness away from a straightforward coat of emulsion.

Stippling

This is a glaze technique in which the colour is broken up into thousands of small dots. You can use it to soften any rich, strong colour, or as a way of counteracting the blandness of a neutral or pale wall colour.

1. The dado line and a small wall shelf are linked by a border stencilled and hand-painted in co-ordinating colours.

2. A disciplined and complex painted golden yellow pattern on the wall makes an interesting Chinese-type background to the grey and gold curtains and tassels.

3. This two-tone yellow wall was created by using a sponging on technique which goes well with the solid furniture and Gothic candlesticks.

4. A warm, yet washable finish is achieved on normally cold bathroom walls using a transparent wash over walls sponged in green and yellow.

5. A colourwash softens the terracotta colour in this warm bedroom.

6. The simple and effective use of a stamp has created the tile-like effect of this grey and yellow wall.

7. A delicate ivy stencil has been used very sparingly to add charming additional interest to this painted yellow and blue cottage-style room.

8. This stencilled farmyard road is just the kind of wall decoration any young child would love.

Spattering

Spattering is a pattern created when a brush loaded with paint is flicked so that dots of paint splatter higgledy-piggledy on to the base coat. It is easy to do but the choice of colours is crucial in achieving a satisfactory effect. Experiment on a board first.

Dry-brushing

Dry-brushing creates a rougher, more dramatic effect than either colour-washes or glazes. A base of matt emulsion is criss-crossed over the wall using a wide, hard-bristled brush, with the brush kept as dry as possible.

Stencilling

A stencil consists of a decorative cut-out in paint-proof material – such as oiled card – through which paint can be dabbed, sponged, brushed or sprayed. Stencils enable a simple, straightforward pattern to be repeated over a wall to create a border or frieze, or you can use them individually to create pictures and motifs or a design over a whole wall. You can buy stencil kits or make your own. They can be large or small, simple or complicated, and used with one or several colours.

Block-printed patterns

These are usually small and simple, and often Gothic in character, with motifs such as *fleur de lys*, shamrocks, hearts and so on. You can either print on to the wall in a random fashion, or mark out beforehand exactly where each print is to go.

Basic techniques: Glazes and colourwashes

Glazing techniques produce a shinier, sharper look than colourwashing. Here, glazing techniques have been used to produce an 'antiqued' look, almost marbled in some places, the darker patches more prominent on the pink wall. The glazing is highly suitable for the clean modern lines of the chairs and table.

Equipment required

The equipment that you will need is much the same as for straightforward painting, and includes good quality decorating brushes for basic painting and for applying glazes and washes. You will also need some or all of the following, depending on the technique that you choose:

- Plenty of old rags and cloths.
- Natural sponges.
- A firm-bristled artist's paintbrush for mixing colours.
- Saucers for test-mixing.
- A white plastic paint kettle with a lid for your mixed colours.
- Additional or specialist brushes (these are specified where needed).
- A varnishing brush, if you are applying a final varnish.

Decorative paint techniques are produced by using a base coat of coloured paint with an application of transparent or coloured paint over the top. The top coat is treated in various ways to create different effects. With most decorative paint techniques it is surprisingly easy to achieve a satisfactory and effective result.

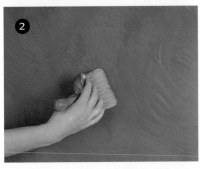

The base coat

Prepare the wall by painting it with your chosen colour of eggshell (for a glaze) or emulsion (for a wash). If you cannot find the colour you require, buy a paint in the colour that most closely matches it and add artist's gouache or poster paint (available from art stores) until it looks right.

The top coat

The way in which the top coat is applied creates the decorative paint effect. If you have not tried a technique before, it is a good idea to practise on a board or part of the wall that is to be painted before committing yourself to the real thing.

APPLYING A GLAZE

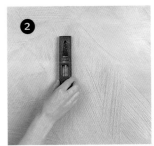

1. Apply the tinted glaze in random strokes over the eggshell base colour. Be sure to cover the walls evenly. **2.** To create a dragging effect, apply the glaze then line up a spirit level vertically on the wall and indent slightly to give a guidemark for vertical strokes. **3.** With a clean brush (about 75mm/3in wide), drag straight down the wet glaze so that vertical strokes are left behind. **4.** The finished dragging effect.

Glazes

Glazes are used to give walls a depth and sophistication that plain paint cannot achieve. Start with two coats of eggshell as your base coat, leaving each to dry. Next, pour some clear 'flat' glaze into a metal (not plastic) container, then tint it with universal stainers or artist's oil paints. Try the colour out on a board already painted with your chosen base coat, and adjust the tinting until you achieve the desired colour. Add the contents of a bottle of paint dryer and mix this in well before painting; alternatively, you can use a ready-tinted glaze that already incorporates a paint dryer.

Even with the delaying effects of a dryer, the paint dries out relatively quickly, so work on an area about 1sq m (1½sq yds) at a time.

For the simplest effect, and to add greater depth to the wall, paint on the glaze with a medium-sized decorator's brush using quick, random strokes and then soften the effect with a short-bristled brush. You can create other effects by dragging the brush through the glaze in various ways – experiment on your painted board first before working on the walls themselves.

Colourwashes

Colourwashing produces a matt, powdery finish and is used to imitate faded plaster and many other effects. Start with a base coat of emulsion paint and leave this to dry. The wash consists mainly of water, traditionally mixed with a little thinned distemper, but you can achieve the same chalky look by using thinned emulsion; use about half a bucket of water to one tablespoon of emulsion. Tint the wash to

1. Apply the emulsion base coat and leave to dry. Use a large decorator's brush to apply the diluted top coat in random strokes.
2. Soften off any hard lines with a dry softening brush while the top coat is still damp.
3. The finished colourwash.

your desired colour with artist's gouache or poster paints (available from art stores).

Try the wash out on a piece of board already painted with the base coat. If you are happy with the result, apply the wash with a large decorator's brush using random strokes, covering about 1sq m (1½sq yds) at a time. Then go over the brushmarks with a dry softening brush to soften the marks and wipe up drips.

Basic techniques: Using glazes and washes

Before you begin painting, work out your colour scheme carefully and test out the paint effects on inconspicuous areas or offcuts of board. Here, colour-washes of mauve and green have been blended to create a textured plaster feel. A green colourwash band creates a frieze. In contrast, the window surround is painted in strong, flat gloss.

Ragging
• Glaze technique

As in all the glazing techniques shown here, the choice of base coat colour and the covering glaze tint is all-important to the success of the finished technique. In the example below, a glaze tinted with yellow ochre is brushed over a warm yellow background to create a rich, earthy effect.

Most of the following techniques are very simple and you will need only a little practice to create your own lively, effective and entertaining wall finishes. These can stand as important decorative elements in their own right or as a means of adding greater depth to a scheme; they can also provide an ideal backdrop for paintings or other decorative elements.

RAGGING

1. Paint on the glaze in vertical strokes. Over large areas, join the strokes at varying levels across the wall to avoid an obvious join line.
2. While the glaze is still wet, blot the surface with a piece of hessian to break up the glaze.

Rag-rolling

• Glaze technique

This is slightly more difficult than ragging as more precision is called for to roll the rag in straight lines up the wall. The glaze is brushed on in random strokes over the base colour. The muslin rag is then twisted into a sausage and slowly rolled up the wall. Reshape the rag after every roll, and overlap the lines at the edges.

RAG ROLLING

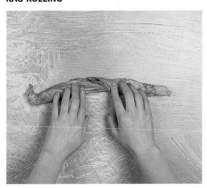

Roll the muslin 'sausage' up the wall over the wet glaze. Take great care to avoid touching the glaze with your fingers.

Stippling

• Glaze technique

Special stippling brushes are available but these are expensive, so you may prefer to use a round headed or square brush which will give a similar effect. Test on a piece of board before working the wall to make sure your brush will produce the right effect.

STIPPLING

Hold the dry stippling brush at a 90° angle to the wall. Dab the wet glaze with a stabbing motion. Do not drag the brush or the glaze will smudge rather than stipple.

Sponging on

• Emulsion technique

For this simple technique you can apply two or three colours on top of one another to create subtle colour schemes. Here, a deep pink is sponged onto a pale pink base coat. When dry, white is dabbed over the second colour to soften the deep pink. Make sure each layer is thoroughly dry before applying the next.

SPONGING ON

Apply the base emulsion and leave to dry. Dip a piece of natural sponge into emulsion paint and dab it across the surface.

When the first sponged layer is dry, take a new piece of sponge and dab on the second colour to soften the first.

Sponging off

• Glaze or emulsion technique

This is similar to ragging except the effect is worked using a sponge, rather than a piece of cloth. A dabbing motion is used to lift paint or glaze off the surface to leave a textured finish with the base coat showing through.

SPONGING OFF

Paint on the base colour and leave to dry. Paint emulsion or a glaze over the base coat and while still damp, sponge the surface to lift off some of the paint.

Spattering

• Emulsion technique; needs practice.

This can be a rather messy technique, so make sure that any areas that you do not want to be spattered are covered up. Do not overload the brush as you want to achieve fine spots not large blobs or dribbles. More than one colour may be spattered onto the base coat. Wait for the first colour to dry thoroughly before applying a second. Here, orange and light blue are spattered over a turquoise background.

SPATTERING

Hold a wooden stick about 46cm (18cm) away from the wall and rap the brush against it.

Basic techniques: Alternative paint effects

A rural cascade of ivy round a French door has been stencilled meticulously onto this warm yellow wall, providing an appropriate introduction to the garden beyond.

In addition to glazes and colourwashes, there are alternative techniques which can enhance the look of your home as well as hiding blemishes, and which are easy and fun to do. The materials for stencilling and block or stamp printing are available in kit form, but you may prefer to make your own patterns and motifs.

Stencils

There are many stencil kits on the market, however, these can be expensive, and it is not difficult to make your own stencil.

Trace your chosen motif. To enlarge or reduce, trace then photocopy the motif, or trace it on to graph paper and scale it to size. Transfer the pattern to a piece of oiled stencil board or acetate. If using board, tape the picture on top with a piece of carbon paper behind it, then trace the outline with a pencil. If using acetate, tape the design under the transparent sheet and trace the outline on to the acetate using an isograph technical pen. Cut along the lines with a sharp craft knife, leaving about 2.5cm (1in) around the cut-outs for strength.

Using low tack tape, stick the stencil to the surface to be decorated. Load a stencilling brush with just a little paint on the tips and fill in the colour with a stabbing motion. Once the paint is dry, a second colour may be applied over the first.

STENCILLING A REPEAT DESIGN

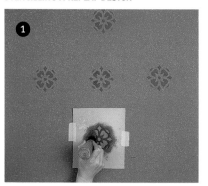

1. Mark the centre position of each motif using a ruler and pencil. Line up the centre of the stencil with a pencil mark and secure with masking tape. With a small amount of paint on the stencil brush, apply paint through the stencil in a stabbing motion.

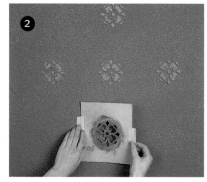

2. Once the first colour is dry, realign the stencil and apply a second colour in the same manner as before.

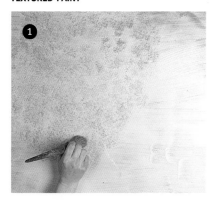

Apply the paint with a brush in the usual manner and ensure that there is a good even

covering. Use a dry brush to stab at the wet paint, raising the surface into small peaks.

Textured paint

This is thickened paint which is used to give a surface texture to the wall. Self-texturing paint automatically creates its own texture as you roller or brush it on. With ordinary textured paint, the pattern is worked into the smooth layer of paint. Different effects can be created with implements such as a plasterer's comb or a stipple brush.

Before you begin, make sure that the wall surface is clean, dry, sound and free from flaking paint and distemper. It is a good idea to experiment on a piece of board before working an entire room.

Decorative stamps

There are many ready-made rubber and foam stamps available, or you can make your own from high-density foam. Draw on a simple motif, cut around it with a craft knife and then glue the sponge on to a small block of

wood. Apply paint to the motif with a small roller or by dipping it into a saucer of paint. Print randomly or in rows on the walls, or use the motif to create a border.

STAMPING A BORDER

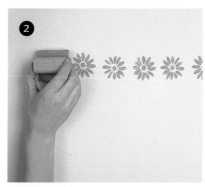

1. Use a spirit level and ruler to mark a straight guideline in pencil. Cover the surface of the stamp with paint. 2. Press the stamp firmly on to the wall. Remove it immediately. Take care not to drag the stamp or the motif will smudge.

Gilding

Gilding traditionally uses gold leaf. Unfortunately this is prohibitively expensive for most domestic situations, but Dutch metal leaf or aluminium leaf can produce an exotic gleam at a more affordable price. The leaf is stuck in place using a size, preferably water-based as this is easier to use.

As the leaf is quite expensive, it is best to limit gilding to small motifs or highlighting on borders. Another option is to make use of the wide range of metallic paints, creams and pens now available quite cheaply from craft stores and specialist suppliers.

GILDING OVER A STENCILLED MOTIF

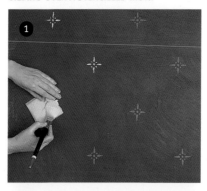

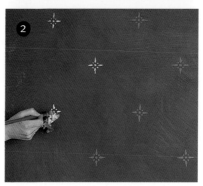

1. With a fine artist's brush, apply a water-based size sparingly over the motif. When the size is tacky, carefully take up a sheet of Dutch metal and place it over the area. Do not touch the metal with your fingers. 2. Rub the back of the leaf with a brush, then gently peel it back. Dust any excess away using a clean, soft artist's brush.

Paper
and fabric

Main picture A simple, monochrome repeat motif framed between battens adds a touch of order to a riot of objects collected from afar. *Right* The pattern on this wallpaper is large and could have been dominating, but its monochrome design and the restrained use of blues and creams in the rest of the room allows it to blend in perfectly.

Using wallpapers and other wallcoverings is a good way of providing pattern and texture in your home, as well as of covering poor plasterwork and other blemishes on the walls. You can co-ordinate them with curtain and upholstery fabrics, and many manufacturers produce complete ranges of fabrics and papers in designs and colourways designed to be used together to create a complete 'look'. However, colours and patterns that you have put together yourself may be more intriguing and satisfying than those designed to go together. Modern wallcoverings fall into three main categories – paper, vinyl and fabric – and within these groups there is an almost overwhelming choice of colours, designs, qualities and prices.

The types of wallcoverings that you choose must depend on the rooms for which they are destined. A covering for a bathroom or kitchen, for instance, should certainly be washable and perhaps have some water-resistant and even insulating properties, particularly if the room suffers from condensation. In a hallway or children's room, pick something that will resist wear and tear, and

A pretty trellis repeat pattern is the perfect 'lining' for this charming attic room with its wooden beams, and it co-ordinates well with the floral fabric used on both the windows and bedhead.

even scrubbing. If you have a dining room that you use mainly for formal entertaining, you could afford to clothe it in a purely decorative fabric.

Remember that colour and pattern in a wall-covering can influence the design and proportions of a room; the wallcovering will also affect and be affected by the furniture and by other fabrics and objects. A room with unfortunate proportions – too narrow, say, or too tall – can have these disadvantages minimized by clever use of wallpaper pattern. Dark paper makes a room seem smaller, while vertical stripes appear to push a ceiling upwards; you can also use borders and friezes to change proportions visually. In general, the busier the room, the more restrained the pattern in the wallcovering should be. Small rooms will benefit from smaller patterns – perhaps overall small floral or geometric designs – whereas large, imposing rooms can take wallcoverings with large designs or wide stripes.

Another important consideration is price. If you particularly like a wallcovering but cannot afford the quantity you need, consider using the expensive paper in a smaller area and complementing it with a paint effect or with a cheaper but co-ordinating paper over the greater part of the wall.

Stripes can add formality to a room, particularly when used in sombre colours such as these reds, blues and greens. They all combine to produce an impression of royal purple which is lightened by the pinks of the fabrics and the painting on the bedhead.

Wallpaper and vinyl

Many wallpapers have matching or co-ordinating fabrics that can be used to create diverse and interesting results. Here, the curtains and upholstery co-ordinate prettily with the wallpaper border without saturating the room with pattern. The pale blue of the print has been picked up and used on the woodwork.

In general, most of the wallcoverings used in the home are made of paper or vinyl. Within these two categories there are wallcoverings to suit practically any situation and style, from the darkest basement to the grandest of drawing rooms, as well as all the vicissitudes of hallway, bathroom or kitchen.

Types of wallcovering

We have available today a great number of choices: cheap, modern and cheerful papers which can be found in any wallpaper store; more specialist papers for the smarter rooms in style-conscious homes, available directly or to order from larger stores, specialist suppliers or interior decorators; and very carefully researched document papers for those who wish to re-create the style of another era. What you choose will depend on your budget, and also on the effect that you are trying to achieve.

Modern wallcoverings

Contemporary papers are primarily manufactured by the modern methods of rotary screen-printing, rotogravure, flexography and ink embossing. Each of these techniques can mass-produce papers at a rapid rate, making the wallpapers and vinyls sold in most stores comparatively cheap.

Wallcoverings include those which are practical in use: for instance, they may be damp-resistant, insulated, scuff-resistant and/or scrubbable; they also vary in the ease with which they can be hung. Vinyl wallcoverings resist steam and water, and can be scrubbed with a soft brush. Some are available ready-pasted, but for non-pasted types you should use a vinyl adhesive con-

Above A fresh, leafy border is used here to accentuate the line of the stairs and the small motifs are echoed in the tablecloth. *Right* Disciplined plaid paper echoes the colour of the cushions and carpet, and also helps to tone down their riotous floral motifs.

taining a fungicide because vinyl will not allow air through and, if it does become wet, it may not dry out.

Hanging ordinary wallcoverings has been made much easier with modern wallpaper pastes, folding tables and other equipment, but there are also ready-pasted papers (the paste is usually fungicidal) which are easier and less messy to hang. All you need to do with these is to fill the small trough (generally supplied) with water, and place it under the strip of wall to be papered. Draw the paper through the water, allow it to soak briefly, and then hang it on the wall.

Manufacturers have also simplified the task of stripping paper by introducing easy-to-strip wallcoverings so that, when the time comes to redecorate, all you need to do is to strip off the top layer of the old covering. Wipe the under-surface clean of old paste with a damp sponge, and it will be ready for the new wallpaper.

A number of different symbols have been devised to indicate whether a covering is ready-pasted, whether the pattern needs matching up and so on. These are printed on the wallpaper packaging, and many stores display large notices showing the symbols and explaining what each of them means.

Traditional wallpapers

The recent upsurge of interest in historical styles, and the attempts by many people to re-create these in their homes, has resulted in a revival of so-called 'document' papers. These are wallpapers reproduced in the same manner, and using the same techniques and colourways, as original papers from the eighteenth and nineteenth centuries which were found in stately homes during redecoration.

There are now many document papers available and, in addition to these, there are reproduction papers and new ranges devised from old archive papers but adjusted in colour and/or pattern to fit in with more modern schemes.

Although modern screen-printing methods are used for the majority of the historic papers reproduced today, a small number are still hand block-printed using the original wood blocks and virtually identical techniques to those used to make the original papers. These include a collection of nineteenth-century papers designed and printed by William Morris in the Arts and Crafts Movement.

Practical considerations

When buying wallcoverings, avoid cheap, thin wallpapers because these will tear easily when handled, especially when they are wet with paste. Always buy an extra roll to allow for miscalculations or accidents during hanging, as the colour of wallcoverings may vary if you buy them from different batches. You can keep the odd extra roll for possible repairs later, or ask the retailer if you will be able to

get a refund for unused rolls. If a roll varies in colour from one end to the other, exchange it for another one. If you buy paper with a selvedge, ask the retailer to trim it for you (selvedges are usually only found on hand-printed wallpapers, but it is a difficult task to trim them precisely and should be done by an expert). Do not stand rolls on their ends when storing, but lie them on their sides.

Plain wallcoverings or small repeat or overall patterns are the easiest to hang, and they are also more economical because they need little matching up. The larger the pattern, the more you will need to ensure a good match.

When pricing wallcoverings, remember that thin paper is the cheapest and that prices rise according to weight, pattern and also the method of machining.

Alternative wallcoverings

Watered silk is best used ungathered so that the subtle patterning in the fabric can be appreciated. This dark green silk has been used as the foil for a very stylish, traditional room interior.

Alternative soft wallcoverings include hessian, grasscloth, silk, woven fabrics, felt and cork. These are generally more expensive than wallpapers and vinyls, but can be worth the extra cost. Remember that you don't always have to cover a whole wall – it may be just as effective to use one of these materials in an alcove or as panels.

Advantages and disadvantages

Most alternative wallcoverings are thicker than paper and are very good for covering flaws in a wall. Many of them also act as good heat and sound insulators and, with special treatments and care, they can remain in good condition for longer than conventional coverings. Most fabrics can be treated with a dirt-resistant finish, and this will not prevent you from being able to spot-clean and vacuum them when you need to.

Disadvantages are that some of these materials – particularly silks – tend to get dirty rather easily, and their delicate texture makes them difficult to clean. With some, it is hard to disguise the seams when hanging them, and a few tend to fray at the seams. Many of these materials are also costly, although there are inexpensive alternatives for most, and it is often worth taking time to hunt around and seek them out.

Using fabric to demarcate and divide

A fabric wallcovering can help to divide a tall wall if you use paint, panelling or more formal wood panels below a dado rail, a section of fabric in the middle of the wall, and a frieze at

picture-rail level (or a section of paint above the picture rail). It can also be used to emphasize one wall or part of a wall, such as an alcove; this is particularly effective in a formal room where something rather more grand than wallpaper is required.

Using the fabric's characteristics

Choose the method of hanging to make the most of each fabric's special qualities. For instance, silk should always be hung where it will be viewed from various angles because it takes on a completely new character in different lights, whereas damasks and brocades are best used flat rather than gathered, to display their intricate patterns. Silk damask was used as a wallcovering in eighteenth-century mansions because the enormous pattern repeat – often as large as 2m (2½ yds) – had a splendid effect in long drops. Other fabrics also have particular qualities to offer.

Above Hand woven traditional kilim rugs can be used as 'pictures' hung on a wall. In this country-style kitchen, the rug adds visual and physical warmth to a basically practical interior. *Below* Fabric has been used in this ultra-chic bedroom as a soft and insulating wallcovering. Its disciplined gathers are held to the wall by a narrow carpet border at the top and a strip of beading is fitted at the skirting.

Toiles de Jouy

These fabrics, which are printed with a pictorial monochrome design on a plain white background, have been popular since they were first introduced in 1770. *Toiles* are suited for hanging as single lengths in straight panels from supporting poles, which can be placed at intervals around the room; they may also be used for emphasis in an alcove or above a fireplace, or fixed to battens as panels. They are particularly effective when used as flat, vertical wall panels because the picture or story can be best appreciated in this way.

Patterned chintzes

Chintzes – particularly those with traditional floral designs – can look marvellous on walls. When used like wallpaper, one of these can make a dramatic backdrop to a room's décor, particularly if a single colour from the design is picked up in a cornice, dado moulding or skirting to define the patterned area. Printed striped cotton fabric – in colours linking with the main fabric – would also make a good foil for floral chintz.

Felt and cork

These materials can provide a certain amount of sound-proofing by 'deadening' loud noises, as well as greatly improving heat insulation in a room.

For this reason they can be particularly useful in basements or attics, which are inclined to be unbearably hot in summer and cold in winter. Cork is available in a number of subtle dyed colours and also looks good in its natural state. It is an excellent wall finish in a room such as a study, where something workmanlike but attractive is needed. Felt is available in a wonderful range of colours, and can look splendid if two colours are juxtaposed to create a vivid effect.

Sheer fabrics

If used on the wall, sheer fabrics such as muslin and man-made curtaining materials should be shirred (gathered with special shirring tape) and hung from special tracking. They can be vacuumed and dusted, and taken down for the occasional wash, and this is important, as such delicate fabrics begin to look shabby very quickly if they are not kept in pristine condition.

Wallhangings

Do not forget textiles such as hand- and machine-woven tapestries, and oriental rugs – particularly flat-woven kilims – when you are considering how to clothe your walls. You can hang heavy tapestries, including antique ones, with barely any fullness by means of a fabric slot sewn to the reverse side of the piece, through which you can run a pole or rod. If you are interested in tapestry hangings, you don't have to buy expensive pieces; you could hang undamaged sections from larger tapestries or a series of smaller tapestries together as separate panels against a wall.

Oriental kilims are woven in exactly the same way as tapestries and also look marvellous as wallhangings. One of the advantages of these textiles is that they are heavy and stiff enough not to need stretching; they also last a very long time and require the minimum of care.

Tools and equipment

Wallpapering tools are not expensive, and if you do a lot of home decorating it will be a good idea to invest in a complete set. The most expensive piece of equipment that you may need will be a steam stripper for removing obstinate papers covering large areas, but you could hire this from a DIY outlet if you wish.

Stripping and cutting tools

You will need a straight and a serrated scraper for removing old paper. A wallpaper scorer is a more sophisticated tool, and is used before soaking the wall and then using a steam stripper so that the water and steam can penetrate the paper and help to remove it.

Cutting tools include a pair of shears with 25cm (10in) blades for making straight, accurate cuts. A trimming knife and a smaller pair of scissors are useful when making intricate cuts around complicated shapes such as electric sockets and light switches, or around a fireplace.

Pasting tools

You will need a soft-bristled paste brush, an old 125mm (5in) paintbrush which does not shed its bristles, and a paste bucket – line the bucket with a plastic bag so that you won't have to clean it, and tie a piece of string across the top for resting the brush on. You will also need a paper-hanging brush for smoothing the wallcovering on to the wall. A folding table is invaluable for cutting and pasting. This type of table is cheap, takes up little space and can come in useful as an extra dining table or for outdoor eating.

For ready-pasted paper you will need a plastic water trough instead of the bucket (this is often supplied with the paper), and a sponge instead of a paper-hanging brush.

Measuring tools

A plumbline and a soft pencil are essential for marking accurate guidelines on the wall before hanging the first length of paper. A chalked string line is ideal for ceilings (you can use this on walls too, instead of the pencil). You will also need a steel tape measure or straight-edge ruler for measuring lengths of paper. Initial accuracy is vital: if the first piece of paper is not straight, the whole scheme will go awry.

Finishing tools

Use a damp sponge for removing excess paste and a small wooden seam roller, if necessary, for pressing down edges on untextured wallpapers.

Pastes

Always choose the paste recommended by the manufacturer for lining paper and for top paper, or use a universal paste designed to be mixed up in various strengths to suit different types of wallcovering. Cellulose paste is suitable for all papers except vinyl wallcoverings, which must be hung with a paste containing fungicide to prevent mould from forming subsequently on the wall. Ready-mixed pastes are only economical for heavy textiles, and cold-water paste is best used on heavier papers.

Additional items

Other useful items include:
• A hand spray bottle to soak paper; this can often be more effective than a sponge.
• Plastic refuse sacks for removing stripped wallpaper and other debris.
• A length of wooden dowel or a stick for mixing paste.

Tools and equipment for wallpapering
1. Scraper
2. Plumb line
3. Craft knife
4. Scoring tool
5. Retractable tape measure
6. Wallpaper shears with 25cm (10in) blades
7. Paste bucket
8. Soft-bristled paste brush
9. Seam roller
10. Paper-hanging brush

Directory of wallpapers and vinyls

Wallpaper has been used with great ingenuity here to create a Gothic interior with ogee arches made from border papers, Gothic motifs on the ceiling and *fleur-de-lys* on the walls.

Wallpapers and vinyls – the most common types of wallcoverings – are mainly used for cosmetic purposes. Being cheap and quick to hang, they can transform an interior very quickly. Some of these papers are plain while others have pre-plastered or self-adhesive backings. Apart from the standard paper varieties, there are a number of specialized types such as embossed and flocked papers which have all kinds of possibilities.

Lining papers

There are four basic types of lining paper available:

- White lining paper: a pure-white paper specially made to provide a smooth surface for painting.
- Off-white lining paper: this comes in different weights and is used as a base for wallpaper. Medium-weight lining is suitable for most papers; heavyweight is designed for thick wallcoverings and vinyls.
- Brown lining paper: this is used under extra-heavy papers such as flock papers.
- Reinforced linen-backed lining paper: a heavy, white lining paper backed with fine linen scrim, which is intended for uneven surfaces.

Standard wallpapers

These are smooth papers with pattern and colour printed on them. Although inexpensive, they are the least resilient of the papers and vinyls. The range of designs, motifs, styles and colourways on standard papers is enormous, from florals and geometrics, stripes and checks to children's pictorial papers and all-over small motifs.

Hand-printed papers

Produced by block- or screen-printing methods instead of by machine, these papers have a unique depth and textural quality. The technique is used to reproduce historical or 'document' papers, and many famous traditional designs are still produced in this way. Designs range from all-over rosebud or geometric patterns to Regency stripes, *chinoiserie* and large Gothic motifs. Roll widths and sizes for these papers are not always standard.

Flock papers

Here, a fine pile is added to selected areas of the paper and this produces a raised-pile pattern not unlike velvet; this is designed to imitate old Italian silk brocades. Flock papers need to be handled carefully while being hung in order to prevent paste from staining the surface. Flocks with a vinyl base are more durable and easier to clean, and some are available ready-pasted.

Borders and friezes

These thin strips of painted wallpaper are usually supplied in rolls, often in designs to co-ordinate with wallpaper ranges. Friezes are usually hung at a picture-rail level and borders at dado level or around doorways.

Wallpapers for painting

The following types of papers are all designed to be painted over, and can be useful for concealing less than perfect surfaces.

Woodchip paper

This ubiquitous paper is designed specifically to cover flaws in the wall. The heavy paper base has a surface of wood chips which creates a porridge-like texture.

Plain, embossed wallpapers

These heavy papers have a texture pressed into them to form a whole range of patterns from basketweave to imitation plaster. Duplex embossed papers are made of two layers of paper. Anaglypta and Lincrusta papers were first introduced in the nineteenth century and are still available – almost unchanged – today. Anaglypta is made from wood pulp which is embossed with a texture or pattern; Lincrusta consists of linseed oil, welded to a backing paper and then embossed with a hessian or tile-like texture.

1. This is vinyl wall-covering at its best, a stylish traditional design imitating old Italian silk damask fabric. Its grandure is matched by the 'gold' decorations.

2. Modern rococo wallpaper creates an elegant background and enhances this stylish staircase.

3. This beautiful wallcovering is a splendid choice, its red and grey pattern perfectly at home with the grey panelling reflected in the mirror.

4. Narrow sand and blue stripes provide a practical, washable and cheerful finish for this child's room.

5. Paint-effect vinyl paper is useful in a bathroom.

6. Gold *fleur-de-lys* on deep red create a Gothic-style interior.

7. This delicate paper is similar to the style of the eighteenth-century hand-painted Chinese papers.

8. A very subtle luxury vinyl, relying on a delicate embossed pattern instead of colour for its effect.

9. An embossed vinyl paper in plain black makes an impressive 'Dutch still life' background for an ancestral portrait and a collection of artefacts.

10. A bold yet subtle wallpaper in varied tones of ocean blue, overlaid with a diaper pattern of tiny gold diamonds.

High-relief papers

These wallcoverings have a pronounced relief pattern imitating stone, pebbles, tiles, plaster or random relief. Good for concealing lumpy surfaces, high-relief papers are also designed to be painted.

Vinyl wallcoverings

These waterproof coverings are tougher than washable papers because they are made from backed polyvinylchloride, not simply from paper with a plastic coating. Vinyls stand up well to dirt, grease, grubby fingermarks and cooking splashes, and so are excellent for use in the kitchen, bathroom, play room and hallway. Since they are waterproof, water cannot escape through the surface, and so vinyls must be applied with a fungicidal adhesive to prevent mould from forming underneath them.

Foamed polyethylene

Also called Novamura, this is a soft, lightweight, easy-to-hang wallcovering available in a wide range of designs.

Foil and mylar papers

These papers are steam-resistant and they are useful in the bathroom and kitchen, as well as in dark areas where they will help to lighten the space. Avoid using them on very uneven surfaces because they will emphasize imperfections, or in sunny situations where they will create glare.

Directory of alternative coverings

Stone can be effective in a rustic interior. Here, it has been used to surround a fireplace, with half-logs on the surrounding wall, giving a country-cottage feel to the whole scheme.

You can use almost any fabric to cover your walls – plain canvas or highly patterned weaves, early or modern hand-woven tapestries, oriental rugs or the finest of muslins and other sheers. Some fabrics are specially prepared with a paper backing, and these are easier to hang or to fix than unbacked textiles. Nevertheless, with a little ingenuity most fabrics can be used in some way to clothe a room. Make sure that the fabric you use is not likely to shrink or distort, and that it can be cleaned. Many fabrics can be lightly sponged or vacuumed, or taken down for washing.

Cork
Cork wallcovering consists of a thin veneer of cork on a paper backing. It can look attractive in a study or in an attic room, where its insulating properties will also be useful.

Cotton
You can use a wide variety of cotton fabrics as wallcoverings, including canvas-type fabrics, muslin and gingham. *Toiles de Jouy* fabrics – with their single-colour printing and pictorial designs – were originally produced for covering walls, windows, beds and furnishings such as screens.

You will be able to stick some cottons directly on to the wall, but it is usually preferable to tack the fabric to battens or to shirr (gather) it with special shirring tape. A thin cotton will need an interlining between the wall and the cloth to conceal what lies directly behind it.

Felt
This soft, non-woven material comes in a range of wonderfully bright colours. Its dense texture makes it a good insulator; it is also reasonably hardwearing, will not fray and can be stuck directly on to the wall. Some felts have a paper backing.

Grasscloth and raffia
Grasscloth consists of natural woven grasses bonded to a paper backing, and needs to be hung with a special adhesive. Raffia can have either a medium- or heavyweight paper backing. One disadvantage of using raffia is that the coarseness of the material makes it rather difficult to hide the seams neatly.

Hessian
This unbleached woven fabric – normally sold in rolls and paper-backed – is easy to hang, although its coarse texture can make it difficult to conceal seams. You will need to use a heavy-duty wallpaper paste, spread on to the hessian backing with a roller. Furnishing hessian is the most economical type to buy. If you would like a more colourful effect, you can paint hessian with thin oil paint.

Linen
Linen is a hardwearing, good-looking fabric made from flax. You can stick a closely woven linen directly on to the wall although, if you are inexperienced, it will be easier to buy it as a wallcovering with a paper backing.

1. Large cobbles, set in cement, accentuate the rather Gothic-like quality of this stained glass window.

2. A Jacobean-style embroidered fabric has been tacked to battens and fixed by wooden moulding at ceiling height.

3. A medieval style tapestry hanging makes a really splendid backcloth for a display of antique books and boxes.

4. A subtle woven brocade in palest sand has been framed with a narrow maroon ribbon with small black and gold rosettes holding it in place.

5. Woven fabric gives a warm quality to this bathroom.

6. Woodchip wallcovering gives a no-nonsense, studious feeling to a library.

7. A machine-woven tapestry in a medieval design is well matched by the tapestry cushions and the 'table carpet' in the corner.

Silk

Woven silk cloth is glued to a background paper for hanging on walls; the walls must first be lined. Silk damasks and other figured silks were originally used in grand houses as wallcoverings. Today, silk is among the most luxurious of all the available finishes and looks superb as a backdrop to polished wooden furniture, but it does have disadvantages: namely that it is not particularly easy to hang, it fades easily under strong light and the seams are difficult to conceal. For these reasons, silk is really only suitable for very special rooms and circumstances.

Tapestries

Hand-woven tapestries are among the oldest of all wallcoverings and were used on the walls of cold and draughty castles during the Middle Ages. Antique tapestries are still available at auction, and new ones are also being produced by modern weavers. These are certainly expensive, but there is no more luxurious way of adorning a wall. Alternatively, you may be able to find machine-made copies of old tapestries, which will be considerably cheaper. You will need to hang tapestries from poles, as they will be too heavy to adhere to the walls.

Basic techniques: Preparation

A simple wallpaper pattern such as this pretty 'hearts' design, requires a perfectly flat, flaw-free wall to look its best. Taking time to prepare the wall is well worth the effort to get a fine result like this.

Although wallpapers are good for covering imperfections, the better you prepare the walls, the better the finished result will be. Strip off any existing wallcovering to leave the walls bare, as joins, blisters and even the pattern in an old wallcovering may show through the new one. If you are papering over sound paintwork, wash down the walls as you would before painting.

Stripping old paper

It is important to take time and care over this. Keep soaking the wall until the paper becomes loose: if you are dealing with an ordinary wallpaper, sponge it with warm water until it is soft enough to scrape off gently; with a washable paper which is stuck fast to the wall, you may need to use a steam stripper. Never scrape at the paper too vigorously or you may gouge out lumps of plaster with it, giving you more holes to fill later. Finally, wash down the walls with hot water to remove old paste and to loosen any last pieces of paper. Fill any holes or cracks.

If the wallpaper comes away too easily, it may mean that the plaster is in bad condition or that the surface is damp. Scrape away any flaking paint, then check and cure the problem and apply a coat of oil-based primer sealer to provide a sound surface.

Stripping standard wallpapers

Using a sponge or a large brush, saturate the paper with warm water. Go all the way around the room, by which time the water will have started to loosen the old paste where you started. If the first soaking has not been enough, go around the room once again with sponge and water. A little detergent added to the water will speed up the process, and a handful of wallpaper paste in the water will thicken it, preventing it from running down the wall and so giving it more time to soak. Finally, gently scrape away the loosened paper, keeping the scraper as flat as possible.

STRIPPING STANDARD PAPERS

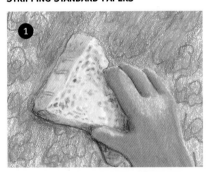

1. Use a sponge to saturate the paper with warm water. Repeat if necessary and add a little detergent to speed up the process. A small amount of wallpaper paste in the water will prevent it from running down the walls.

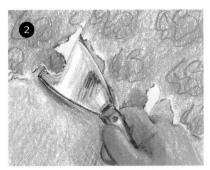

2. Scrape the paper away carefully, with the scraper held as flat as possible. Wait until the paper is really soaked so that you don't damage the wall.

Stripping difficult papers

Washable papers are made to withstand water, so soaking their surface will have little effect. Score the surface with a wallpaper scorer, wire brush, serrated scraper or sharp implement to allow the water to seep in, and then use a steam stripper; the holes that you have created in the surface will allow the steam to penetrate.

STRIPPING DIFFICULT PAPERS

1. Score the paper with a special scorer, wire brush, serrated scraper or other sharp tool.

2. Hold a steam stripper over the scored wallpaper, where the steam will be able to easily penetrate the paper. Scrape off old paper.

Stripping vinyl wallcoverings

Easy-strip wallcoverings are widely available and can be removed by releasing the bottom edge of the paper with a fingernail or a stripping knife. Pull each length upwards (not outwards). A layer of backing paper will remain on the wall to act as lining paper for the new wallcovering. If this backing starts to come away in places, you should remove it completely.

EASY-STRIP WALLCOVERINGS

Peel away vinyl by releasing the bottom edge. Pull the length upwards (not towards you). The backing paper is then left on the wall. If the backing paper begins to come away, remove it completely.

Sizing

On a bare plaster wall, you will need to apply a coat of glue size or diluted wallpaper paste to seal the surface; this is to prevent it from absorbing water contained in the paste on the back of the wallpaper. Sizing also leaves the surface slippery, which will make it much easier for you to slide the paper around when butting up adjoining lengths.

Basic techniques: Calculating quantities and cutting

Hanging wallpaper is a little more tricky than simply painting walls, so make sure that you have all the necessary tools and equipment to hand before you begin, and study their instructions carefully. The easiest papers to hang are plain, textured and woven wallcoverings, and miniprints. Large patterns need care in matching up all the repeats.

Calculating quantities

1 Measure the height of the walls and add 10cm (4in) as overhang allowance, and one length of the paper's pattern repeat (if you need to match a pattern); this is the length you will need for each drop. Divide the total length of a roll – usually 10.5m (34ft) – by the length of the drop to calculate how many lengths you will get from one roll.

2 Measure the distance around the room and divide the measurement by the width of a roll – usually 52cm (21in) – to establish how many drops you will need to paper the whole room.

3 Divide the number of drops needed to paper the room by the number of drops you will get from one roll to calculate the number of rolls needed to cover the room. Round this figure up to the next whole roll, and add an extra roll in case of miscalculations or accidents.

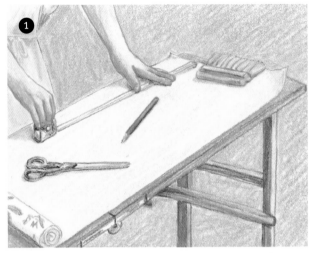

1. Measure the paper on a pasting table, allowing an extra 10cm (4in) before cutting, to give 5cm (2in) for trimming at the top and bottom.

Measuring

Measure the height of each wall at either end and in the centre to find the maximum length for the strips of paper, then allow an extra 10cm (4in) before cutting. This will give you an extra 5cm (2in) for trimming top and bottom, at ceiling and skirting. Measure the ceiling in the same way, allowing an excess of 5cm (2in) for trimming at either end.

Cutting

Unroll a short length of paper to check that you have the pattern the right way up. Trim the end of the roll so that it is square, then use a steel tape measure and pencil to mark out lengths; use wallpaper shears to cut the paper. Cut off individual lengths as you go, or cut several lengths at a time so that one can be soaking while you are hanging another. Mark consecutive numbers on the back and make a note of which end is the top.

When using plain or randomly patterned paper, you can cut the whole roll into lengths at once. However, if there is a pattern repeat, it is advisable to cut out and hang the first piece of paper before matching up the second against it. If you are pasting a large pattern, always try to position a complete motif at the top of the wall. With

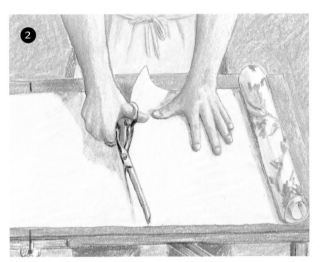

2. Unroll a short length of paper to check that the pattern is the right way up. Trim the end square, mark out the length and use wallpaper shears to cut the paper.

a diagonally matching paper, try to work from two or three rolls at a time to minimize waste in pattern-matching; drape lengths over a table and align them carefully before cutting. Keep all the odd lengths, as they may well come in useful for papering around doors or under windows or, later on, for small repairs.

MATCHING PATTERNS

Match up the pattern at the top of the new length before cutting. This is easily done with a small pattern.

Large or diagonally matching patterns will create bigger offcuts. Work with two or three rolls at a time to minimize wastage.

Basic techniques:
Pasting and folding

The secret of successful wallpaper hanging is patience and thoroughness – not just when matching patterns, but throughout the whole process. Don't forget to mark a vertical on the wall before hanging the first piece, and be sure to match up a pattern carefully on the next length before cutting. Paper the ceiling first, to prevent paste from splashing on to finished walls.

Pasting

Having cut each length, lay it decorative side down on the pasting table with the long sides parallel to those of the table. To avoid pasting the table, let the short edge of the paper overlap the end of the table by about 2.5cm (1in), and let the long edge nearest to you overlap the table edge by about 5cm (2in).

1 You must cover the paper thoroughly with paste because bubbles will form under any dry patches, so paste the paper in two halves lengthways. Divide the paper into three imaginary long strips. Load the brush and paste the central portion, then work towards the edge furthest from you.

2 When these portions are thoroughly pasted, pull the paper towards you, allowing it to overlap the table edge by 5cm (2in). Brush the paste outwards towards that edge.

3 Keep the brush well coated with paste, and continue feeding the paper along the table until you have pasted about half the length. Fold the top edge over to the centre line.

4 Paste the second half of the length in the same way. Fold the other short edge of paper over to meet the first one in the middle, taking care not to crease the fold.

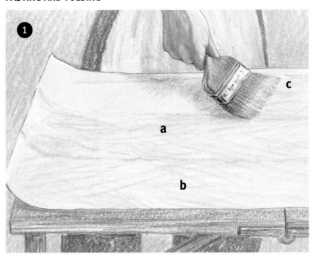

1. Divide the paper into three imaginary strips and paste in the following order: a. middle strip; b. edge furthest away from you; c. edge nearest you.

2. Paste the paper to about half its length and then fold it edge-to-middle.

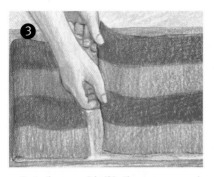

3. Paste the second half in the same way and fold the other edge to the middle.

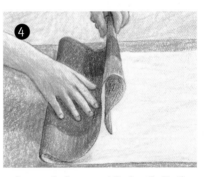

4. Once soaked, open out the length. Starting at the top end, fold the paper back on itself in concertina folds.

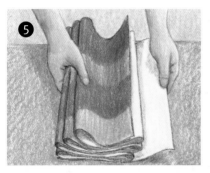

5. Continue in this way for the whole length, taking great care not to crease the folds.

Soaking

Place the length of pasted paper on a clean, dry surface to soak until it is supple, while you paste or hang another length. You will need to leave a medium-weight paper for about five minutes, and a heavyweight paper for 10–12 minutes before hanging. Keep the soaking time constant for each length to avoid variations in stretching (and therefore pattern-matching).

When it is ready to hang, unfold the soaked length and then fold the paper back on itself concertina-style. This makes the length easier to carry to the wall and hang.

Hanging lining paper

Hang lining paper horizontally, using long pieces to avoid the difficulty of achieving perfect joins. Mark a guideline for the first length, starting at the top of the wall and overlapping the first length on to the ceiling by about 2.5cm (1in); trim this off after hanging. Overlap each corner by about 12mm ($\frac{1}{2}$in). Horizontal lengths should butt up: overlaps would show through the eventual wallcovering.

Marking guidelines for wallpaper

Mark a vertical line on the wall as a guide to hanging the first length of paper by using a plumbline and a soft pencil; alternatively, suspend a plumb bob on a chalked string from the top of the wall and snap it against the surface to leave a vertical line. Draw a new guideline as you come to each wall, and check the vertical again after hanging a few lengths. On the ceiling, measure equal distances from the wall at each end of the ceiling, and snap a chalked string between the two points to provide your guideline.

MARKING A VERTICAL GUIDELINE

Use a plumb line on a chalked string from the top of the wall and snap it against the surface to leave a vertical line. Check the vertical every few lengths and make a new line at each new wall.

Basic Techniques: Hanging wallpaper

Hanging ready-pasted wallpaper

Cut a length of paper, roll it up loosely with the pattern facing inwards (top edge outside) and immerse it in a water trough, following the manufacturer's instructions. Continue as for ordinary paper.

Papering around corners

To ensure a neat finish, the corner length needs to be cut and rejoined.

- Internal corners: Measure from the edge of the last length to the corner and add 12mm (½in). Cut the corner piece to this width. Hang this strip with its uncut edge next to the last piece of paper. Hang the offcut to overlap the cut edge.
- External corners: Measure as for an internal corner but allow a 2.5cm (1in) overlap. Paste the strip and smooth it around the corner. Position the offcut close to the corner, lining up the pattern.

When papering a room, start in the corner next to the window sill and work outwards from the largest window, away from the light in both directions. On the ceiling, begin by working parallel with the main window and then work away from the light.

Hanging ordinary wallpaper

1 Unfold the top half of the pasted paper and position the edge against your vertical guideline, leaving a 5cm (2in) edge at the top.
2 Run a paper-hanging brush firmly right down the centre of the paper length, and then in an outwards direction to expel air bubbles and smooth the paper.
3 At the ceiling and skirting joins, run the back of your shears along the paper, peel back the edge, cut along the creaseline and then brush the paper back into place.
4 Align the second length of paper, sliding it in place with your fingertips. Brush the join with the paper-hanging brush, and press the edges with a seam roller, if necessary.

DIRECTION OF HANGING

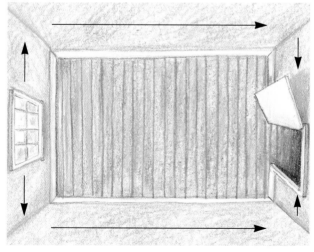

Work from the window in both directions, towards the door.

HANGING ORDINARY WALLPAPER

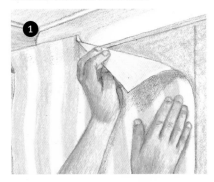

1. Place the top half of the pasted paper and position the edge against the vertical guide-line, leaving a little at the top for trimming.

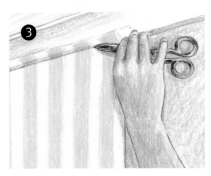

2. Brush flat down the centre of the length with a paper-hanging brush.

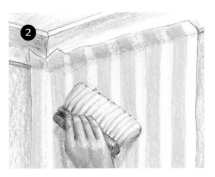

3. Run the back of the shears along the paper, peel back the edge, cut along the creaseline and brush paper back into place.

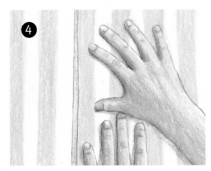

4. Slide the next piece into position with your fingertips to butt up to the first piece.

INTERNAL CORNER

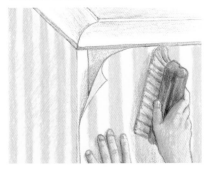

Hang the first strip with its uncut edge next to the last full piece. Hang the second piece so that it overlaps the cut edge of the first strip of wallpaper.

EXTERNAL CORNER

Allow a 2.5cm (1in) overlap. Paste and smooth round the corner. Position the offcut close to the corner, lining up the pattern.

SQUARE LIGHT FITTING

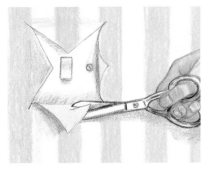

Cut out from the centre to the corners. Trim off the flaps and smooth edges into place.

Papering around doors and windows

Hang complete lengths until you are less than a full width of paper from the frame. Rub the back of your shears across the overlap with the frame to make a creaseline. Ease the paper away from the wall, trim and brush into place.

Papering around a fireplace

Cut into the paper at each change in angle, and then smooth and trim each flap against the solid part of the fireplace, working downwards.

Papering around a light fitting

Switch off the mains electricity. Loosen the cover plate and then hang the length of paper up to the fitting. Cut a hole in the paper, about 5mm (¼in) smaller than the plate, and smooth the paper on to the wall beneath the plate. Finally, carefully replace the plate.

For square sockets and switches, press the paper against the switch and make small cuts, radiating from the centre of the fitting to 12mm (½in) beyond its edges. Brush the paper around the block and trim the flaps.

Papering an archway

Paper the outer wall first, allowing a 2.5cm (1in) margin with small cuts in it to allow for the curve. Fold and smooth the flaps around it. Carefully paper the inside of the arch using two pieces of paper cut to the exact width of the arch.

Papering a window reveal

For a window reveal, paper the reveal first, aligning the paper with the edge of the wall. Then paper the outer wall, allowing a small margin to cover the papered reveal.

Basic techniques:
Friezes, borders, covings and cornices

The attractive cornices and ceiling rose in this tall, traditional room have been painted white to match the woodwork and ceiling, and they are divided by narrow bands of gold that matches the ornate gilded mirror frame. The whole room has a sumptuous, but tasteful appeal.

Friezes, borders, covings and cornices are the finishing touches which can make a room look as though it has been professionally designed. Most manufacturers now produce friezes and borders to compliment their wallpaper ranges, while covings and cornices are available in various designs, from plain, concave shapes to sophisticated mouldings.

Applying a frieze

Friezes are available as pre-cut designs which you can use at cornice, picture-rail or dado level – with or without a matching wallpaper. You can use a border in any position where you would like to frame something – perhaps a piece of wallcovering, a door or even around a window.

To apply a frieze, measure around the walls at the height at which you wish to fix it. With a pencil, draw a soft line to mark where the bottom edge of the frieze is to be, using a spirit level to make sure that it is straight.

APPLYING A FRIEZE

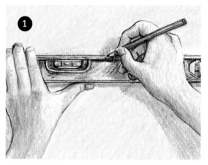

1. Make horizontal guidelines using a spirit level and pencil.

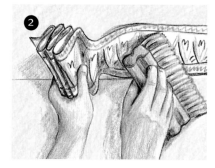

2. Concertina frieze loosely after pasting, line up the bottom edge with the pencilled guidelines and smooth into place.

Lay the frieze pattern side down in the middle of your pasting table and brush on the paste, making sure that the adhesive reaches right to the edges. Concertina the frieze loosely and then stick it to the wall with the bottom edge lining up with your pencil guideline. Smooth into place with a paper-hanging brush.

Applying and mitring a border

Borders devised to be used with ordinary wallpaper paste will not stick on to vinyl wallcoverings, so you will need to use self-adhesive vinyl borders, or special overlap adhesive to apply ordinary paper borders.

To apply a border, first mark out the desired shape of the panel on the wall, using a spirit level and pencil. Cut each piece of border paper 10cm (4in) longer than the exterior of the panel. Paste the strips and then stick them to the wall, making sure that they run accurately along your guidelines, and leaving a 5cm (2in) allowance at each end to overlap with the adjoining strip at the corner.

To mitre the border, place a ruler diagonally at one corner through the parts where the border pieces intersect on the outside and inside edges. Using a craft knife, slice through both layers of paper along this line to create a mitred corner. Carefully, peel off the overlapping border strips and remove the offcuts, and then brush down the join with a paper-hanging brush. Repeat with the other three corners.

MITRING A BORDER

1. For mitres, use a craft knife to carefully slice through both layers of paper along a diagonally-placed ruler.

2. Peel off overlapping strips and remove offcuts. Brush down the join.

Fixing coving and cornicing

Make sure that the walls and ceiling are dry and dust-free. Temporarily support the lengths of coving or cornicing with masonry nails at top and bottom, and mark their position with a pencil. Allow extra for mitred joins at external corners, and use the templates supplied to cut the mitres. Remove the nails, then sand any rough edges on the moulding and on the areas of wall and ceiling to be covered.

Mix the adhesive and spread it on the top and bottom coving or cornicing edges with a filling knife. Press the moulding in place between the guidelines, and replace the masonry nails temporarily to hold it while the adhesive dries. Remove the excess adhesive with a filling knife and fill in the joins.

FIXING COVING

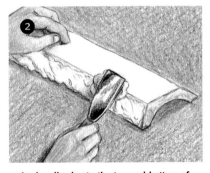

1. Temporarily support the coving with masonry nails and lightly mark the position with a pencil.

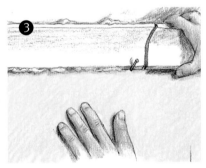

2. Apply adhesive to the top and bottom of the coving edges with a filling knife.

3. Press the moulding in place and replace masonry nails temporarily to hold in place until the adhesive dries.

Basic techniques: Fabrics

Fabric wallcoverings usually have a backing and can be stuck straight on to the wall. Here, this silk covering makes an excellent background for paintings.

Thick or heavy fabrics – such as grasscloth, hessian and felt – will help to disguise irregularities in a wall; thinner materials tend to emphasize them. For this reason, if you are using finer materials you must hang lining paper and, if the covering is sheer or semi-transparent, apply a coat of neutral emulsion before hanging.

Sticking fabric to a wall

As has been discussed, most fabric wallcoverings – even silk – are backed with paper to make them easy to hang. However, with care you can hang even an unbacked fabric, provided that it is of a reasonable weight and has a firm weave. When securing an unbacked fabric, it is important that you apply the adhesive to the wall, not to the fabric. It is also a good idea to choose fabrics which are mildew- and stain-resistant and, of course, stretch- and fade-resistant. If any edges become frayed during the hanging process, you could cover them with braid or with a trim of chrome or brass.

There are two excellent ways of hanging an unbacked fabric other than pasting: the first is battening and the other is by hanging the fabric as though it were a curtain.

Stretching fabric over battens

Stapling fabric directly on to the walls is a satisfactory way of dealing with children's or other rooms, where the overall effect – rather than the detail – is what is important. However, it is easier to achieve a better-looking and more professional finish if you stretch the fabric between battens, which will give an altogether smoother look. You can also work with smaller widths of fabric if you wish, to create a more panelled effect.

If you intend to hang paintings, prints or anything else on the walls, you must work out where they are to go before you hang the fabric so that you can position any battens to hold the picture hooks or fixtures. Once the fabric is in place, it will be quite easy to feel where the battens are and to hammer hooks or nails through them. Interlining the fabric with a layer of polyester wadding (available in various weights from craft stores and department stores) will give the panels a plump, upholstered look.

GLUING FABRIC TO WALLS

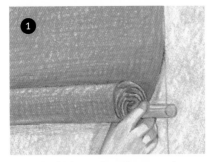

1. Roll the fabric round a pole, secure the top to the top of the glue-covered wall and then, keeping the fabric taut, unroll it by degrees down the wall on to the adhesive.

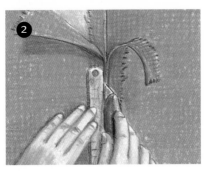

2. Overlap the fabric edges and then slice through both layers to get a neat seam with a sharp blade.

Hanging fabric on a wall

You can suspend a closely woven linen or wool, or a heavy hanging, from a rod or pole (using loops sewn to the reverse if necessary) and allow it to hang free at the bottom. Another way of fixing fabric to a wall is to use long plastic strips with 'jaws' to hide jagged edges and an adhesive strip to hold the fabric taut.

ATTACHING FABRIC OVER BATTENS

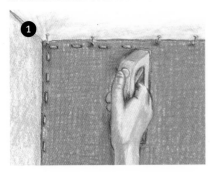

1. Turn the fabric under at the edges and tack it in place, then staple at regular intervals with a staple gun.

2. Use decorative braid, glued in place, to cover over the top of tacks and staples.

Shirring fabric (gathering)

For shirring, you will need approximately three times the width of the wall in fabric in order to produce a really effective result, so use a relatively cheap one such as muslin; this will also readily form tiny pleats.

   You can create a shirred effect by gathering the fabric with shirring tape before attaching this to the walls, or by slotting the fabric on to flat wooden rods at the top and bottom of each fabric length. The rods are then attached below the ceiling and above the skirting. To do this use either hanging wires or screw the rods to the wall, placing a 6mm (¼in) rubber washer between them and the wall to prevent crushing the shirring.

SHIRRING FABRIC

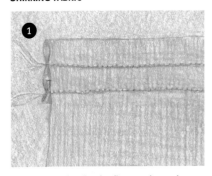

1. Stitch a casing for the flat wooden rod, making the channel just large enough to slip the rod through easily.

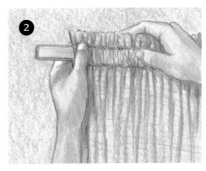

2. Iron the fabric then pull the rod through so that the length is evenly gathered.

3. Secure the rods to the top and bottom of the walls, or at the top of obstacles such as door and window frames.

Tiling, panelling and alternative wall finishes

Ceramic tiles and wood panelling can, between them, cover a multitude of sins, including poor or damaged plaster; wood can also have insulating material packed in behind it to prevent heat loss. Both are very attractive materials – tiles lending a particularly colourful decorative quality with the possibility of bright, sharp colours, and wood bringing a calmer, warmer look to a room. They are also extremely durable and will retain their good looks for generations.

Ceramic tiles are the most popular form of wallcovering after printed wallpaper, and are produced in a wide range of sizes, shapes and colourways. They can be hand- or machine-made, hand- or machine-decorated, plain or patterned, glazed or unglazed. The obvious use of tiles is in wet areas, and they can create beautiful yet hygienic finishes in the bathroom, kitchen, utility room and cloakroom, where they are especially good as splashbacks behind sinks and basins. In a hot climate, where the cool surface of the tiles is refreshing and welcome, they can be used in living areas as well. You will be able to produce interesting effects by using plain colours with borders, by mixing patterned tiles as friezes or randomly among plain tiles, or by buying a series of tiles to make up a complete mural.

Above The kitchen mixer tap sprouts directly from the tiled wall – a neat and practical idea. *Centre* A frieze of pictorial tiles adds interest to the earthy colours of the diagonally-set tiles. *Below* A patchwork of plain-coloured tiles complements the bright colours of the plate and fruit.

Main picture Green and white tiles set diagonally behind a worktop make a practical and interesting finish to this Provençale kitchen. *Left* Wooden tongue-and-groove 'match-boarding' has been used to line this bathroom completely and to box in the ceramic basin. Wood panelling provides insulation and has a warm feel. Pale blue paint adds lightness to the whole room.

Wood creates a warm, smooth and attractive surface, and has sound- and heat-insulating properties. Modern finishes on wood make it easy to maintain, so it is an ideal covering for walls and ceilings in most rooms in the house (wooden panelling in all sorts of colours and finishes is specifically manufactured for covering walls, and panelling suitable for both walls and ceilings is sold in board form or as sheets). Wooden boards are easy to fix and can make a good wall surface in rooms such as the bathroom. When varnished, sealed or covered with a gloss paint, they will be impervious to water. You can apply wooden boards vertically, horizontally or diagonally. Panelling often looks its best when run from the floor to dado level, with paint or wallpaper above.

Sheet panelling is usually made of thin plywood with a real wood veneer or a printed plastic or paper surface, simulating various types of decorative wood. It is more expensive than board panelling. Embossed panels with deeply textured wood effects are also available. Solid wood panelling has a wonderful quality but is very expensive indeed, although you may be able to find old panelling in an architectural salvage yard.

Tiling and panelling

Ceramic tiles and wood panelling are special and sometimes expensive materials, and it pays to find exactly what you want. Handmade tiles cost more, but their colours and texture have attractive slight variations that will give your walls greater depth. The choices in wood panelling are between whitewood (which is best painted), various types of pine and more unusual decorative woods.

This unusual modern Gothic interior combines many design ideas successfully. The cupboard doors are panelled and painted white, matching the white of the wall panelling and the tiles are in contrasting black. The Shaker idea of lifting chairs off the floor onto pegs is both practical and an effective way of keeping this small room uncluttered.

Choosing wall tiles

Wall tiles differ from floor tiles in that they are thinner, smaller and less robust (they are not strong enough to be used on floors). They are generally made of earthenware or white china clays and have a decorative glazed surface that may be hand-decorated, printed, moulded or plain. Colour options are almost limitless, and patterns range from floral and figurative to geometric. Although there are standard dimensions, tiles do come in a variety of sizes from tiny, mosaic-sized tiles on a mesh backing to 10 or even 15cm (4 or 6in) square. They are also available in rectangular and other original shapes, and as small insets or drop-ins for use as an integral part of the design.

Wall tiles are available in much glossier finishes than floor tiles, which for safety must be matt or semi-matt and non-slip. On walls this is obviously not a problem, so there is an enormous choice of glaze qualities as well as of pattern, shape and colour.

Tiles may be sold singly, in boxes or made to order. If you are buying them in boxes, take the first available opportunity to check that none of the tiles are chipped or cracked.

Using plain tiles

You can lay tiles to form geometric patterns and *trompe l'oeil* effects by carefully planning colours and shapes: use them horizontally, diagonally or vertically, or cut them diagonally to produce triangles. You can also design the tiling so that the colour changes gradually as it runs down the wall. Working with two plain colours can produce a very stylish effect.

Using patterned tiles

You could use occasional decorative tiles to liven up an area of plain tiling, or add a border or dado edge to finish off a run of tiles. However, you will achieve more interesting effects by running a row of matching decorative tiles as a frieze through a wall of plain tiles. This does not have to form a straight line, but could create a frame or an angled pattern in the wall.

Alternatively, position tiles so as to build up a pattern to cover a complete area. If you are bringing a Victorian flavour into your home, reproduction period tiles are widely available; there are also reproductions of older Delft

Above Small navy blue tiles have been used with panache to contrast with the purpose-built shelving units, then built up into a decorative pyramid in the centre and finished off with a mosaic border. *Right* Tiny mosaic tiles are finished off with a tiled border of wave motifs in a crowded bathroom that is unified by the generous use of white.

tiles as well as contemporary hand-painted floral tiles from parts of the world where their production has never ceased. Sets of colours, known as panels, create a complete picture when fixed to the wall.

A recent development is the appearance of numerous 'paint-effect' tiles, including stippled, marbled, dragged, water-splashed and shadow-strip effect; these can make an attractive alternative to solid-colour or heavily patterned tiles, and can be a softer way of treating walls in a small bathroom than white or plain colours.

Choosing wood panelling

Wood panelling is an excellent choice for many of today's interiors. It is easy to attach, looks good, and is available in a wide range of woods, grains and colours. Alternatively, you can paint the panelling any colour you like, or stain it so that the natural grain will still be visible. There are many stain colours now available, including not only the most obvious wood colours but bright primary shades as well.

Types of panelling

There are two types of wooden boards: tongue-and-groove and shiplap. Both can look decorative if used as panelling, although tongue-and-groove is slightly more sophisticated. Pine boards are inexpensive and can take varnish, seal, paint or stain. They will mellow with age, and it is not necessary to paint them – their colours and grain will look best if waxed or sealed with a matt seal. Tongue-and-groove boarding was used by the colonial Americans to help insulate their homes. It would be taken to dado height – or slightly higher – and was

often painted in plain, positive colours, becoming an attractive backdrop to the furniture. Paints similar to the milk-based paints used by the colonialists are available, and this type of panelling suits the disciplined informality of many homes today.

Buying wood

When buying any decorative wood for your home, check that it has been ecologically grown and not taken from the world's rapidly depleting rainforests. Many desirable woods are now being carefully 'farmed' to ensure that future supplies and the environment will not be endangered.

Choose pieces that will be sufficiently long to stretch the whole of the desired height or width in order to avoid ugly joins. And you must allow the wood to lie in your house for two or three weeks to acclimatize, as this will prevent the boards from shrinking once they are up on the wall.

Other wall finishes

There are a number of other possible finishes for walls, in addition to ceramic tiles and wood panelling. Although less versatile, these have useful specific functions and can be very attractive and decorative when used in the right places. The options here include mirror tiles and panels, cork tiles and plastic laminates.

This spectacular patio room has been decorated in a patchwork of broken tiles worked into a haphazard mosaic of wonderful lively colours, giving the impression of a bright, floriferous climbing plant. The table too, has been covered in a more formal mosaic, using rose motifs from broken tiles.

Mirrors and mirror tiles

Mirrors have an invaluable contribution to make in the home, because they bring in extra light and can appear to double the space. In fact, mirror is probably the most effective way of making a small room seem larger, and in constricted, narrow and dark areas of the house it can often fundamentally alter the quality of the space. Framed mirrors are decorative in their own right and, depending on the frames you choose, can contribute to the chosen style of the interior. For instance, heavily carved gilded frames will add to the formality of a grand room, whereas a wide, flat wooden frame will complement a modern one.

If you are mirroring over a whole wall, you could consider framing the mirror with shelves on either side, with architraving above and a low bookcase or seat at the bottom; this arrangement can look particularly effective if it is reflecting a French window and a garden. However, large-scale mirroring does not necessarily require a frame at all. In a bathroom or in alcoves you could run mirroring from wall to wall, enhancing the feeling of space and light, and using the mirror as a protection from water – just like ceramic tiles. Make sure that

the mirror is facing something worth reflecting: in a small bathroom, for instance, a wall of pretty ceramic tiles, a mural, a bath with panelled sides or a four-legged Victorian bath would add to the pleasure of a mirrored wall.

Mirror tiles are comparatively easy to stick to the wall, while plastic mirror is ideal for a bathroom because it does not steam up to the same extent as glass mirror tiles will do, and is less likely to break while being applied to the wall. Mirror sheeting is much more expensive; it is also very heavy and needs screwing to the wall. If the surface is not completely flat the image will be distorted and, as most walls do have some irregularities, you should think in terms of lining them

Below Sea blue and green mosaic has been used on the walls and floor of this small bathroom, echoing the watery theme of the remarkable aquarium wall. *Right* Brick walls can make a pleasant interior surface, particularly for a cottage or country look. Here, the bricks have been painted white and used as a background for the wicker bedhead.

with plywood set on battens. Having said this, mirror sheeting does have the advantage over tiles of giving an unbroken reflection, so it would be a better choice for use in a living room or dining room.

Miscellaneous tiles

There are a number of alternative wall tiles and each has different characteristics, making some more suitable for the kitchen, bathroom, utility room and work room, and others for the living room. Most are easy to fix, provided that you use the correct techniques and adhesive. Into this category come metallic tiles: these are heatproof, so their most obvious use is behind the cooker in the kitchen. They are washable but will show up any splashmarks, so you will need to wipe them frequently. Also available are vinyl and plastic tiles: these can do much the same job as mirror tiles and are easier to apply to the wall, but will not give clear reflections. Brick tiles can be useful: for example, for the area of wall behind a free-standing fireplace and in other areas where you would like a natural, cottagey finish.

Mosaic tiles are often more effective than standard tiles in a very small bathroom, being more in proportion

with the size of the room. Cork tiles, like cork wallcoverings, have good insulating qualities. They are produced not only in the natural colours that you would expect – from light honey to rich chestnut – but also in a number of lightly patterned styles.

Plastic laminates

Plastic laminates (such as Formica and Corian) are tough, durable and heat-resistant, and can create an effective wall finish in a bathroom, kitchen, utility room, shower room or corridor. However, they are inclined to give a room a somewhat hygienic look.

Floor materials on walls

Rubber flooring makes an insulating, resilient and tough wall finish; it comes in a great many colours and several different textures, and is particularly suited to a minimalist décor. Some home stores and department stores have a selection, and they are worth considering.

Vinyl tiles or sheeting are appropriate for the bathroom and kitchen, but never use them as a substitute for damp-proofing. Always get any damp problems treated and resolved before covering the walls.

Tools and equipment

Right Ceramic tiles are brittle and will snap comparatively easily along any score mark you have made. Avoid using felt pen on the underside when tiling because it may permeate and appear as a stain under the glaze.

It is absolutely essential that you have the correct tools and equipment for applying wall finishes. The materials are often heavy and need firm fixing, and the tools cannot be improvised. Tiles must have the correct adhesive, while for wood panelling you will need several types of saw (unless you ask the supplier to cut the wood).

Tools and equipment for tiling
1. Rubber grouter
2. Tile file
3. Tile saw
4. Tile pincers
5. Tile cutter
6. Serrated spreader
7. Notched plastic adhesive spreader
8. Tile clippers

Tools for ceramic tiles

For ceramic tiling you will need a trowel or spatula for applying adhesive to the wall, and a notched plastic spreader to draw the adhesive over the tile in a series of ridges on which to bed the tiles. You will also need at least one type of tile cutter: there are many of these to choose from, and some incorporate a measuring gauge for very accurate cutting. Tile clippers are handy for cutting

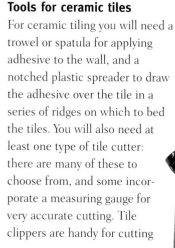

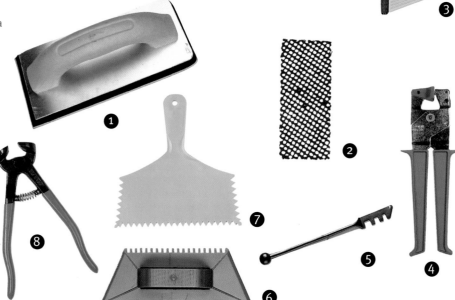

tiles to fit around pipes and other awkward protuberances and, if you wish to smooth the rough edges of cut tiles, a tile file will be useful. You will also need a rubber grouter or sponge for filling joins with grout and a large sponge for wiping the tiles clean. You will have to find a true horizontal and mark it with battens to support the first row of tiles, so you will need a spirit level, pencil, hammer and masonry nails for fixing the battens.

Adhesives and grout

When tiling in a bathroom or kitchen, or in any damp area such as a shower cubicle, choose waterproof adhesive. In other situations, thin-bed adhesive – which is spread about 3mm ($1/_8$in) thick – will be easier to manipulate. Cement grout is supplied as a powder to be mixed with water into a creamy paste. Plain tiles can look very stylish if given a grout in a contrasting colour. If you would like a coloured grout, add a powdered pigment or use a ready-mixed coloured grout.

Equipment for wood panelling

You will need several types of saw for cutting wood panelling, some of which can be hired from DIY outlets (if you prefer not to do the sawing at home, measure up very carefully and ask the supplier to cut the wood specially for you). For cutting sheet materials you will need a circular saw with a fine blade or a cross-cut handsaw, preferably one with eight teeth to 25mm (1in). When cutting individual boards and battens, use a tenon saw. You will also need a pad saw or a power jigsaw for cutting holes.

Other necessary wall finish equipment includes masonry nails, claw and pin hammers, a nail punch, a drill, a steel tape measure, a spirit level and a set square; panel clips are useful for holding boards. For fixing the panels, you will need a mastic gun and adhesive cartridges.

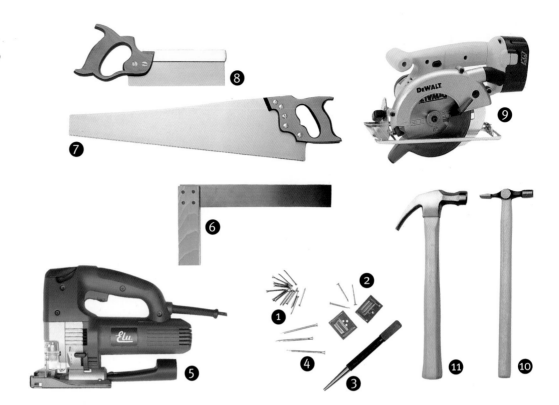

Above Tools and equipment for panelling
1. Round wire nails
2. Lath nails
3. Nail punch
4. Panel pins
5. Powered jigsaw
6. Try-square
7. Cross-cut hand-saw
8. Tenon saw
9. Circular saw
10. Pin hammer
11. Claw hammer

Left This collection of tools illustrates the main essentials that you will need when working with wood panelling. Make sure that your saws are sharp and kept in a place where their teeth will not become damaged. When nailing close to the end of a piece of wood, use oval nails with their longer side along the grain.

Directory of tiles and wood panelling

Pine boards often look their best when painted. These very simple planks have been painted the same colour as the fireplace, giving a unifying background to a collection of old-fashioned tools.

Choosing tiles can prove to be a real problem, because there are literally thousands on offer. The first step is to decide whether you would like plain or patterned, large or small, handmade or machine-made tiles, and then to think specifically about colours and designs. Do not rush into a decision, and remember that the simplest solution is often the best. Make the most, too, of the wonderfully lucid colours that glaze gives to tiles – if you are simply after a neutral colour, you will be able to achieve it more cheaply with a washable wallcovering.

Panelling poses less decision-making problems because there is a limit to what is available. In this case perhaps the most difficult question is how to finish off the panelling, which you could paint or varnish, seal or stain.

Ceramic tiles

The two basic aspects to consider with tiles are their shape and design, and many combinations are available.

Shapes

Modern ceramic wall tiles consist of slabs of clay decorated on the front with a coloured glaze. They are fired to produce an extremely good-looking and durable heat-, stain- and water-resistant surface. Most wall tiles are square or rectangular, and the most common type – known as a 'field' tile – has square edges, sometimes with spacer lugs to allow space between the tiles for grouting. 'Universal' tiles, with one or two rounded, glazed edges, are produced for shelving and for finishing off half-tiled walls.

Also available are interlocking hexagonal tiles, ogee-shaped 'Provençales' and smaller infill tiles so that, just by shape alone, you can create different effects. However, bear in mind that square and rectangular tiles are, on the whole, easier (and also much cheaper) to lay. Quadrant tiles are round-edged, pencil-shaped tiles designed for use as border tiles on window sills and other edges.

Designs

Plain tiles are manufactured in an almost endless selection of wonderful, clear colours. The solid colour of most plain tiles is created by the glaze or by natural clays that lend their own colour to the tile (terracotta, for example). Patterned tiles take their inspiration from all eras and parts of the world. Straight or diagonal stripes, chequerboard designs, squares and shaded squares, floral motifs and patterns, dots, diamonds and checks are all available.

Figurative tiles may consist of small floral or other motifs taken from nature, while Mexican-style tiles have a naïve simplicity and bright, uninhibited colours. Dutch tiles are often blue and white and may depict children playing, ships at sea or other simple motifs, usually with a small triangular decoration in each corner. French-style tiles are also often blue and white, with hand-drawn floral or geometric shapes, or tiny pictures within a circle. Art Nouveau tiles with their characteristic curvilinear, floral motifs are widely reproduced today and can also occasionally be found second-hand, although they are no longer cheap. Many overall tile patterns have special co-ordinating round-edged border designs to give a finished look to a half-tiled wall. Other border tiles can be set in rows or alternative configurations within the main tiled area.

Mural tiles are available as ready-manufactured sets or are designed to order, and can depict anything from a vase of flowers to trees, animals or an elaborate picture over a whole wall. Tile murals are made in most countries and are produced by factories or by individual artists.

Last but not least, mosaic tiles are tiny in size and are usually supplied on a backing so that a larger tile-shaped group can be hung as one piece.

1. Decorated tiles form a pretty surround to a bathrom basin and are finished off with a matching border.

2. Tongue-and-groove panelling gives an elegant and restrained finish to the walls of this small kitchen.

3. This panelling has been taken up to just above window level. A display shelf breaks the hard divide between the panelling and the painted wall.

4. Ceramic tiles need not be square and these rectangular white tiles add to the Victorian feeling of this 'unfitted' bathroom.

5. Traditional Provençale tiles meet deep blue tiles, but are neatly divided by a length of moulding.

6. A motley collection of old Victorian tiles adds character to this purpose-designed aga area.

7. Just a few strips of pine panelling match the door and give a sense of unity to this small garden entrance.

8. Uniform mauve mosaic tiles form a practical and attractive splashback.

9. Dark wooden panelling looks warm and attractive, particularly when it is used with the dark carved oak of the fireplace and ornate mirror frame.

Wood panelling

The choice here is more limited than with tiles, but you still need to select carefully with your chosen room in mind. When panelling a small room, choose a light wood because dark panelling can be quite claustrophic.

Tongue-and-groove boards

These boards are made from planed planks designed to interlock to form a broad, gap-free area of panelling. Most have chamfered (symmetrically bevelled) edges, forming a decorative V-joint with a channelled or scalloped face. Shiplap boards are similar except that the top edge of each board fits under a rebate in the edge of the previous board. Wood panelling – which is fixed to battens at ceiling and floor level – needs to be treated and sealed.

Plain tongue-and-groove boards are usually sold in whitewood (spruce) and knotty pine (deal, Scots pine and red baltic pine), parana pine, Douglas fir and Western red cedar; the more elaborate boards are often available in a range of unusual species such as black walnut, cherry, rosewood, meranti, African mahogany and so on.

Sheet panelling

Sheet-panelling wallboards consist of thin plywood or hardboard sheets with a variety of different surfaces. The best-quality sheets have a veneer of real wood that may be grooved to simulate tongue-and-groove boards; cheaper varieties have a photographic image of a wooden surface printed on paper or plastic and bonded to the plywood backing. One sheet is usually tall enough to cover a wall from floor to ceiling without horizontal joins.

Basic techniques: ceramic tiles

Small black-and-white wall and floor tiles give a startling stylishness to this tiny kitchen, softened by the collection of pictures on the wall. The blue of the cupboards and wall and the Gothic wooden chair also help to soften the whole effect.

Careful planning is important for tiling. Make a scale drawing on graph paper, marking in windows and doors, and remembering that you do not necessarily have to lay tiles in horizontal rows one above the other: you could stagger them, or set them at an angle instead. Avoid using patterned tiles in corners where the breaks in pattern may look odd; instead, if your design includes plain and patterned tiles, plan it so that the plain ones will be in the corners. From your plan, calculate the number of tiles to buy, including those you will have to cut; from this you can estimate the exact amount of adhesive that you will need.

Preparation

You can tile on to any flat surface but it must be sound and clean, with no flaking paint. Seal bare plaster and plasterboard with a PVA sealer, or coat with emulsion. If necessary, fix battens to the wall, clad with marine plywood and then tile. To provide a good surface for the adhesive, key ceramic tiles and painted walls with glasspaper.

Marking out the wall

Mark the tile widths plus a small gap for grout on a narrow piece of wood about 2m (2½yds) long, and hold it vertically and horizontally (or at 45 degrees) so that you can see how the tiles will end up from any given starting point. Few rooms are square, so do not use windows, door frames or skirtings as a guide for the first row of tiles. Instead, establish a vertical pencil line using a plumbline and a true horizontal with a spirit level, and nail a wooden batten to the foot of the wall as the base for the first row.

Applying tiles

Working from the bottom left-hand corner, smooth a layer of adhesive over about 1sq m (1¼sq yds) of wall, then draw even ridge lines through this with a notched spreader. Place the first tile on the batten, lined up with the vertical pencil line, and press it in place. Continue in horizontal strips, using plastic spacers or matchsticks (if there are no lugs) to allow for the grout. After completing this first section, check with a spirit level and make any necessary adjustments. Spread adhesive over a further 1sq m (1¼sq yds) of wall and continue.

APPLYING TILES

1. Apply tile adhesive to the wall using a notched spreader, covering about 1 sq m (1 sq yd) at a time.

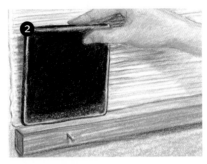

2. Place the first tile onto the wall on the inside corner of the batten and press this firmly in place.

3. Put a spacer at the top corner and position the next tile alongside, so that it sits tightly up against the spacer.

4. Use a spirit level to check that the tiles are correctly aligned. Remove spacers once the adhesive is thoroughly dry.

GROUTING

1. Apply grout to the surface, working it well into the spaces using either a squeegee or a damp sponge.

2. Draw a small rounded stick through each join to press the grout home.

Grouting

Spread the grout on to the tiled surface, working it into the cracks with a squeegee or damp sponge. Draw a small rounded stick through each join to press the grout home.

Cutting and shaping tiles

Hold each tile up to the wall, measure it against the gap and pencil the cutting point. Place the tile on a flat surface (decorative side up) and score a line through the glaze, using a try-square as a guide. Position a matchstick under each end of the tile in line with the score mark, then press down on either side of the tile until it snaps.

For an L-shape, make a paper template and trace this on to the tile. Cut the tile with a tile saw or make deep criss-cross scores over the extra piece. Trim to the main line with clippers. To cut around a pipe, make a template, trace on to the tile, cut the tile in half and chip or saw an arc from each half.

CUTTING A STRAIGHT EDGE

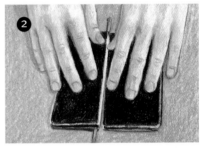

1. Place the tiles on a flat surface, decorative side up, and score a line through the glaze.

2. With a matchstick under each end of the tile in line with the score mark, press down on either side until it snaps.

CUTTING AN L-SHAPE

1. For an L-shape, make deep criss-cross scores over the surplus piece and trim with tile clippers.

2. Snip away through the criss-cross scores by degrees, using tile clippers.

Basic techniques: more ceramics

There are variations and additions to ceramic tiles that can add to the practicality and attractiveness of the home. Mosaic tiles are used in the same way as standard ceramic tiles, but the method of applying them is a little different. You must fix any tile accessories – such as a soap dish – carefully and securely or they may work loose over time.

Fixing mosaic tiles

Ceramic mosaic tiles are generally supplied in sheet form on a mesh backing, and are fixed to the wall using ordinary ceramic-tile adhesive. First of all, mark horizontal and vertical guidelines as for ceramic tiles (see page 102). Spread the adhesive over 1sq m (1¼sq yds) of wall as for the ceramic tiles, and then – having made sure that the arrows on the backs of the sheets are facing the same way – press each sheet firmly into place.

When you have covered the main area of the wall with whole sheets, cut smaller pieces for the borders and to fit around obstacles. Measure the area to be filled, then turn the sheet over, mark cutting lines on the back and slice through the mesh backing with a craft knife. When applying, make sure that each border or cut piece is correctly aligned with the adjacent sheet.

1. Mosaic tiles usually come on a mesh backing. Cut through the backing to get the right size for a particular area.

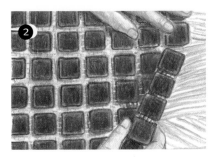

2. Spread adhesive onto the wall as for tiles. Make sure the arrows on the backs of the sheets face the same way. Press each sheet firmly into place.

Fixing ceramic-tile accessories

Ceramic tiles are often available with matching accessories such as soap dishes, toothbrush holders and towel rings. You can either glue these to the wall or fix them with screws. Some accessories are made with a ceramic base in the shape of a tile, and you can therefore fix these with ordinary ceramic-tile adhesive.

When using adhesive, fix one or two tiles (depending on the size of the accessory base) temporarily in position. After 48 hours remove the tiles, spread adhesive on the back of the accessory and push it firmly into place. Secure it there with adhesive tape for a further 48 hours, then remove the tape and fill the join around the edges neatly with grout.

When fixing with screws, use a masonry drill bit in a power drill. Stick a piece of masking tape over the hole position before drilling, as this will prevent the drill from slipping around over the tile surface.

FIXING A CERAMIC-BASED ACCESSORY

For ceramic accessories, fix a tile temporarily in position. After 48 hours, remove it, spread adhesive on the back of the accessory, fix firmly and secure with adhesive tape for another 48 hours.

FIXING A SCREW-IN ACCESSORY

When fixing with screws, stick a piece of masking tape over the hole position to prevent the drill from slipping.

Finishing off

Even the best-laid tiles may allow water to seep behind baths, basins and sinks. To prevent this, finish off by running a bead of silicone rubber sealant along the edges. This will remain flexible and so keep the gap permanently sealed in spite of heat changes and movement.

At external corners – for example, on a window sill – use special plastic beading to form a neat, rounded finish to the edge tiles. Bed the flat strip well down into the adhesive with the larger lip resting on the sill edge; the last course of tiles on the sill will butt up against the rounded lip.

SEALING EDGES

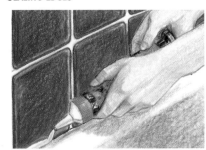

Finish off by running a silicone rubber sealant along the edges. Squeeze while drawing the nozzle of the sealant along the tiles.

NEATENING EDGES

At external corners, use special plastic beading to form a neat, rounded finish to the edge of the tiles.

Directory of alternative wall finishes

Cork has excellent insulating properties and its warm brown colours can make it attractive as a wall covering, particularly when used in a restrained interior with natural wood and white paint as its foils.

The following possibilities for covering walls are used less frequently than conventional wallpapers and vinyls, tiles and wood panelling, but each has its own merit in terms of interior decoration. One advantage of almost all these finishes is that they are easy to apply – only plastic laminate (and possibly large pieces of sheet mirror) will require battens, as used for wood panelling.

Mirrors and mirror tiles

Mirror tiles are hardwearing, waterproof and stain-resistant, and are manufactured in plain and tinted varieties. Plastic mirror tiles are cheaper than glass tiles. They do not steam up as easily as glass mirror will do, and so are particularly good for the bathroom. Many mirror tiles are self-adhesive and they should be applied to a clean, shiny surface.

Sheet mirror comes in a greater variety of colours, from clear to almost black. When buying large pieces of sheet mirror, remember that you will have to manoeuvre it through doorways, and also that it becomes more expensive and more difficult to install, the bigger it is. You will need to screw it into – rather than stick it on – the wall, and, if the wall is not perfectly vertical, you will have to use battens and a hardboard backing if the mirror reflection is not to be distorting.

Brick tiles

These are made of tile-depth layers of real or synthetic brick. They are available in many colours and cut to the same size as real bricks to give the wall an authentic brick appearance. They are hardwearing, stain-resistant and can be used for small areas around a fireplace or around another feature where they would be appropriate. You will need to apply these tiles with special brick-tile adhesive.

Metallic tiles

These are usually either aluminium or stainless steel, or may be made of some other metal coloured gold, silver or copper in a matt or shiny finish. They are heatproof, fire resistant, waterproof and washable, but will show water marks so are not ideal for splashbacks. Being expensive, metal tiles are generally used over a small area; they are most often produced as squares, although other shapes and designs are available. The tiles have hollow backs and can be cut to shape with scissors (trim them well away from light switches because they are good conductors of electricity), or bent around corners. They are fixed to the wall with self-adhesive pads.

Vinyl and plastic tiles

These are made from thin plastic or vinyl sheeting. They are warm to the touch and so help with heat retention in a room, and also provide slight insulation against noise. Like metallic tiles, they have hollow backs and can be cut with scissors. They are fixed with self-adhesive pads.

Cork tiles

Cork tiles are produced in a wide range of natural and dyed colours and patterns. Cork is not a naturally washable material, so you must seal it carefully if you are using it in a wet area. Many varieties of cork tiles are supplied with a self-adhesive backing; otherwise they are easily laid using a special cork-tile adhesive.

1. Glass bricks provide a strong wall while still letting in light. Here, they make a useful partition in a bathroom.
2. Ceramic tiles lend an unusual rustic flavour to this small bathroom.
3. Mosaic tiles and glass bricks combine to create a hygienic, light and very unusual curved shower cubicle.
4. This remarkable bathroom is entirely lined with plain wood, including the bath, giving a feeling of being in a clipper at sea.
5. Marble tiles make a sumptuous finish for a bathroom and here, they are carried from the floor to the bathroom divider, round the bath itself and used as a splashback.
6. Stainless steel has been used on the walls in this highly modern kitchen to complement the cooker and kitchen units.
7. Thin metal strips tacked to the wall make an interesting contribution to a modern working space, softened by a wood block floor.

Cork's insulating properties make it an ideal covering for rooms that are very hot or very cold, such as attic rooms or basements. It is also good in bathrooms where its comparatively warm surface can often help to reduce the amount of condensation.

Plastic laminates

Plastic-laminated panels for walls are durable, heat-resistant and also stain-resistant. They are thinner than the hardwearing laminates used for surfaces in work rooms and kitchens, and should be glued on to chipboard or plywood. You will easily be able to cut them with a fine-toothed saw. Plastic laminates are not cheap, but they are generally a less expensive option than the equivalent area covered in ceramic tiles would be; they should be fixed with a contact adhesive.

Synthetic rubber sheeting

This is a hardwearing flooring that is very often used in airports, for example, where it gets punishing treatment. It is usually made with a raised pattern and is available in many vivid plain colours. Rubber sheeting can make an attractive and practical finish when extended from the floor to the walls of a small kitchen or bathroom. A selection may be found in DIY or department stores, but it is worth looking at the wider range available through a design or architectural office.

Basic techniques: non-ceramics

Mirror tiles can help to make a bathroom seem larger than it really is. Decorative objects and foliage strategically placed to reflect in the tiles help to give the room a pleasant, relaxing ambience.

Most of the techniques used for fixing alternative wall finishes are comparatively simple. As always, read the instructions on the packaging because different manufacturers may have slightly different guidelines for their products. If a particular adhesive is recommended for a product, be sure to use it – this will help you to achieve the best results. The wrong adhesive may not secure the tiles properly, and could even cause them to discolour.

Preparing surfaces

As with conventional wallcoverings, it is important to start with a sound, clean, well prepared wall surface. Very absorbent wall surfaces can be sealed and sized; all holes should be filled and if you suspect damp, make sure you get the problem treated first before applying the wallcovering.

Fixing mirror tiles

It is particularly important with mirror tiles that the surface to which you stick them is flat and even, or the result will be a distorted reflection. If necessary, fix a sheet of 12mm (½in) chipboard or plywood to battens on the wall. The surface must also be sound and dry: seal porous materials such as plaster or wood with a coat of oil-based paint and leave to dry for three days; if you have new plaster, you will need to let it dry out for several weeks before applying the tiles. In cold weather, and especially if the walls are cold, heat the room a little as this will encourage the tiles to adhere firmly in place.

Mirror tiles must be perfectly aligned, so mark your guidelines as for ceramic tiling (see page 102). Most come with self-adhesive tabs on the

FIXING MIRROR TILES

1. For mirror tiles, remove the coating paper from the self-adhesive tabs before sticking the tile firmly to the wall.

2. Mark the guidelines as for ceramic tiles and position them carefully before pressing them against the wall.

reverse but, if not, you can buy these separately. Mirror tiles should be cut in the same way as glass; you may need to get a professional to do this for you. Place the tiles in horizontal rows, starting from the bottom. Try to align them accurately, and leave a narrow gap between each one; they do not require grouting.

Fixing metallic tiles

Since the surface of these tiles is not highly reflective, it does not matter if the wall surface is slightly uneven. Set out the tiles as for ceramic tiles (see page 103) and fix all the complete tiles first. Any tiles that need cutting can be trimmed with an old pair of scissors or with tin snips.

Fixing brick wall tiles

The important part of the planning with these tiles is to achieve a realistic pattern. Arrange several courses of tiles on the floor so that you can work out the best brick-bond pattern, staggering the joins, and then pencil this on to the wall as a guide. Spread each tile with adhesive and press it firmly on to the wall, placing 19mm (¾in) wooden spacers between each brick course. Cut bricks where necessary with an electric grinder or circular power saw fitted with a masonry disc. After 24 hours, remove the spacers and fill the joins with mortar or pointing compound, using a small pointing trowel or a filling knife.

FIXING BRICK TILES

1. Arrange several courses of brick tiles on the floor so that you can work out the best brick-bond pattern, staggering the joins.

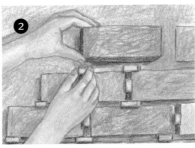

2. Spread each of the tiles with adhesive and then press them firmly onto the wall. Place wooden spacers between each brick course.

Fixing cork wall tiles

Cork tiles are not at all difficult to fix but, as always, check that the wall is flat, smooth, dry and not flaking. Fix a horizontal batten and draw a vertical guide as you would do for ceramic tiles (see page 102). Proceed as for ceramic tiles, but use a special cork-tile adhesive (if the tiles do not have a self-adhesive backing) and butt join the tiles closely. Cut cork tiles on a flat surface using a sharp craft knife held against a metal rule. If the tiles are not pre-finished, apply two coats of sealer with a clean brush, allowing 24 hours between each coat.

When using the thick, crumbly sort of cork tile often needed for insulation, it is best to protect the exposed edges (for example, at the corners of a chimney breast) by pinning slim wooden beading to the angle before starting to fix the tiles. Tile up to the beading as if it were an internal angle.

CUTTING CORK TILES

Cut cork tiles on a flat surface using a sharp craft knife held against a metal rule.

Basic techniques: wood panelling

Wood panelling completely lines the walls of this house from top to bottom; different coloured paints have been used to create the dado line and demarcate the various rooms.

Adding panelling to a wall will hide the wall completely, so it is important to make sure that the surface is thoroughly prepared and free from damp before you begin. You will need supporting battens, which should measure 5 x 2.5cm (2 x 1in) and can be unplaned. To allow for the battens, you will need to remove the skirting board and possibly any picture rail; if you plan to use insulation material under the panelling you should insert this once the battens are in position.

Preparing a wall for panelling

Loosen each section of skirting using an old chisel before levering it away with a hammer claw. You will only need to remove a picture rail if it stands proud of the battens and will obstruct the panelling. In this case, make a cut in the rail close to one of the nails and then break it away.

LOOSENING A PICTURE RAIL

Loosen a picture rail with a chisel and prise it off with a claw hammer.

LOOSENING SKIRTING

Use an old chisel to loosen the skirting and then lever it away with a claw hammer.

Estimating quantities

Measure the height and width of the area you are going to panel. With tongue-and-groove and shiplap panelling, you will need to allow for the overlaps. For vertical panelling, divide the exact width of one board into the total room width, multiply the result by the room height, and add 10 per cent for wastage and joins.

Fixing battens

For vertical boards, fix horizontal battens at about 40cm (16in) intervals, placing hardboard packing pieces behind the battens if you need to level them. Fix them with masonry nails (or wall plugs and screws). If you have removed skirting and intend to replace it after panelling, fit short lengths of batten vertically to support it, marking their positions so that you can locate them when you replace the skirting.

For horizontal panelling, fix vertical battens about 40cm (16in) apart. The lowest board should fit behind where the skirting will be, but need not go right down to the floor.

FIXING BATTENS FOR VERTICAL PANELLING

For vertical boards, fix horizontal battens at 40cm (16in) intervals with masonry nails or with wall plugs and screws.

FIXING BATTENS FOR HORIZONTAL PANELLING

For horizontal panelling, fix vertical battens about 40cm (16in) apart.

Fixing tongue-and-groove panelling

Fix the first board vertically with its groove pointing into a corner, and pin it to each batten about 12mm ($\frac{1}{2}$in) from the groove edge. Drive each pin below the surface with a nail punch. Hammer pins at an angle through the shoulder of the tongue (the groove of the next board should hide the pins). With the subsequent boards, you should only need one pin in the shoulder of each tongue. Use a wood stopper to hide the holes made by the nail punch. Alternatively, you can use clips instead of pins; different systems are available for this.

At a junction with another wall, cut the last board to fit, snap the last two in place and face nail the final board. Butt join internal corners and neaten them with a length of moulding; at external corners, plane off the tongue to butt square. Finish the top edge of the panelling with beading, moulding or a dado rail.

Negotiating doors and windows

With a door, prise up the architrave, fix a vertical batten to the wall and, when you have fixed the panelling, conceal the batten and the join with beading. Finally, pin back the original architrave. Most windows have no room for battens, so you will need to stick the panelling to the wall or stop it about 6mm ($\frac{1}{4}$in) from the turn and finish off with strips of beading.

NEGOTIATING DOORS

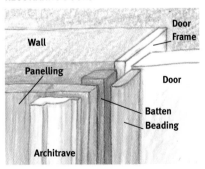

At a doorway, fix a vertical batten to the wall and when the panelling is fixed, conceal the batten and join with beading.

FIXING TONGUE-AND-GROOVE

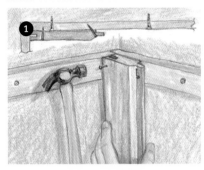

1. For tongue-and-groove panelling, fix the first board vertically, with the groove towards the corner, and pin it to each batten using at least two pins.

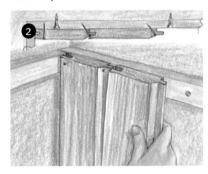

2. Fit the second board into the first, then the third and so on. You should need only one pin in the shoulder of each tongue.

NEGOTIATING WINDOWS

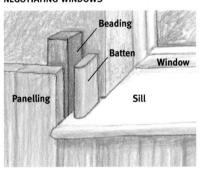

At a window, fix the last panel about 6mm ($\frac{1}{4}$in) away from the turn and then finish off with beading.

Doors and windows

Before doing any decorating, you should make sure that your doors and windows are sound and performing their functions efficiently. The purpose of windows is to let in light, to enable you to enjoy the view (if any) and to provide ventilation. You do not have to be able to open all the panes to achieve satisfactory ventilation, and many windows are made up of both fixed panes (or 'lights') and opening ones.

A home can lose a wasteful amount of heat through the glass in its windows, but double-glazed equivalents of most types of window – including traditional sash windows – are now available and will improve insulation enormously. Some are available as DIY kits and can be perfectly satisfactory, although the best insulation will always be provided by professionally installed double glazing.

If you need to replace a window, you could opt for an exact copy of the original or for a double-glazed replacement window. Many manufacturers will only provide made-to-measure windows that they install for you, but you will also be able to buy replacement windows that you can fit yourself, whose frames may be made of timber, aluminium, unplasticized polyvinyl chloride (uPVC) or steel.

Various types of glass are used in windows. Standard 'float' glass is the most common, but there are also several kinds of toughened glass, patterned and tinted glass, and – if you wish to give a really authentic look to a period house – you will still be able to find handmade glass panes that are slightly distorting (as the originals would have been).

Doors are available in many different materials including wood, metal, glass and plastic; the majority are made of wood and hang on hinges. Panelled doors have a framework of solid wood filled with solid wood, plywood or glass; flush doors have a much lighter framework covered on both sides with facing sheets of hardboard or plywood.

In a dark, narrow entrance, fitting glass panels into the top half of the front door is a good option and immediately makes the space seem less overbearing.

Paint is used on both doors and windows not just to decorate them but also to protect their surfaces; it needs to be used with a primer and undercoat.

Doors

These doors have been turned into Moorish portals with a cut-out MDF board and marvellous red and gold painted decoration. Through the open door lies a modern interior that is lit up with bright sunshine-yellow paint. The tiled floor, though quite plain, reinforces the Moorish theme.

Doors are often forgotten when an interior scheme is being planned but, like windows, they take up a fair amount of space and deserve some thought. Your choice of decoration for doors is, of course, important, but you should also consider the style of the doors themselves and the way in which they open into the rooms.

Finding a door to suit the space

A standard door needs about 2m (2½yds) of clear space for opening into a room. However, in the very small bedrooms, bathrooms or kitchens common in modern new-build homes and conversions there may be no room for the door to open once the furniture is in. In this case, half-width double doors take up half the space, while vertically divided folding doors (bi-fold doors) – which fold as they open – can save enough space to make a small room perfectly practical.

Sliding and concertina sliding doors can also save space, but do be sure to choose a sturdy mechanism so that the doors do not slip out of their tracking or rattle about loosely in it. If you are using the door to divide a room, concertina, multi-fold or louvred bi-fold doors are the best solution.

Door style

The modern, flush, unpanelled door almost always needs some form of decoration to disguise the fact that it is of flimsy construction with a thinly veneered surface. You could paint *trompe l'oeil* panels on to this type of door, or fill it with painted *chinoiserie* or other motifs. Some flush doors have a moulded facing that makes them appear to be painted; alternatively, you can buy self-adhesive mouldings to create realistic-looking panels, and paint them as a panelled door.

Another idea is to paint a door and frame in contrasting bright colours to blind the eye to the door's flimsiness but be sure to choose stylish handles with a panache to match the colours.

and magazines, but not so big that a burglar could reach inside to open the door. A box on the inside of the door for holding letters will also act as a draught excluder.

If you have panelled doors leading from an enclosed porch or hallway into your home, stained glass fitted in the top panels of the interior doors can be attractive while allowing a little extra light into the hall; these will not affect the security of your home provided that the exterior doors are solid and have satisfactory locks.

Door furniture

You can change the look of a door fundamentally by simply painting it and choosing different fittings: there is a huge choice available, and it is surprising what a difference such seemingly trivial alterations can make. Door fittings include handles, hinges, knobs, catches, knockers and fingerplates, hinges, escutcheons (to prevent draughts from penetrating keyholes) and letterboxes; all are made in many different styles and you will need to choose carefully to complement the style of your door and interior.

Traditional-style fittings are often made of brass, iron, wood or china.

Covering a flush door with suede, leather or fabric will completely conceal its basic construction and provide a solid-looking and stylish finish; these materials are most suitable for a work room or for a book-filled study, but not for children's rooms or other places where they could become dirty, as cleaning may be a problem. Steel or aluminium doors can look functional and stylish in a high-tech home, but will look bleak if they do not co-ordinate with their environment.

In the space above the door you may be able to insert a stained-glass panel or fanlight or you could paint a *trompe l'oeil* fanlight to give a feeling of greater height. If you prefer to get rid of flush doors altogether, you could buy new ready-made panelled doors, or you should be able to find them secondhand in furniture and junk stores, and at architectural salvage depots. They can be stripped for a reasonable price, then sealed or painted.

Exterior doors

Exterior doors should always be made of hardwood (or possibly aluminium), and need to be very strongly constructed for security reasons. Letterboxes are sold in a variety of period and modern styles; they should be sufficiently wide to take large envelopes

Ceramic fingerplates may be in plain white or decorated with floral or other motifs. Modern handles may be made of metal – such as chromium-plate or stainless steel – or in plastic in bright colours; these may have clean, uncluttered lines or be moulded into unusual shapes such as seashells. Shiny brass or gold-plated metal fittings usually look best on gloss-painted or varnished panelled doors (particularly front doors); wood, china and plastic will be more in keeping on interior doors. As always, traditional styles are in keeping in a traditional interior, while cleancut, modern-style fittings in bright colours will be most effective in a modern, minimal and high-tech interior. For a neat finish, always fix door fittings in position after painting, staining or varnishing the door surface.

Above An extremely solid cantilevered door divides the kitchen from the dining room and fits in well with the simple 'cut-through' arch. *Below* Large, double, panelled doors lead directly onto an ultra-elegant and traditional staircase.

Windows

This splendidly shaped arched window, with its stone reveals and beautiful solid wood, provides a fascinating frame for the view of tree-tops outside, as well as for the venerable rocking horse, whose wooden base echoes the wood of the window frame.

You can either consider windows and doors as separate features, by picking on a colour that contrasts with the rest of your decoration and acts as an eye-catching device; or you could use them to co-ordinate and unify a scheme. When choosing your window decoration, it is important to consider their shape and style.

Window style

If you have rather grand, stately and well-proportioned windows, you will probably decide to dress them with suitable blinds and/or curtains which will emphasize their shape.

Colours for woodwork

If you intend to dress up a window with lots of drapes, swags and frills, the colour of the woodwork need not stand out. However, if you are going to fit a simple Roman or roller blind, you can use the window frame as an important visual element in the room, painting it to contrast directly with the walls or to form an integral part of the view beyond.

Modern architects very often choose white for the woodwork in a house, including window frames, doors and door frames, skirtings and mouldings. White has always been popular for woodwork, and in general gloss paint is the preferred choice because it is hardwearing and resists knocks; it also catches the light, creating a sharp, hard-edged contrast to other colours in the room. Some modern gloss paints are water-based, and so do not present the problems of slow drying and smell associated with oil-based gloss. However, white is by no means the only answer to decorating doors and windows, and modern homes often have these painted in bright and lively colours to match an uninhibited décor.

Historical colours

Historically, the native hardwoods used to make windows and doors were usually left unpainted, and instead were simply varnished or polished so that their natural colour and grain would show through. However, during the eighteenth century, deal (pine and fir) was introduced as a cheaper alternative to native hardwoods, and the poor quality of this wood – which was full of knots – in comparison with the sleekness of the hardwoods meant that it was never left in its 'raw' state but always painted. Window and door frames were white, while doors were often painted dark brown or black.

Graining was also popular, and remained so until the early twentieth century; this was easy to do and very hardwearing. The Victorians often favoured black woodwork, and the Edwardians black woodwork with thin lines of aluminium silver – all in the newly formulated high-gloss paints. In contrast, the search for 'good taste' in the 1920s and '30s favoured white or matt-grey woodwork combined with white, cream, yellow and buff walls.

Today we have an enormous choice available for woodwork, from the ever-popular white through the traditional natural hardwoods or ebony black to pale 1930s' shades, and finally to modern primary colours or paint effects. There is also a huge range of paint types, from high gloss through eggshell to matt paints, all of which can be quite satisfactory in practical as well as visual terms.

Dealing with shutters

If you are lucky enough to have original shutters on your windows, make the most of them. In eighteenth- and nineteenth-century homes shutters were common on the inside of the house, and were folded back by day into storage recesses at the sides of the windows; at night, or when the house was unoccupied, they were unfolded and secured by strong iron bars. They were usually panelled and folded back concertina-fashion, or

could be pulled up and down on pulleys. Shutters like this provide good security and they are usually very attractive in their own right. They can either be stripped, sealed or varnished, or painted.

If you do not have original shutters, ready-made louvred 'plantation-style' shutters can make an attractive alternative to curtains or blinds, or can be used in conjunction with them. You will need space on either side of the window so that you can open the shutters right back from it and, ideally, the window will have a deep reveal. If the shutters are made of narrow panels, hinged in the middle, they can work in a more confined space. Plantation-style shutters have louvres that you can open to let light filter into the room, while fixed louvre folding shutters will fold neatly into a reveal.

Right **The delicate stained glass of this small Gothic window casts fascinating shadows over the wall and floor of the landing.**
Below **Two sets of double doors with glass panes create a pocket of space between garden and home, while still allowing light to enter.**

Tools and equipment

If you want to get really good results, it is worth investing in good quality paints and brushes, and in a range of stripping tools that will allow you to deal with mouldings and narrow areas, as well as large flat areas. Always make sure you have everything you need and that it is readily to hand before you begin work.

Many of the tools that you will need to prepare and paint doors and windows will be the same as for walls and, as always, if you choose good-quality brushes and care for them properly, they will last a long time. There are, however, a few items that you can usefully add to this basic collection.

Paintbrushes and pads
You will need a 75mm (3in) brush for flush doors and similar large areas of gloss paint, a 50mm (2in) brush for skirtings, a 25mm (1in) brush for window and door frames, panels and mouldings. A 19mm (¾in) cutting-in brush with angled bristles is ideal for window frames and door mouldings, and a thin 12mm (½in) brush is useful for small areas where you need to be precise. Small paint pads can also be used on window frames.

Preparation paints
Primer is a thick liquid designed to seal bare surfaces and reduce their absorbency. Water- and oil-based primers, intended for wood or metal, are available. Undercoat is thick and opaque, and designed for use on primed surfaces (or to obliterate other colours) and to provide a good surface for the top coat. Water- and oil-based versions are available. Undercoat is not intended as a finish and will not last well unless it is finished with a matt varnish.

Glasspaper
You will need glasspaper to remove flaking or cracking paint or varnish, as well as to create a key on finishes that you intend to paint over. Glasspaper will also level dried filler, and is useful after each new coat of paint has dried to create a key for the next coat.

A wire brush and sugar soap
This type of sturdy brush is ideal for removing flaky paint and rust from metalwork; sugar soap (or washing-soda crystals) will remove dirt and grease from existing paintwork.

A hot-air gun

This very useful tool is used for stripping paint: it will melt several layers of old paint very efficiently, which you can then scrape off with a scraper. Always wear goggles to protect your eyes when using a hot-air gun.

Chemical paint strippers

These are available in paste or liquid form, and are quick and effective. Whichever type you use, always protect your eyes and hands because they are all caustic, and be sure to follow the manufacturer's instructions carefully. Special strippers are also available for removing paint from metal window frames.

A shavehook

This is a triangular tool for scraping narrow surfaces. A shavehook with a combination of straight, convex and concave sides is ideal for scraping paint from window frames, the curved profiles of mouldings and glazing bars.

Rust killer

This will smooth the surface of metal window frames where rust has left pit marks, and inhibit further rusting. You will need to clean the areas and remove all existing rust thoroughly before application.

Filler

Designed for use on wood or metal frames, this is usually applied after the priming stage. Be sure to choose the right sort of filler for the material you are working on and, if you are not using a ready-mixed filler, follow the manufacturer's instructions on preparation carefully.

Liquid sander

This is useful for cleaning surfaces before applying a new finish, and is particularly helpful on mouldings and corners where glasspaper is not flexible enough to get into all the nooks and crannies.

Knotting solution

This is a sealant made from shellac and methylated spirit. The oils in the solution prevent the knots in timber from weeping, which is particularly important when working with pine.

Masking tape/Paint shield

Masking tape is essential for protecting glass panes from paint splashes and marks. A paint shield does a similar job, but you will need to hold it firmly against the glass to prevent paint from creeping beneath it.

Tools and equipment
for painting doors
and windows
1. Gloss paints.
2. 25mm (1in)
   decorating brush.
3. 75mm (3in)
   decorating brush.
4. Hot-air gun.
5. 19mm (¾in)
   cutting-in brush.
6. 12mm (½in)
   decorating brush.
7. Wire brush.
8. Triangular
   scraper.
9. Shaped scraper.

Directory of doors

This simply manufactured door has been given a really grand presence with the addition of a Gothic arch, together with Bohemian painting and stained glass.

Doors are available in wood, metal, glass and plastic, and in many different styles and sizes. Interior doors are often made of a honeycomb core that is sandwiched between two sheets of facing material and are comparatively cheap. Panelled doors are more expensive but often more attractive and more solidly constructed. Most doors are made of wood and hang on hinges, but sliding doors may be more convenient where space is at a premium; folding doors also take up less space when open and are particularly useful where a room has been opened up and the door acts as an openable divider.

Panelled doors

Panelled doors have recessed panels, often edged with moulding. In the eighteenth century, doors had two or six panels, while doors in the late nineteenth century usually had four panels. Interior panelled doors may be made of redwood or Douglas fir, and can be sealed, stained or painted. Less grand doors made of tongue-and-groove panelling and hung from simple iron hinges can look appropriate for a country cottage décor, and may be sealed, varnished or painted.

Flush doors

Flush doors are comparatively modern, and are much lighter and also cheaper than panelled doors (the actual cost will depend on the quality of the facing panels and internal core). Plywood is a common facing material. Some flush doors have a moulded facing to make them resemble panelled doors; DIY kits of self-adhesive moulding (usually enough to create four panels) are also available. Fire doors are required by law in some situations, and are usually flush doors with a core of fire-retardant material.

Flush doors are often given a mock mahogany finish, but can be decorated in exactly the same colour as the walls (or in matching wallpaper), or the same colour as the rest of the woodwork. They often look best when dealt with dramatically, as their very basic and cheap make-up does not respond well to subtle treatment.

Stable doors

These are made in two halves which open independently, so that you can open the top half to let in light and air without allowing children or pets to escape. Stable doors are particularly suitable for country kitchens and they can be painted to match the rest of the woodwork.

Louvred doors

These make cheap and good-looking doors for cupboards, and are available in a wide range of sizes. They can be painted, or sealed to give a natural wood effect.

Sliding doors

These doors are especially useful for wardrobes in a bedroom where the bed leaves no room to open a hinged door, or in a cloakroom or other small room where a hinged door would take up too much space. Sliding doors should be fitted with appropriate sliding equipment, usually consisting of rollers and tracks. Make sure that this is of good quality, as doors that do not slide or fit well will be a constant source of aggravation.

Bi-folding doors

These are made of two vertical parts connected by a hinge. As the door opens, it also folds so that it takes up half the space of a complete door.

Door accessories

The choice of door accessories today is extensive; department stores and DIY outlets usually stock a good selection.

Knobs

These either twist to operate the door's opening mechanism, or are designed to be pulled (as on cupboard doors). They are traditionally made of china, wood or brass, but may be glass or plastic; they are often elaborately decorated or moulded, and may be mounted on a backplate.

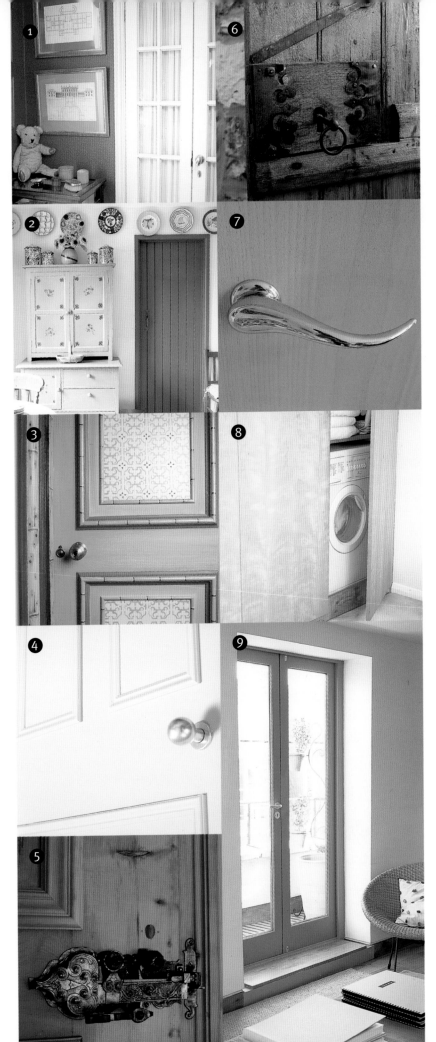

1. Double glass doors can be a good way of dividing interior spaces, letting in light and giving a feeling of space.

2. A tongue-and-groove door fits in nicely with a 'cottage' or 'rural' look.

3. This panelled door has been painted and papered to give it an exotic quality which might fit well into a library.

4. A flush door has been given a more solid look by attaching moulding from an inexpensive kit to form panels.

5. A marvellously ornate metal latch gives this panelled door a heavy Gothic quality.

6. A rough wooden door has been fitted with an ornate lock and ironwork in a suitably unsophisticated manner.

7. A most elegantly shaped stainless steel door handle, suitable for almost any modern interior.

8. Flush veneered pale wooden doors cleverly conceal the washing machine.

9. A neat double patio door, with bolts fitted at top and bottom, is painted a sea blue and gives a view out to the garden.

Handles

Door handles are usually made of iron, brass, plastic or enamelled metal. A wide range of designs is now manufactured, including some very attractive sturdy modern handles in simple shapes and primary colours, as well as in black and white.

Latches

Three types of latch are available. A rim latch is a metal box fitted on to the door which holds the door's opening mechanism; a mortise latch is fitted into the thickness of the door and hidden from view; and a thumb latch is a traditional, very simple mechanism (appropriate for tongue-and-groove and other country-style doors), where pressing down on a thumbplate raises the snib that lifts the bolt.

Fingerplates and escutcheons

A fingerplate is a narrow rectangular panel, often made to match the door knob, which is fixed above or below the knob to protect the door from dirty fingermarks. Escutcheons are tiny plates designed to prevent draughts from coming in through the keyhole. Traditional fingerplates and escutcheons were often made of glass or china; modern ones may be plastic or metal (particularly stainless steel).

Portières

A portière is a hinged metal curtain pole that is attached to the top of the door and is wider than the door. A curtain can then be hung from it to exclude draughts.

Espagnolettes

An espagnolette is a long bolt often found in French windows; it consists of a handle fitted to one of a pair of windows that sends the bolt into the top and bottom of the window frame.

Directory of windows

A floor to ceiling picture window allows light to flood into this narrow kitchen to create a bright working environment. The light, airy atmosphere is further enhanced by doors opening out onto the patio.

Your treatment of any window will depend to a large extent on the shape of the pane or panes and the materials of the frame. Where shutters exist, they are an important part of the window decoration and should be treated in a way that conforms to the rest of the window; wooden shutters are very attractive whether painted white or given a stronger character of their own with brighter, more positive colours. Metal window frames are not always the most attractive part of a window and often look best when painted white or black, although a deep blue can also work well.

Casement windows

These are the most common type of window, and usually have a fixed pane (or 'light'), a side-hinged casement and a smaller, top-opening pane called a ventlight. Larger windows may have more than one casement; the panes may also be joined together in a curved shape to create a bow window, or in a rectangular or angled shape to make a bay.

Sash windows

These are the windows that are most often seen in older buildings. They consist of two sliding sashes, one set in front of the other. Each is counter-balanced by a hidden weight or by a spring-balance system.

Pivoting windows

These are often used in upper floors and as windows in a roof. They are convenient, but in a family home a safety stop should always be fitted to prevent a child from being able to push the window open and crawl out.

Louvred windows

These windows are made of horizontal slats of glass in a metal frame which can be opened all together with a single pull on a lever, and often come as part of modern, double-glazed windows. The louvred pane is sometimes the only part of the window that can be opened.

French windows

Glazed double doors are normally fastened by top and bottom bolts, with the inner edge of one door overlapping the other to give a good fit.

Patio doors

These often have metal frames, or may have uPVC frames that require no maintenance. The doors should be double-glazed and fitted with laminated glass to make them secure. Commercial-quality patio doors – which can only be opened from the inside – are very secure indeed.

Double glazing

Double glazing will reduce heat loss, increase the comfort of a room, cut down condensation, lower noise levels and add value to your property. If you intend to install double glazing, do so before you decorate. Aluminium and uPVC are the most commonly used materials for secondary glazing, but wood can also be used. Metals can form a cold bridge between the outer and inner units and cause condensation, whereas wood and uPVC are less likely to do so, although new designs of aluminium frames are made with a thermal barrier so that heat loss and the risk of condensation are reduced.

Sealed units

These are made with insulating glass, which consists of two sheets of glass spaced apart and hermetically sealed. In a window the visual effect is very similar to a single pane and there are only two surfaces to clean, and each sealed unit replaces a single pane so that windows and patio doors can open and close in the normal way. The units are usually fitted into the window with synthetic or rubber gaskets. Some have heat-reflecting qualities.

1. A dull view through a casement window can be concealed by a louvred blind which can be adjusted to let in more or less light.

2. Traditional window with deep reveal and leaded lights. The owner is making the most of the wide sill to display light-loving plants.

3. This tall Georgian window, with its deep reveals and rounded arch, looks out onto a farmhouse setting. The white-painted woodwork and yellow walls are in keeping with the whole style of the architecture.

4. This sash window looks out onto the houses opposite which are screened from view by hanging ivies.

5. Well-proportioned corner windows can be screened by white-painted, louvred blinds, adding security as well as elegance.

6. The tiny windows in this converted Umbrian farmhouse are designed not to let in too much of the hot sunlight.

7. A curved window looks out onto a small green garden area surrounded by a grove of trees. Use has been made of the depth of the curve to fit a window seat and cupboards.

8. An interesting angled, modern window looks out onto a very small area of space; the light and shadows creating optical illusions.

Secondary panes

With this type of double glazing, a second pane in its own frame of metal, wood or plastic is secured to the existing frame or to the inner or outer sill; the existing window is left in place to form one half of the double glazing. Secondary panes cannot easily be opened for normal ventilation, although they can be removed for cleaning or storage during the warmer months of the year.

Coupled windows

More substantial than other double-glazing systems, these usually consist of sheets of glass or plastic with aluminium or plastic frames (although they can be made of wood). They can be fixed in position, or hinged or sliding so that they open independently of the main windows.

Made-to-measure glazing

If your window sizes are not standard, you will be able to have secondary casement or sash systems made to measure. Some companies now specialize in making wooden double glazing for sash windows, in which the glazing is virtually invisible.

Basic techniques: doors

You should paint doors after painting all the walls and windows, but before painting the skirting boards. Use a gloss or oil-based silk finish for protection against wear and tear (modern water-based gloss paints will be suitable if you prefer these to the oil-based variety). If possible, paint in one continuous session to prevent dried paint lines from forming.

Preparation

Remove all handles, keyhole plates, hooks and other door furniture before painting so that you do not cause smudges and runs; this will also speed up the work. Store all the fittings in a safe place, together with their screws, and loosely replace them between coats so that you can open the doors.

Thoroughly clean the top edges of doors and the keyholes so that your brush does not pick up and spread specks of dust and dirt (there is no need to paint the top edge of a door unless it is visible from the stairs, although a painted edge will collect less dust). Fix hinges if necessary, deal with any squeaks and sand down doors that are prone to sticking before painting them.

Always use at least one undercoat, even if the existing paint surface is sound and the new colour is darker than the old. Use two undercoats when covering a dark or strong colour with a paler shade, and sand the surface with glasspaper between each of the coats.

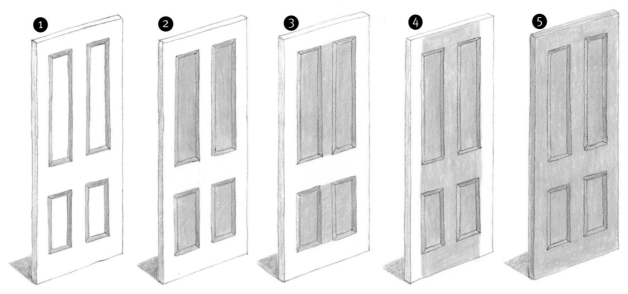

1. Use a 25mm (1in) brush to paint the mouldings.

2. Paint the panels using a 50mm (2in) or 75mm (3in) brush.

3. Next, paint both of the vertical centre sections of the door.

4. Paint the top, middle and bottom horizontal sections of the door.

5. Finally, paint the vertical outside sections and edges of the door.

Painting a panelled door

The following sequence of working will minimize the number of wet edges and so avoid any noticeable ridges in the paintwork.

1. Use a 25mm (1in) brush to paint the mouldings, being careful not to overload it or you will create runs and spoil the finish.
2. Then paint the panels with a 50mm (2in) or 75mm (3in) brush.
3. Paint the vertical centre sections.
4. Next, paint the top, middle and bottom horizontal bands.
5. Paint the vertical outside sections and edges.
6. Finally, paint the door frame.

Painting a flush door

Cover the area fairly quickly with a 75mm (3in) brush. Start at the top corner of the hinge side and work in small sections towards the bottom corner on the handle side, working quickly so that you can cover the edge of each section before it dries. Begin

with vertical strokes, then cross-brush to spread the paint and lay off with light, upward strokes.

When painting the edges, use a 50mm (2in) brush. Do not allow the paint to build up into ridges and, where you can, take it around corners for a neat finish. Many people make the mistake of applying too much paint to the top of the door and too little to the sides, so try to avoid this.

PAINTING A FLUSH DOOR

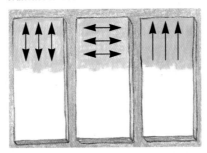

Start at the corner of the hinge side and work in small sections towards the bottom corner.

Painting skirtings

Masking tape or a piece of card will prevent any paint from getting on the wall. Use a 50mm (2in) brush, and dab a lightly loaded cutting-in brush into the crevice of the skirting to draw away excess paint.

PAINTING SKIRTINGS

Use masking tape or a piece of card to prevent the paint from getting onto the wall.

Basic techniques: windows

Interior windows will probably suffer from temperature changes as well as from condensation, and are therefore the most likely pieces of interior woodwork to deteriorate. For this reason, it is very important to repair any damage, to re-putty if necessary and generally to prepare the surface carefully before painting. The order of working for individual parts of a window will depend on its type. For best results, follow the instructions given here for sash and casement windows, and, on wooden frames, always finish your painting by following in the direction of the grain.

Painting a sash window

When working on this type of window, be careful not to get paint on the sash cords as this will make the window difficult to open.

1. Push the bottom sash up and the top sash down until there is a 20cm (8in) overlap. Begin by painting the bottom meeting rail of the top sash, followed by as much of the vertical sections as you can reach.
2. Almost close the window and paint the rest of the top sash.
3. With the sashes almost closed and matchsticks inserted between them to prevent sticking, paint the bottom one. Leave to dry.
4. Paint the rest of the window frame apart from the covered parts of the runners and the sill.
5. Open the windows and paint the exposed parts of the runners. Finally Paint the window sill.

PAINTING A SASH WINDOW

1. Paint the bottom meeting rail of the top sash and as much of the verticals as possible.

2. Next, paint the top part of the top sash of the window.

3. Paint the bottom sash of the window.

4. Paint the rest of the window frame, except the sill.

5. Open the window and paint exposed runners. Finish off by painting the window sill.

Painting a casement window

If one window is fixed, begin with the opening one. Should paint overlap on to the hinges, wipe it off before it dries or it will be very difficult to remove. Leave the window sill until the end or you will smudge the wet paint, and paint the stay last of all so that you can still adjust the window during the painting process.

1. Remove the catches and handles, and put them aside in a safe place.
2. Paint the rebates.
3. Paint the crossbars.
4. Paint the crossrails.
5. Paint the side verticals and edges.
6. Paint the frame.
7. Paint the window sill and the stay.

Cutting in

This technique produces a fine line on glazing bars, frames and edges. Place a loaded cutting-in brush about 3mm ($\frac{1}{8}$in) from the edge and carefully push it towards the join. Press lightly down and then draw the brush quickly along to make a long, clean line. Practise this technique; in the meantime, use masking tape or a paint shield to protect the glass.

PAINTING A CASEMENT WINDOW

1. Paint the rebates.

2. Next, paint the crossbars.

3. Paint the crossrails of the window.

4. Then paint each of the side verticals and edges.

5. Finally, paint the casement frame, window sill and stay.

USING MASKING TAPE

Fix masking tape over areas where you do not want the paint to go. Carefully remove once the paint is thoroughly dry.

General tips

- Paint windows that can be opened as early in the day as possible to allow enough time for them to dry before the evening.
- Scrape off any dried splashes and smudges using a razor blade or craft knife. Clean the surface with white spirit on a clean rag.
- Allow the paint to overlap 3mm ($\frac{1}{8}$in) onto the glass to prevent moisture seeping between putty and glass and causing the wood to rot.

Flooring

The floor always has a tremendous impact on the overall appearance of an interior. It is also a major expense, so consider your choice carefully in conjunction with the rest of the scheme, and do not leave it to chance or the last minute, or to an impulse buy that bears no relation to your décor. Nor should you rush out and buy something new and expensive before thinking about whether you can resuscitate an existing floor: you may find that sanding the floorboards, or cleaning a carpet that is old but in good condition, will give you just as attractive and appropriate a floorcovering as a new one.

When buying carpeting, remember that it comes in various qualities in similar colourways. If you are buying a carpet for the bedroom, for example, it will not need to be particularly robust and may therefore be cheaper, while outside in the corridor or on the staircase you could choose the same colour but in a tougher quality to withstand heavier wear.

When choosing tiles or other hard flooring for the bathroom, kitchen and hallway you must make sure they have a non-slip finish, as many hard floors become slippery when wet and can be dangerous.

Flooring

Floors work harder than any other part of the house: they have to withstand the weight of furniture and the constant tramp of shoes and boots, the abrasion caused by particles of grit and damage from spills. The harder the wear your floor is likely to receive, the more robust it will need to be, so ask for advice when buying.

Flat woven rugs, such as kilims, are remarkably versatile and can be used as upholstery; some are even flexible enough to use as curtains. They are versatile aesthetically as well, and will complement a wide variety of styles. This room is a good example of how they can be used on the floor, bed and cushions without being overbearing.

Choosing a floorcovering

The look of a floor and its relationship to the rest of the interior decoration matter a great deal to the final look of a room. However, there is a flooring suitable for every conceivable situation, and the most sensible course to take is to decide what flooring you actually need in each room or area and then to look for what you like best in that category. Warm floorcoverings such as seagrass matting are better for children's rooms than thick carpet that is no good for building bricks or doing jigsaw puzzles; you can use certain types of carpet in the bathroom, but it is usually better to choose a smooth, hard flooring that will be easy to mop and clean; and smooth floorings are best in rooms where pets sleep and in the hallway where dust and mud are brought in (you can always soften them with small rugs that will be quick to vacuum or to shake out).

In a hot country, a quarry- or ceramic-tiled floor is a welcome relief from the heat of the sun, whereas in a cooler climate it may be more welcoming to use some sort of matting or carpet, or a warmer finish such as linoleum. In centrally heated homes, tiles are often the favoured finish for kitchen floors; these are particularly pleasant when the heating comes from under the floor so that, since tiles conduct heat well, the floor itself acts as a large and pleasantly warm radiator.

Above **The machine-woven tapestry fabric used on the sofa and curtains makes an intriguing contrast with the very large, dramatic diamonds painted in purple and sand onto the floorboards.** *Below* **Polished terracotta tiles give a lovely warm and solid finish to this elegant conservatory and make a good foil for the wicker furniture.**

Linoleum and vinyl floors are suitable for kitchens and bathrooms. Vinyl is available in a vast range of designs and can emulate marble, brick or ceramic tiles, or be self-coloured. Linoleum feels softer and is sold in interesting colours and geometric patterns that have many possibilities.

If you have decided on a soft flooring such as natural-fibre matting or carpet, you will have a wide choice. Decide what will be the most practical and the nearest to your budget.

The existing floor

You may have a concrete or a suspended timber floor as your basic surface. Solid concrete floors are laid over the building foundations and are found in newer properties. They are usually finished with screed (floor-levelling compound) and may have tiles or wooden flooring or other semi-permanent flooring on top.

Suspended timber floors are found upstairs in many houses and, in older properties, on many ground floors too. They usually consist of floorboards, sometimes tongued-and-grooved, supported on timber joists, which are con-

nected to the walls of the house or held up by brick walls laid over a concrete foundation. Often the joists are not sturdy enough to support a heavy floor, so if you have set your heart on a heavy material for an upstairs room, check that this will be possible.

Preparation

Before laying new flooring, check the existing floor or sub-floor to ensure that it is level, clean, smooth and damp-proof. You may have to use a screed: this is mixed on site and poured over the floor, and will be self-levelling. It is best to have the screed laid professionally (although there are some DIY types available); one type can be 'feathered' at the edges and is suitable when a sub-floor is very uneven or where there are likely to be problems at skirtings and doors.

Old floorboards and some other floors can be covered with hardboard, chipboard or plywood to give a smooth, level finish and to draught-proof them. This makes them suitable for many kinds of flooring — or you could paint or stain and varnish them.

If you are preparing for ceramic tiles, you must make sure that the floor is absolutely solid because, if it moves, the tiles will crack and break.

Treating damp

Deal with damp problems before laying new flooring on top, or the damp could affect its surface or even creep up the walls. The most effective remedy is to have a damp-proof course installed professionally. Various types of damp-proof membrane are available: some are poured on as liquid and allowed to harden, some are in sheet form and others are painted on. There are also various vapour barriers, which are recommended for use with specific floorings such as rubber.

Damp proofing should always be professionally installed, but remember to discuss your chosen flooring with the installer so that the correct type of damp-proof membrane is laid.

Hard and semi-hard flooring

The floorings included under this heading are the most durable types available, and will stand up well to wear and tear. Hard flooring is expensive and a major part of the decorating budget, so take time to consider carefully before deciding on the flooring that you need for each room.

This sensational floor is custom-made of MDF, painted with wood stain and floor paints, then lightly sanded and finished with several coats of satin gloss varnish.

Qualities of hard flooring

Hard floorings include floorboards, parquet and woodblock flooring, wood-strip flooring, ceramic and quarry tiles, stone, brick, slate and marble. These are the most durable types.

Wooden floors have a warmth, colour, texture and grain that no imitations can achieve. They look stylish, are hardwearing, blend with traditional and modern furnishings and are comparable in price to other floorcoverings, but their surface is vulnerable to damage. Wooden floors of all types look marvellous in living rooms as well as in hallways and bedrooms, and can be varnished, sealed, painted, stained or polished. Rubbing the surface with a dry mop will improve its sheen. Wooden flooring is available in light, honey colours or in rich, warm tones, so choose the one that will go best with your furniture and decoration.

You may well be able to sand and seal existing floorboards to provide a completely new look. However, boards are often cut up to allow for laying central-heating pipes in the space underneath them, and are subsequently re-laid in small pieces. These will wobble and squeak and never really provide decent flooring again, but in this case you could easily lay wood-strip flooring to take their place.

Stone, marble and slate floors are porous in their natural state but can be sealed. There is a very wide colour range available, so choose carefully.

Refurbishing a hard floor

Most existing hard floors can be refurbished if necessary, so, if you live in an older property and have an uneven or worn stone floor, don't immediately feel that you must take it out. Such floors – including granite, sandstone, or York or Portland stone – can be extremely attractive. Some cement or concrete floors can be painted to make them look more attractive: you will need to buy a special industrial floor paint, or a deck paint for use on boats.

Ceramic tiles always look attractive on floors, although they are fairly hard on the feet and would need rugs in an area where you have to stand or walk around a great deal. Cracked or broken ceramic or quarry tiles can be replaced and re-grouted. Most ceramic tiles have a permanently glazed surface, but some quarry tiles are porous and can be sealed. A special dressing is available to help preserve old slate, and badly scratched marble can be polished up again. Wood can be stripped, sanded, varnished, stained or painted and, if necessary, re-sealed.

Pattern on floors

Beware of introducing too much haphazard pattern on a floor, and remember that plain tiles always look stylish. If you do use patterning, make it an overall disciplined geometric design or put in the occasional patterned tile at specific distances. Don't be seduced into using pretty wall tiles for a floor, as these need to be flooring-grade tiles (some manufacturers do make 'universal' tiles for wall and floor use).

You can cover any hard floor with rugs or small mats to soften the look and give a more comfortable area where the floor is most used. All rugs should have a non-slip backing, and the floor underneath them should not be highly polished.

Semi-hard flooring

Semi-hard floors include cork tiles, linoleum tiles, vinyl sheet and tiles, rubber sheet and thermoplastic tiles.

Hardboard and plywood are often used as sub-floors for other types of flooring but, if used in flooring grades, can also be used as semi-hard floors in their own right.

Although semi-hard floors are not as durable as truly hard floors, they will stand up to fairly heavy wear. They are usually fixed to the sub-floor, so are not easy to remove. You may sometimes be able to cover a semi-hard floor with a different type of flooring which can be laid loose on top, stuck down with adhesive or pinned into position. It is also possible to cover a semi-hard floor with a latex compound in order to put another type of flooring on top. If in doubt, seek expert advice.

Cork and linoleum are both natural floorcoverings. Cork comes from the bark of a tree and linoleum consists mainly of linseed oil and sawdust. Linoleum largely went out of use with the advent of vinyl, but has come back into fashion because of its hardwearing, quiet, warm and fairly bouncy qualities; it is good for kitchen and bathroom floors as well as children's rooms. Rubber, vinyl and thermoplastic tiles are all easy to maintain and suit to modern interiors, although vinyl is also available in designs that mimic natural floorcoverings.

Below A mosaic floor is ideal for a garden room like this and the variations in the colours soften the effect. It also looks good when used with a rug.
Right A stylish sense of ceremony is apparent here in the use of ceramic tiles laid in an enormous Greek key design in a grand entrance hall.

Directory of hard and semi-hard flooring

A multitude of different coloured tiles spill across this floor, around the bath and up the side of the washstand unit. The muted tones of the woodwork and bath prevent the tiles from overwhelming the room.

When choosing a hard flooring it is just as important as with soft flooring to get the colours and textures right for the colours and style of interior you have chosen. Do take samples of wallcoverings, upholstery, curtain materials and paint (or your complete sample board – see pages 28–9) with you when going out to buy floorcoverings to be sure that everything matches up or co-ordinates. There are many specialist flooring companies selling colours and textures of floors not available in all stores, so don't make up your mind until you have seen and compared as many options as possible.

Hard flooring

The varied options for hard flooring will allow you to create a range of finishes – from very traditional to bright and modern – to complement the rest of your décor.

Bricks

These are special bricks designed for indoor use, produced in shades of red, blue, brown, purple and yellow; they can be sealed.

Quarry tiles

Unglazed, high-fired clay tiles, these are impervious to grease and liquids (they can also be sealed). They are made in square, rectangular or interlocking shapes in yellow and terracotta through to dark blue.

Ceramic tiles

These good-looking glazed clay tiles will stand up to almost any wear, stains and spills, and are made in innumerable colours, shapes, sizes and patterns. Disadvantages are that they are cold in winter, and that anything dropped on them is liable to break.

Mosaic tiles

Elegant, waterproof and easy to maintain, this flooring may be made of glass silica, clay or marble. Mosaic floor tiles are sold in a wide range of colours and textures, and are generally backed on to squares of peel-off sheets for ease of laying.

Marble tiles

These attractive natural-stone tiles are usually sold in squares. They look best as a single colour (perhaps with a border), so that the natural patterning in the marble will stand out.

Terrazzo

This consists of marble chips set in a concrete base, and is available as tiles or slabs of varying colours. Terrazzo is expensive and probably not worth laying in a small area.

Slate

Slate is a stone flooring available in grey, blue-grey or green; it is impervious to water and heat.

Hardwood

High-quality woods used for floors include oak, maple and teak, all of which are resilient, warm and hard-wearing. These woods are available as parquet and as woodblock or wood-strip flooring.

Semi-hard flooring

This is a good option and can produce a warmer look and feel than some types of hard flooring.

Softwood

Spruce, fir and pine are all softwoods used to make floorboards, and will need sealing. Tongue-and-groove boards provide a handsome background for rugs; butt-joined boards may shrink unless you season them well (by letting them lie in your house for two to three weeks to acclimatize) before laying.

Plywood

This can resemble parquet, although it will deteriorate quickly in areas of heavy wear. It must be sealed and, if laid over floorboards, will require a plywood base.

1. Tiles in two shades of blue with a sea-green bath, acid pink walls and yellow ceiling decoration make this one of the most cheerful bathrooms you could hope to find.

2. Venetian marble steps lead up to a ceramic tiled floor. The earthy brown colours are very easy to live with.

3. Slate makes a particularly attractive flooring and it can be given a gentle sheen just by rubbing it over with a cloth dipped in milk.

4. Narrow hardwood boards make a friendly and elegant floor that particularly suits traditional furniture and panelling.

5. Cleverly chosen vinyl tiles in a disciplined design have been so arranged as to give the impression of a woven check fabric.

6. Large stone slabs suit an ancient interior and are well matched by antique rugs and furniture.

7. An unusual colour combination of chestnut brown and marble, laid diagonally to make an interesting floor of vinyl tiles.

8. Terrazzo flooring is an excellent material for a large and imposing room. It is good-looking and practical, but also rather expensive.

9. Modern parquet hardwood flooring with a darker border round the walls is the epitome of elegant design.

10. Ordinary floorboards have been painted in a large chequerboard design for maximum effect and to conceal their true identity.

Chipboard

This makes a good covering for concrete prior to carpeting, or can be used as a base for a hardwood floor; it must be sealed. Chipboard is a good insulator against noise.

Hardboard

This is a cheap, short-term flooring that should eventually be covered with a permanent flooring. Stain or seal it when in place.

Cork

Compressed cork is produced as tiles or in sheet form, and provides a quiet, resilient surface. It is usually available in a range of browns, or sometimes dyed; it needs to be sealed.

Vinyl

Vinyl is made in sheet form or as tiles, usually backed with latex. It can help with sound insulation, and is made in a wide range of qualities, designs and patterns including ceramic-tile and other imitations. Cushioned vinyl is the most comfortable flooring surface on which to walk.

Linoleum

This traditional type of flooring is hardwearing, flexible, resilient and quiet (the thicker the better for hard wear and sound insulation). It is available in sheet form or as tiles, and can be sealed.

Rubber

Made from a combination of natural and synthetic materials, rubber flooring is hardwearing, resilient, quiet, non-slip and stain-resistant. It comes in tile or sheet form in a range of interesting textures; narrow tiles are available for staircases.

Soft flooring

Soft floorcoverings such as carpets, rugs and natural matting are popular in many homes because they give a warm, soft finish that is comfortable to walk, sit or play on. These floorings are available for almost any situation – special carpets and carpet tiles are even manufactured for use in the kitchen and bathroom.

Carpet

Carpet is the most popular soft floorcovering. It comes in a wide range of types, materials, styles, qualities and prices, and can be fitted or loose-laid. Carpets and rugs are often placed on top of hard or semi-hard floorings, although fully fitted carpeting can be laid directly over the sub-floor provided that it is smooth and even, clean, dry and damp-proof.

Carpets may be either woven or tufted, the former being the hardest wearing. Modern carpets are made in many different fibres and blends of fibres; each gives its own distinctive character to the finished carpet, and affects its durability and resistance to staining and abrasion. Fibres range from wool and cotton to several types of man-made fibre.

Wool is still the most luxurious fibre for carpets: it is hardwearing, good-looking, takes colour well, does not attract dirt and is easy to clean. Many synthetic fibres are also hardwearing and stain-resistant, but they lack natural resilience and tend to flatten after a few months. For this reason, many carpet manufacturers now blend a natural and synthetic fibre to give the best of both worlds: a mix of 80 per cent wool and 20 per cent

Above Natural matting makes a good stair carpet and the black edging on this one adds definition and style. *Below right* A luxurious soft carpet made from pure wool is perfect for a bedroom and as a background for a hand-knotted rug.

nylon is a common blend. Acrylic carpet is hardwearing and looks very like a wool blend. Polypropylene is cheap, hardwearing and resistant to stains, but it is easily crushed and so often combined with wool. Polyester is a bulky fibre that is often used in bedroom carpets.

Loose-laid carpet

Some carpets are produced as squares (these are in fact usually rectangular rather than square). They may have borders, or bound or fringed edges, and they look attractive where floorboards that are in good condition will show around the edges of the room.

Oriental rugs are the *crème de la crème* of loose-laid floorcoverings; they have been made by tribal weavers for centuries and are still woven by hand in many parts of the world including Turkey, Iran, India and China. Motifs and designs have been handed down through the generations, and have crossed borders from country to country. Many of these rugs are now woven in workshops where they may lose some of the individual charm of the tribal weavings but have acquired a perfection that it is hard to beat. In spite of their often bold colours and positive designs, oriental carpets and rugs have a way of fitting into almost any interior scheme.

Always lay rugs over a non-slip underfelt: this will save them from becoming damaged between shoes and the hard floor, as well as preventing them from slipping dangerously or creeping across the floor.

Laying fitted carpet

Fitted carpets should always be professionally laid – particularly in the case of stair carpet, unless you intend to use stair rods or grippers. However, you can lay some tufted or felted carpet and carpet tiles yourself. If you are having a carpet professionally laid, ask for an itemized estimate, and check whether or not underfelt is included. Discuss with the layer where the seams should fall to avoid heavy wear and so that they are least noticeable. He will expect you to remove any furniture before the carpet is laid. Never be tempted to lay new carpet on top of old underfelt.

Laying carpet tiles

Carpet tiles can be laid on most floors, and are particularly useful for areas that may become grubby because individual tiles can be lifted and replaced if necessary. These tiles are sold by the box, so buy a box extra rather than a box too few. They should generally be laid loose although you may need to stick one or two tiles down, particularly on an uneven floor. In this case, use double-sided tape especially made for carpet tiles, or a spray adhesive.

Matting

Natural floorcoverings – such as seagrass and jute – are more basic than carpet but make good flooring for down-to-earth rooms such as a garden room or children's bedrooms, where something warm and natural is wanted without the expense of carpet. Oriental rugs look good when laid directly over these coverings.

Directory of soft flooring

Natural mattings is versatile and looks good in a number of different situations. Here, it works well in a formal living room where it suits the other natural objects such as baskets and oatmeal upholstery.

Carpets are graded for different uses and colours can often be matched in different qualities to provide continuity, so you can save money by buying cheaper carpeting for areas that will receive less wear. Carpet samples have labels on the back telling you the type of carpet and its recommended use. For example, a hallway will need an extra-heavy grade, while the bathroom and kitchen may be better suited to carpet tiles.

Woven carpet

The two main woven carpet types are Axminster and Wilton. They use high-quality materials and tend to be expensive, and the pile yarn and the backing are integrated during weaving to give a smooth, stable and durable finish. Wilton carpet is usually plain but occasionally has very simple, all-over designs; Axminster lends itself to intricate designs. Brussels weave is a very expensive variation on Wilton.

Tufted carpet

Here the yarn is stitched into a ready-made backing, secured with latex and strengthened with jute, polypropylene or foam. Tufted carpets come in a great many qualities and prices. They are often produced in plain colours but, when patterns are used, these are either incorporated during the tufting process or will be printed on.

Bonded carpets

Fusion-bonded carpet consists of fibres bonded to a pre-woven backing. The result is not very flexible, and so is unsuitable for use on stairs. Fusion-bonded carpet is less common than woven or tufted carpet; it is cheaper than woven but more expensive than tufted carpet.

Fibre-bonded carpet is another less common method of carpet construction, in which loose, synthetic fibres are felted on to a synthetic backing. Fibre-bonded carpets are hardwearing and inexpensive but rough underfoot and difficult to maintain; for this reason they are usually found in the form of carpet tiles.

Carpet tiles

Carpet tiles are available in a range of sizes. They are usually square in shape and are very easily laid even if you have no experience of carpet laying. The tiles can be made in the same ways as carpet and from the same fibres or blends of fibres. Many are designed specifically for use in kitchens, where their strong, rot-proof fibres will withstand dirt and liquids; as they are usually loose-laid, very stained squares can also be changed for new ones. Carpet tiles sometimes need to be stuck down around the edge of the room and at doorways: this is very easily done using heavy-duty double-sided tape specially designed for carpet-laying.

Natural fibres

These include coir, jute, seagrass and sisal. Natural fibres are subject to colour variations depending on the growing season and are liable to have knots and other minor imperfections, although these may be considered part of their charm and will not affect their wearing qualities. Colours range from light porridge to warm brown and pale green, and many different weaving patterns are available. These materials have a backing which makes them easy to clean and helps to prevent them from stretching.

Coir

This by-product of coconut is available in 4m (4½yd) widths, or as rugs; it is sometimes combined with sisal.

1. A natural wool carpet acts as a neutral base for a bold modern rug in a child's room.

2. A hand-knotted Oriental pile carpet is something to cherish. Such a carpet will complement a great many decorating styles.

3. Hand-woven kilims can be mixed and matched with each other and with many different interior styles.

4. This pure wool carpet in a lavender colour makes an interesting contrast to the surrounding warm yellow walls and green table.

5. Modern rag rugs can brighten up a bedroom or child's room with their uninhibited random colours.

6. Natural coir matting looks good with a hand-knotted Oriental carpet and Chinese vase.

7. A soft camel coloured carpet is a good match for the pretty sculptured desk and slender chair in this room.

8. An interesting, subtle tile effect is produced by this elegant white carpet in an all-white room.

9. A pretty and unobtrusive pattern in this Axminster carpet echoes the greens and blues in the furniture and furnishing fabrics.

Jute

Made from an Indian plant, jute is often used as a backing for carpets and, as a flooring in its own right, is a popular choice for bedrooms. It may be dyed in pastel colours or it can also be self-coloured.

Seagrass

Seagrass is a tough, flat fibre that is very resilient to stains and dirt and therefore often used in hallways, conservatories and children's playrooms. It needs to be sprayed with water from time to time to keep it supple, and makes a suitable base flooring for oriental carpets or rugs.

Sisal

Made from the leaves of the *Agave sisalana* plant, sisal is hardwearing but much smoother than coir. Wool-and-sisal mixes are available.

Oriental carpets and rugs

These floorcoverings are woven, usually from wool and sometimes from silk, or from a combination of both. New rugs are cheaper than their antique counterparts, and many shops import handmade rugs of great charm, woven in various parts of the world. In general, the denser the weave, the better the finished carpet will be.

Soft furnishings

Soft furnishings will be the icing on the cake of your decorating scheme: they make an important addition and can liven up, tone down or complement a room in a meaningful way. Even if you are not able to decorate the rest of the room immediately, a change of colour in the upholstery and curtains will transform the space and give the existing décor a new lease of life.

Your soft-furnishing scheme will take as much planning and thought as any other part of the decoration. There is such a wide choice of fabrics and styles available that it is easy to get carried away and find that you have bought wonderful fabrics that simply do not go together, or that

over-ride your carefully planned ideas. Whether you are starting afresh or livening up an existing scheme, remember that, as with all other design elements, soft furnishings have much greater impact and create a far better overall impression when they give a co-ordinated style to a room.

Making your own soft furnishings can be quite easy, and will give you the opportunity to create loose covers, curtains, cushions and cushion covers that are inexpensive, yet give your home a very personal touch.

Just one cushion cover can make all the difference to a scheme that needs a little pepping up and a change of curtains can transform a room. Even tie-on covers for chairs are suitable for beginners to tackle.

Soft furnishings

Much energy and colour flair has gone into furnishing this room, with its deep blues, bright reds and oranges and rich fabrics. These are complemented by the floorboards, stained red, and the pale kilim.

The choice of fabric is crucial to the final look of a room. However, fabrics are expensive and, unlike paint, if you don't like what you have chosen you cannot simply change it once you have turned it into curtains or upholstery, so your initial choice is very important.

Types of fabric

You should never choose fabrics simply for their colour and/or pattern – you must also consider whether a particular fabric will stand up to wear, whether it should be sheer or heavyweight, whether it will fade in the bright light of a window, whether it will drape well, whether it will stretch and whether it will crease easily.

Practicality and suitability are therefore the primary considerations. Upholstery and loose covers require fabrics with a high rub test (used by manufacturers to ascertain how well a fabric wears). Sofa and chair covers, window seats, seat cushions and other items where a fabric will undergo a lot of wear need a minimum rub test of 35,000 and preferably 50–60,000. The type of yarn used to weave the fabric will also affect its durability: for example, linen, cotton, wool and some man-made fibres are very durable, whereas silk and viscose are less robust. If a fabric is closely woven (with a high thread count), it will be less likely to pull out of shape.

Loose covers and upholstery must be heavy enough to withstand constant friction from sitting and, in a family home, must be sufficiently resilient to cope with the attentions of children and the dog or cat. Chair and sofa covers are expensive items, and should be chosen to last for many years. Piped edges wear quickly, so make sure that any material used for piping is at least as tough as the cover fabric itself (piping of the same fabric or of a different colour of the same range is a good idea). Bed and table linen also needs to be robust, as it will be continually washed at high temperatures. Only with small, decorative pieces of furniture, or accessories such as a bedroom chair cover or a display cushion that will receive little wear, can you indulge any yearning to choose a covering fabric for its beauty rather than for its practicality.

When it comes to curtains, drapes, throw-overs and fabrics that do not suffer from constant frictional wear you will have a wider choice of the sheers and more exotic fabrics, although kitchen curtains and others that may become dirty and need frequent washing should be made of cotton or other washable material. Sheer curtains will also need fairly frequent laundering, but can usually be given a cool wash and will dry without needing to be ironed. Heavily lined and interlined curtains in the dining room, living room and bedrooms, which will only need cleaning once a year, are candidates for more exotic materials. Bed covers will not receive much wear, and so can be either washable fabrics or sultry silks and satins.

Colours for fabrics

Fabrics that will take an important place in the room – such as for seating covers and curtains – should be in a colour that will match or complement the main colours of the walls. Remember that pale-coloured chair covers will become grubby very quickly, particularly in well-used rooms such as a playroom or the family living room, so it will be best to keep yellows, whites and other pastel shades to rooms where they will retain their original freshness.

Rooms that receive little natural light usually liven up when filled with warm colours such as oranges and orangey-reds. Blues and greens can look marvellous in a very sunny room, and a glazed or sheer fabric will respond well to the light.

Pattern and style

When choosing and mixing patterns, keep in mind the scale of your room as well as the main design and balance of colours. You can pick up on the main

colour in the room in the background colour of your fabric, or in any of the other colours in the upholstery design. Mix and match patterns if you wish, but make sure that they always relate to each other in some way – perhaps by having the same design, or similar colour tones.

The pattern itself should relate to the general style of the room. A *toile de Jouy* fabric, for example, would go well in a frilly French-style bedroom, whereas a more formal plaid or check pattern would work well with striped wallpaper in a smarter setting. If you are aiming for a more Gothic style, rich fabrics with Medieval motifs – such as a heavy velvet with a *fleur-de-lys* repeat design, work well.

When choosing fabrics, it is often a good idea to concentrate first on the main fabrics for upholstery, loose covers and curtains, and to choose the fabrics for the finishing touches – such as cushion covers, table cloths and so on – once you have completed the main scheme.

Above A range of reds in matt and shiny fabrics makes a truly rich and exotic impression. *Below* Co-ordinating colours, but in different fabrics, create an understated, yet confident elegance.

Directory of soft-furnishings fabrics

Here, a rich mix of woven fabrics including sheers, damasks and linen, contrast effectively with the tiny prints on the cushions.

Woven fabrics can range from plain weaves such as calico and gingham through to twill (which has greater weight and firmness), satin weave (which has a definite front and back) and doublecloth (a strong, reversible material); while computerized looms can also produce very complex tapestries, damasks and brocades. However, pattern is often added by printing rather than during weaving and, in general, printed fabric is lighter in weight.

Woven fabrics

These provide a wide choice of colours and designs, and will be suitable for a range of soft-furnishing requirements.

Plain weaves

These fabrics include basic plain cotton weaves such as calico and cambric, as well as canvas which is heavier and more durable; you must wash them before use to prevent shrinking later. Plain-woven stripes and checks are available in different colours and qualities, including Madras cottons, ginghams, tartans and mattress ticking. The harder-wearing fabrics will make seat covers; the more delicate are suitable for curtains and blinds.

Textured weaves

Single-colour twill weaves are available in herringbone, ladder stripe, floral, brocaded and other textures. They are often sufficiently robust for upholstery, and the texture changes subtly in different lights. Coloured motifs are sometimes woven into the fabric and these can break up the plain colour on, say, a large sofa, without distracting from larger patterns in the room.

Silk weaves

Plain and patterned silks are versatile and change colour when viewed from different angles. They are good for rich curtains, covering small chairs and twining round curtain poles.

Damasks and brocades

A true damask is reversible, with intricate patterns in one colour and a shiny satin-weave surface contrasting with a matt surface. Brocade is similar but has extra colours woven over the surface like embroidery. Both fabrics are suitable for formal furnishings, heavy curtains, bed covers, and table cloths and napkins.

Tapestries

These heavy, hand-woven pictures were originally used to clothe Medieval walls, and antique and modern tapestries still make marvellous wallhangings. Hand-woven kilim rugs use the same technique and can be used for upholstery, cushions and wallhangings. Tapestries made on computerized looms are softer and more pliable, and they are good for curtains and throws.

Velvet and chenille

These fabrics are hardwearing, heavy and luxurious with a raised pile. Velvet can be used for upholstery, although the pile will flatten where it is sat on. Corduroy – a ridged velvet – is a practical choice for cushions.

Ikat

This is a hand-woven fabric in which the weft threads are dyed before weaving, producing delicate and subtle patterns. Being lightweight, ikat is generally best used for cushion covers, curtains and bed covers.

Sheer fabrics

These are open-weave fabrics – such as muslin, organdie and lace – which allow light through. Some sheers incorporate a delicate embroidered pattern. They can be used on their own as single curtains or blinds, or behind a main set of curtains, and are fine enough to be draped over poles.

Printed fabrics

These fabrics can add a whole new dimension to a plainly decorated room, but you will need to use them judiciously to maintain an overall balance and harmony.

1. Rich and rare: chenille fabrics with gold *fleur-de-lys* motifs woven in.

2. This damask fabric with its contrasting matt and shiny surfaces is a rich complement to an elegant sofa.

3. Simple blue and white gingham and seersucker have been used here to provide a fresh, pretty look.

4. Two luxury woven damask pillow covers add a touch of the exotic to this bedroom.

5. The choice of damasks, brocades and other woven fabrics is enormous and exciting.

6. The traditional floral prints on these two spectacular chairs is amply complemented by the enormous bold floral motifs on the wall and curtains.

7. Woven paisley throws and hangings can add grandeur to a scheme.

8. Here, woven kilims and striped rugs create a warm and comfortable interior.

9. Blue and white always has a fresh look. Here, it contrasts prettily with the greenery of the conservatory plants.

10. Pale fabrics are given added interest by their different textures in this traditional room.

Pictorial designs

These fabrics are epitomized by the eighteenth-century *toile de Jouy* designs, with their pastoral scenes printed in one colour on a white or cream background. Other pictorial fabrics are inspired by classical architectural elements, by pictures of fruit and vegetables or boats and fish, or by favourite storybook or TV characters. They are best not draped so that the pictures can be appreciated.

Flora and fauna

Flowers and foliage and, to a lesser extent, birds and animals are the most popular themes of all for printed fabrics. These may be formal with stripes, grand with large motifs, or informal with rambling plants or cottagey with tiny flower buds and sprays. Chintz is a cotton fabric with a floral design printed in several colours on either a white or light ground; glazed chintz has a shiny finish.

Arts and Crafts patterns (many designed by William Morris and his contemporaries in the 1880s) are perennially popular and were probably influenced by Persian textiles. Informal Provençal prints, with their bright floral motifs, were seventeenth-century copies of imported Indian prints, and today look best in country-style interiors. Printed paisley uses a motif taken from Kashmir in the eighteenth century. It will add to a sophisticated scheme.

Geometric and abstract designs

The inspiration for these fabrics, which were popular in the 1950s and '60s, derives from the Middle East, China, Japan and India.

Curtains and drapes

Windows bring light into a room. Tall, well-proportioned windows do this particularly effectively, providing an airy, well-lit space that enhances the decorations inside. However, even the smallest window will bring in some light, and you should exploit this to the full.

It is important not to conceal any of the window panes or to block any light with heavy curtains that you cannot draw right back. In overlooked rooms where you need some privacy, you may need to add sheers – muslin or very light lace would be ideal as it will not block out light.

Another role of windows is to offer a view to the outside. This may simply be a view of clouds and sky through a rooflight, an outlook on to a bustling street, or even a wonderful vista of sea or a beautiful garden. Whatever view you have, keep it in mind when choosing curtain fabrics and styles. For instance, you may best do justice to a

startlingly beautiful view by not curtaining the windows at all, or you could frame a view attractively with well-chosen drapes or curtains; keep the style simple or the viewer's eye will stop at the curtains and go no further. At the other extreme, you can screen or diminish a less attractive view with curtains that provide their own area of interest.

The way in which you dress a window will affect the mood of the room, the amount and quality of the light entering it and its relationship to the outside world. In Holland few people have curtains at all, so their windows provide little vignettes of home life for passers-by. In France, by contrast, lace is often used to conceal interiors. The patterns in the lace often feature subjects such as cottages and the fabric is used in a restrained manner that gives it great interest and style.

When choosing curtains, consider how the windows will appear from outside. For example, townhouse windows often look better with restrained styles – maybe blinds or draped curtains – with ruched curtains and blinds reserved for the back of the house. Elaborate styles are best kept for flamboyant houses, such as Victorian Gothic edifices, or country homes where they will echo flower borders in the garden.

Main picture Deep blue silk certainly suggests formality and these gathered curtains, with their self-fabric tie-backs and brass rosettes, give a definite formality to this dining room, with its mahogany tables and elegant chairs. The blue-and-gold scheme is reinforced by the blind.

Left Sheer curtain fabrics provide a stylish solution to old-fashioned net. This one has simply been stitched at the top, leaving a wide enough channel through which to slot the curtain rod.

Curtains and drapes

You can have enormous fun with curtains and drapes. In a formal setting, you should make and line the curtains carefully, and hang them from suitable poles or tracking with appropriate headings; but for a more informal interior you can create stunning but inexpensive effects by simply folding, draping, looping or scrunching fabrics around your windows.

White can be a very restful colour. In this bedroom, the chair, stool and bed are all in white and the choice of sheer white curtains adds to the calming atmosphere here.

Curtains for privacy

For anyone confident enough to leave their homes open to public view, or in the countryside where privacy is not a problem, the undressed window can be enchanting from outside and also allows maximum light for those inside. However, if you prefer some privacy, you could curtain the lower window with lace. Lace is often best left ungathered so that the pattern can be more appreciated.

Billowing muslin or sheer fabric running down the whole length of a tall window can be attractive when heavier curtains frame the window, but remember that even the sheerest of fabrics will keep out some light. A blind may enable you to cut out glare from the sun while still allowing light in through the bottom of the window.

Curtain length

The length of your curtains will be crucial to the final look of the room. Usually these end just below the window sill, or at floor level; occasionally they may come to the top of the sill or trail on the floor. Floor-length curtains

Right This grand and unusual bathroom scheme follows its midnight blue-and-gold theme through really well. The glazed chintz curtains are held back by a golden sun and the carpet, panelling, wallpaper and even the bath itself are all in keeping with the style. *Below right* This simple window treatment is given a touch of glamour by the use of satin finish fabric swept up with a tie-back.

look generous, make a strong statement and help to give a unified look. Curtains that end below sill length look more cottagey and will suit small windows. In the kitchen, blinds may be more practical but, if you want curtains, leave them open with blinds fitted behind them.

Matching fabric to style

You may wish to match your curtain style to the period of your house and, certainly, curtains will look better if they are in keeping with the architecture. Elegant Georgian windows always look good with fabrics draped from a curtain pole and perhaps drawn back with ties. During the eighteenth century, fabrics were expensive and many people used Roman blinds made of waxed and printed linens, but a Rococo look could be acquired quite cheaply with festoon and drapery curtains which use less fabric. Festoon curtains are made by attaching lines of brass rings to vertical strips of tape, sewn to the back of the fabric; cords passed through the rings are then used to raise the curtains in looped swags. Drapery curtains work the same way but the rings are lined up diagonally to

pull the curtains up and aside. The idea was to use as little fabric as possible, so the ruches are restrained. Only the rich could create Rococo effects with heavy velvets and satins, adorned with lambrequins, swags and fringes.

The Gothic interiors of the Victorians harked back to the architecture of the Middle Ages. Windows had ogee arches, and fabrics were heavy velvets and brocades. Today's version is less heavy, with lighter fabrics and colours and hints of the Medieval in looped curtain headings, ogee furniture shapes and in the heraldic *fleur-de-lys* and Tudor rose fabric motifs.

Country style spans many centuries and in general the curtaining in this case is simple, with pleated fabric hanging from a pole. The fabric itself would often be a printed floral or striped cotton, or a glazed chintz in a tiny diaper (overall) pattern or with a larger design of garden flowers. There

might be a simple pelmet, and the fabric would usually be lined.

1960s and '70s homes were often severely square, and had large 'picture' windows running from one end of a wall to the other. These windows are best treated simply, with curtain tracking running along one wall and curtains rigidly gathered and falling to the floor so that, when drawn, they form a curtained wall. Picture windows often leave little wall space, so the fabric chosen should not be heavy or bulky.

Matching poles and tracking to style

Simple poles with a large diameter are suitable for eighteenth-century styles as well as for an Arts and Crafts interior, while metal or elaborate wooden poles with finials, curtain clips or castellated loops are more in keeping with Gothic style. Tracking can be used to hang the disciplined pleats that will be best for picture windows.

Directory of poles, tracking and accessories

An elegant, narrow black metal pole with painted gold finials makes a gracious support for this elegantly draped white calico. It is important to use such fabrics generously to get a good effect.

The main difference between curtain poles and tracking, stylistically, is that poles are intended to be seen as part of the overall effect whereas tracking is designed to be as discreet as possible and is usually completely hidden by the curtain heading or by a pelmet. A pole consists of a rod made of wood or metal, with decorative finials and curtain rings. Tracking is fitted with runners.

Curtain poles

As poles are intended to be seen, you need to choose a style to complement your decorating scheme. Poles are available in various diameters and are usually sold by the metre (yard). Pole kits (consisting of the pole, brackets, rings and finials) are widely available and the poles can be cut to length.

Wooden poles

These can be painted, stained, oiled or waxed. Natural wood suits a modern interior, as do plain, bright colours; white works well with a simple floral scheme; and mahogany-coloured poles look elegant in a formal room. Carved, painted and gilded poles will complement a Gothic or an ethnic look.

Metal rods

Narrow metal poles of iron or steel, in black, steel-grey or with a greenish patina, are often very sculptural and are suitable for modern Gothic or minimalist interiors; use these with rings, or, alternatively, with cased or looped curtain headings.

Slender rods

Cheap but strong enough to carry lightweight curtains and sheer fabrics, these rods may be made of wooden dowelling, plastic-covered net rod or brass café rod and are suited to small windows or to the bottom half of windows facing the street. You can fit slender rods into a window recess or where the top of a window is near the ceiling. Lightweight rods with a bracket and hinge fitted at one end are also quite useful in deep-set windows, where you can pull curtain and rod back against the reveal.

Curtain tracking

This comprises a plastic or metal rail with sliding runners to hold the curtain hooks; different weights of tracking are available for different fabrics and situations. An overlap arm enables one curtain to overlap the other when drawn. Metal tracking is strong and durable; plastic is easier to fit and is perfectly adequate for most domestic curtains; and plastic tracking with a metal core is easily bent around curves. *Faux* poles (or corded poles) are pole-like casings with tracking set inside; a hidden pulley system opens and closes the curtains.

Accessories

Accessories are widely available to suit all types of curtains; department stores and DIY outlets usually carry a good selection of designs.

Curtain rings

Rings are used with curtain poles and curtain heading tape. Make sure that they fit over the pole loosely so that they are easy to draw across, and allow for a separate ring at either end of the pole, between bracket and finial, to keep the outer edge of the curtain in place. To hang lightweight curtains, you can simply sew small brass, metal or plastic rings at equal intervals to the curtain top.

Curtain clips

These provide a quick, easy and very effective method of hanging curtains: they are small curtain rings attached to decorative clips, which you simply clip at equal intervals along the top of the curtain.

1. Silk fabric deserves special treatment and these curtains have been meticulously gathered and hung from wooden rings on a large wooden pole with extra draping at the top.

2. A matt blue rod and finial with gold decoration gives a bright finish to a white curtain.

3. A very simple method of hanging curtains is from a metal rod with wire rings that fit through eyelet holes in the top of the curtain.

4. Black wrought iron finials and a rod give this charming sheer fabric a whole new dimension.

5. Disciplined pleating, using a special curtain heading tape, gives these track-hung curtains great formality and restraint.

6. If a bed can have a sheer canopy, why not a bath? This one has been simply draped over a short brass pole attached to the wall.

7. A choice of narrow poles and finials in metal. All these would look good with sheer or unlined curtains.

8. A fixed, sheer curtain hangs over a circular window without concealing its shape or the view outside.

9. A metal curtain rod has been bent to follow the curve in the deep recess of this window so that the curtains can be drawn completely back from the window panes.

10. The gun metal of this simple, elegant pole is echoed by the grey edging to the unlined curtain.

Finials

Finials are decorative finishes designed to be fitted to each end of a curtain pole. A huge variety is available, but make sure they are in keeping with the style of your curtains and in proportion to the pole.

Curtain hooks

In addition to the usual curtain hooks, which slot into heading tape and runners, several specialist hooks are available. These include a combined hook and slider, and a combined valance hook and glider which draws the valance back with the curtain during the day. You can buy valance tracking either with tracking, or separately to add later.

Cording sets and draw rods

A corded pulley system makes it easier to draw curtains that are difficult to reach, and without handling the fabric. Plastic draw rods attached to the leading edge of the curtain provide a simpler alternative. Electric curtain track will draw the curtains at the touch of a button, and computer mechanisms can draw the curtains at specific times (a useful device for making the house look occupied at holiday times). For neatness, wind the excess cord around a cord tidy before tucking it into one of the tape pockets.

Curtain weights

Weights help curtains to hang well, and they are available in two different forms. Buttons are circular and they need to be sewn into place individually; lead weight tape consists of small cylindrical weights and runs in a continuous line along the inside of the curtain hem.

Basic techniques:
fixing poles and tracking

It is important to fix curtain poles and tracking securely to the wall. Long curtains of heavy fabric and lined curtains in particular weigh a great deal and are constantly being pulled backwards and forwards, so will certainly dislodge any fixings that are not secure.

These curtains, though imposing, were easy to make by gathering the tops evenly and hanging them from a simple brass pole with brass hold-backs fitted at window level.

General information on fixing

Poles are usually fixed to a wall on brackets, one at each end and, for a long pole, one in the middle.

A bracket will prevent the rings from moving any further so their position depends on how far you want to pull the curtain back. The outer curtain ring fits between bracket and finial to hold the curtain in place when it is drawn.

Lightweight rods can be slotted into small metal brackets with integral sockets. You can also get telescopic rods with an internal spring which can expand to fit the window. Track should be fitted at least 5cm (2in) above the window and 15–40cm (6–18in) beyond the sides of the window.

If possible, screw the holding brackets for tracks and poles directly to the wall. Battens can be useful in some situations to help the curtain clear the window frame but they can look clumsy.

If you want the curtains to fall from ceiling to floor, some track can be screwed to the ceiling. In this case, make sure you can fix the brackets into the joists or fix timber between joists to provide a secure fixing.

Marking the position

Decide where the pole or tracking is to sit between the top of the window and the ceiling, use a spirit level to check that the line is horizontal and measure carefully to make sure that it is centred on the window. Mark the line with a pencil. (If fixing the brackets to a batten, mark where the top of the batten is to go).

Fixing brackets to the wall

To fix the brackets for tracking, drill holes to take the screws and wall plugs at about 15cm (6in) intervals. Poles will need only two brackets, one at either end (if you have long windows, the poles must be strong enough to support the curtains without sagging). When you mark the positions for the holes, use a spirit level to check that they are level, then use a screwdriver to ensure a tight fixing.

Fixing to a solid or hollow wall

With a solid wall, you must drill holes so that you can fit plastic wall plugs to grip the screws in place. Most curtain tracking comes with the brackets, screws and wall plugs that you will need to put them up; if not, you can buy these separately.

When fixing to a hollow wall, use special expanding plugs that will grip the inside of the wall and become tighter as you screw them in.

Fixing brackets to a batten

Drilling the wall and putting in wall plugs should be simple with a hammer drill and a masonry bit, unless there is a concrete lintel above the window that is too hard for drilling. In this case, the best solution is to fit a planed softwood batten and to fix the brackets to this. The batten should be longer than the lintel so that you can drill into the brickwork at either end, but shorter than the tracking so that it will be hidden directly behind the curtain heading.

Mark the position of the batten as you would do for fixing to a wall, then take the batten down and drill pilot holes at either end (the diameter of the holes should obviously match the screws that you are using). Reposition the batten and mark the position of each hole with a bradawl, drill the holes, insert wall plugs, screw the batten to the wall and secure the central part with contact adhesive. Position the brackets at 25–37cm (10–15in) intervals to hold the tracking along the length of the batten.

FIXING A BATTEN FOR BRACKETS

1. Use a spirit level to mark the position of the wooden batten.

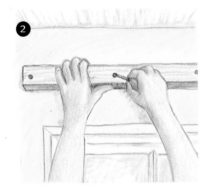

2. The batten should be longer than the lintel. Mark the position of each screw carefully with a bradawl.

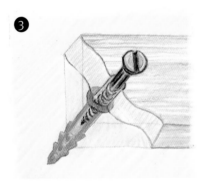

3. Finally, secure the bracket to the wall using wall plugs.

Directory of window treatments

This round window has been treated as though it were a painting in an exhibition, with a pristine white fabric and gold 'frame' pole and cords.

There are almost limitless ways of treating windows, from elaborately gathered, pelmeted and draped curtains to wisps of muslin or lace. Curtains can be interlined, lined or unlined, and can hang sedately from tracking or richly from decorated poles. If you have an arched window you can give it arched curtains, and there are many options for pelmets, lambrequins and tie-backs.

Informal curtains

These types of curtain are very easy to make – even if you have no previous experience – and can create beautiful effects in the right setting.

Unlined curtains

The simplest form of curtains, these are cheaper and easier to make than lined curtains, and are simpler to wash. If you choose the right fabric, unlined curtains will look charming in an informal bedroom or child's room, as well as in the kitchen or bathroom (if necessary, you could add detachable linings to darken a child's room in summer). Suitable fabrics for this include gingham, lace, muslin and light floral cottons.

Ungathered curtains

You can hang fabric with a picture motif or lace with a strong design from a narrow rod or plastic-covered wire without gathers so that the picture is visible. This is a suitable treatment for small windows, for the lower section of windows where you wish to retain some privacy, and for the bathroom; it is also a very cheap way of making curtains because of the small amount of fabric needed.

Tie-on curtains

These look stylish – particularly in a modern interior – and are very easy to make. The top edge can be left ungathered when drawn, giving the curtains a picture-like quality. Tie-on curtains can look particularly interesting if you line the fabric in a contrasting plain colour and use the contrasting fabric as heading and for the ties, which can be wide or narrow.

Sheer curtains

These have an important part to play in today's home – not just for privacy or to keep out the sun, but to give a light, airy and romantic feeling to a bedroom or breakfast room. Very often one width of fabric is sufficient, and you can hang this from a pole or drape and knot it loosely around the pole before tying it back on one side. There are many sheer fabrics from which to choose, including muslin, voile and cotton lace.

Informal drapes

Window treatments can be both informal and dramatic: the secret is to use a lightweight fabric that will drape easily and hang prettily. Use plenty of it and wind it loosely around a curtain pole, drawing it into fold-backs or tie-backs. This sort of curtaining can be particularly effective in some situations: for example, used in front of a bow window where you need to position the curtain some way in front so as not to detract from the window's attractive shape.

Formal curtains

These curtains are time-consuming and costly to make, but the extra effort will be well worthwhile in a more formally decorated room.

Curtains with hand-pleated headings

Tall, elegant windows deserve special treatment. Lined and generously full-length curtains give a feeling of luxury, and hand-pleating can produce intricate headings that will allow the fabric to hang perfectly. You can use hand-pleating either on the curtains themselves, or on a valance above them to lend extra body and dignity.

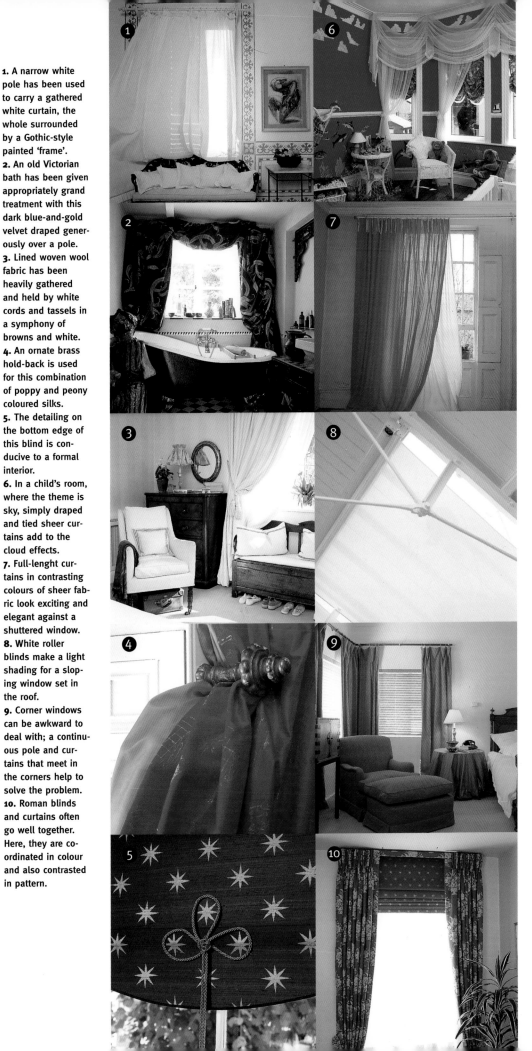

1. A narrow white pole has been used to carry a gathered white curtain, the whole surrounded by a Gothic-style painted 'frame'.

2. An old Victorian bath has been given appropriately grand treatment with this dark blue-and-gold velvet draped generously over a pole.

3. Lined woven wool fabric has been heavily gathered and held by white cords and tassels in a symphony of browns and white.

4. An ornate brass hold-back is used for this combination of poppy and peony coloured silks.

5. The detailing on the bottom edge of this blind is conducive to a formal interior.

6. In a child's room, where the theme is sky, simply draped and tied sheer curtains add to the cloud effects.

7. Full-lenght curtains in contrasting colours of sheer fabric look exciting and elegant against a shuttered window.

8. White roller blinds make a light shading for a sloping window set in the roof.

9. Corner windows can be awkward to deal with; a continuous pole and curtains that meet in the corners help to solve the problem.

10. Roman blinds and curtains often go well together. Here, they are co-ordinated in colour and also contrasted in pattern.

Dramatic headings

You will transform lined curtains with simple gathers into objects of luxury by adding interesting pelmets or heading drapes. Make use of co-ordinating fabric ranges to create really dramatic results, with curtains edged in different fabric and a deep lambrequin or pelmet which you could also edge in the co-ordinating fabric. The pelmet could be spectacularly shaped – for example, in a deep zigzag – or could run straight across with contrasting deep fringing. Lambrequins can be deep with scalloped or other interesting edges. Swags and tails will also give style and dignity to curtains.

Tie backs

These add a definite touch of style to a formal pair of curtains. You could make them in the same or a contrasting fabric to your curtains, or buy thick, rich velvet ropes with tassels or any of the other ready-made tie-backs now available.

Blinds

Blinds may be the best answer where there is no room to draw a curtain back from a window, or where something neat, cheap and unobtrusive is required. They are easy to use, cheap to make or buy, available in many fabrics and colours, and can be used on their own or behind formal curtains. Roman blinds are sophisticated and stylish, lifting into neat folds; roller blinds are cheap and cheerful; and ruched blinds are ideally suited to a dramatic or deeply romantic interior.

Tools and equipment

A comprehensive sewing kit consists of dozens of bits and pieces which can be fun to collect and kept in various containers, not necessarily in one sewing box or basket. As well as the absolute essentials such as scissors, needles and thread, you will find it useful to have a collection of braids, trims, buttons, embroidery threads, beads and pieces of lace. A 'rag bag' of offcuts and short lengths of fabric can also be invaluable for trimmings and for trying out new ideas.

If you are an experienced dressmaker or sewer, you will probably already have many of the items that follow in your sewing box. If you are a beginner, you will find it worth investing in them: the majority are quite inexpensive and will take up very little storage space, and they will all be invaluable for making your own soft furnishings.

A sewing machine

If you do not already have a sewing machine, this will obviously be your biggest outlay. A basic electric machine will usually do straight stitch, zigzag (together with a few more elaborate stitches), and buttonholes, and will be ideal if you wish to make curtains, plain cushions, and table and bed linen. More sophisticated electronic machines will produce a wide range of embroidery stitches, cope better with different weights and thicknesses of fabrics, and have automatic adjustment of pressure and stitch depth.

When buying a machine, ask for a demonstration and ask the advice of the salesperson about whether the machine will be suitable for what you require of it. Make sure that the speed control and bobbin-winding mechanism are easy to operate, that the machine is easy to thread, that you can control the stitch length and tension, and that it is not too heavy if and when you need to carry it.

Sewing needles

You will need to buy a good selection of machine needles for work with different fabrics. These may include fine needles for lightweight fabrics, all-purpose needles for general work, heavy-duty needles for heavy fabrics and bulky items, ballpoint needles for jersey fabrics and knife-point needles for leather.

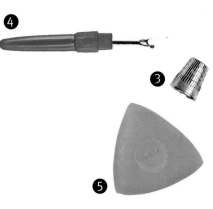
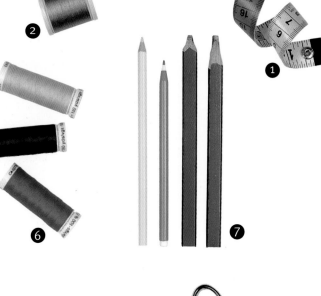

Needles for hand-sewing include sharps for tacking and hemming; 'betweens' for running stitch and other short stitches, milliner's straws for decorative stitches, embroidery needles, darning needles for carrying heavier yarns, and a bodkin with a bluntish point and large eye for threading cords, elastic, ribbons and so on. Long, curved upholstery needles are also useful for specialist work; you can use these to stitch fabric seams and pleats from the right side once the fabric is fixed in place.

Sewing threads

You are likely to need a range of sewing threads for different tasks. Useful threads include cotton for work on natural-fibre fabrics, synthetics for synthetic fabrics, embroidery threads and strong button thread. Heavier weight threads are available for heavy fabrics such as denim and wool, although these may not be suitable for your sewing machine (check the instruction booklet first).

Cutting tools

Good cutting tools are essential for making soft furnishings, and should be reserved for this purpose.

Dressmaking shears

These should have angled handles and long blades for cutting out large pieces of fabric.

Light trimmers

These are for cutting smaller items and for trimming seams.

Embroidery scissors

These small scissors are perfect for cutting threads, for cutting into the centre of stitched buttonholes, and for clipping into seam allowances.

Miscellaneous tools

The following are all inexpensive items that you will need in your sewing kit.

A stitch ripper

This is a tool for removing wrongly placed lines of stitching; it is quick and easy, and will remove the thread without damaging the fabric.

Measuring tools

You will need a tape measure that will not stretch for measuring curved shapes such as lampshades and arms of sofas, a short ruler for measuring short lengths and straight lines, a retractable steel measure for measuring windows, doors and beds, and a metre rule (or yardstick) for measuring up large fabric pieces.

Marking tools

Tailor's chalk or a dressmaker's marker will be useful for marking shapes of pattern pieces, positions of pleats and so on; these are easily brushed off the fabric. Water-soluble markers are also available, but can obviously only be used on washable materials. You will also need pencils and a notebook for noting and checking measurements and calculating fabric amounts.

Other equipment

Additional items that you will need include dressmaking pins, safety pins in different sizes for pulling cords through casings, and a thimble to protect your finger while hand-sewing.

Tools and equipment for making soft furnishings
1. Tape measure
2. Cotton threads
3. Thimble
4. Stitch ripper
5. French chalk
6. Polyester threads
7. Assorted dress-maker's markers
8. Pinking shears
9. Dressmaking shears
10. Embroidery scissors
11. Light trimming scissors

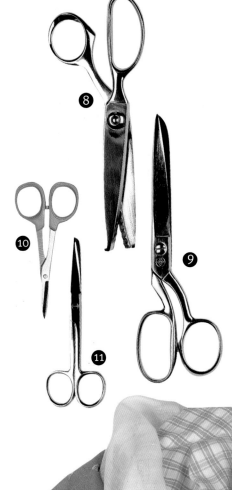

Basic techniques: curtains

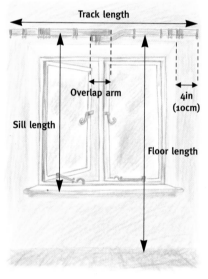

The simple, but effective, tie-on heading for these elegant curtains is easy enough for beginners to tackle.

MEASURING UP FOR TRACKING

Track length

Overlap arm

4in (10cm)

Sill length

Floor length

Measure the width of the track not the window. Remember to measure any overlap arm and add this on.

Curtains are not difficult to make and, if you do sew them yourself, you will have a much wider choice of fabrics and styles. Unlined or small curtains are a good introduction. Heading tapes are commercially available to create a range of different effects, including simple gathers, pinch pleats, pencil pleats, box pleats and goblet pleats.

Measuring up

Standard heading tapes require 1½–2½ times the curtain width; for pencil pleats you will need 2½ times the width. Follow the manufacturer's instructions for the length of tracking that is needed.

1. Measure the width of the pole or tracking – not the window (when using an overlap arm on tracking, measure this too and add it on). Decide how full you would like your curtains to be – remembering that, even when drawn, they should be gathered – and multiply the finished width by the amount needed for fullness. Divide the total by the width of your fabric, and round this up to the next whole figure to give the number of widths of fabric required for two curtains.

2. Measure the drop from the bottom of the curtain rings or tracking to the level at which you wish the curtains to hang. Add 23cm (9in) for hems and headings.

3. Multiply the drop by the number of fabric widths to calculate the total length of fabric.

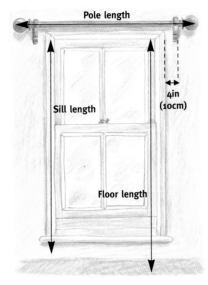

Measure width of pole and drop from bottom of curtain rings to level curtain should fall.

Making unlined curtains

1. Turn in the long sides of curtain twice and machine-stitch. Join any lengths using flat fell seams, as these make strong joins and enclose the raw edges of the fabric without creating a ridge.

2. Mitre the corners of the hem: unfold a corner hem, make a diagonal cut across the corner where the inner fold lines meet. Press under raw edge then fold the hem back again. Oversew the mitre and hand-stitch the hem.

3. Sew pencil-pleat tape 3mm (⅛in) below the top (turned-in) edge of the curtain. When stitching the tape to the curtain, work both rows

of stitching in the same direction to avoid puckering.

4. Insert hooks at 7.5cm (3in) intervals and hang the curtains on either a pole or tracking.

Curtain headings and tapes

Curtain tapes come in tremendous variety, offering many different effects. The simplest of all is standard tape 2.5cm (1in) deep, which gives a simple gathered curtain. Headings for more sophisticated triple pleats, goblet pleats and lattice pleats require deeper headings. All of these will give varying amounts of fullness to the curtains, ranging from twice the width of that needed for standard tape to three times as full for some pencil pleats.

Curtains should look generous, but not too full. Heavy fabric does not need to be as full as finer fabric and lined and especially interlined curtains can afford to be less full than unlined counterparts. Sheer, unlined curtains need not necessarily be very full, particularly if you don't want them to completely obscure a view. For extra privacy, you could add a blind for use at night. Curtains can, of course, be pleated, or gathered without tape.

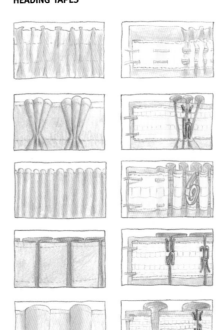

A selection of different heading tapes are illustrated here showing the front on the left and the back on the right. From top to bottom they are; simple gathered heading, triple pinch pleat, pencil pleating, box pleating, goblet pleating, detachable lining tape.

They will have to be folded and the pleats sewn into place by hand which takes more time but, if well done, can give an *haute couture* effect which is very effective.

FLAT FELL SEAM

Trim one seam allowance; turn other seam allowance to enclose fabric's raw edges; topstitch.

MITRING HEMS

1. To hem, turn in the edges twice. Press, then baste.

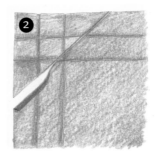

2. Unfold the corner. Cut diagonally 3mm (⅛in) from the point where the fold lines cross.

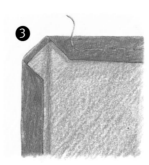

3. Press under 3mm (⅛in) turning across the corner. Refold the hem. Tack, then stitch.

Basic techniques: blinds

Roman blinds, which pull up into large pleats, are among the most elegant forms of window treatments. They are not difficult to make, although some precision is required.

You can use blinds as an alternative to curtains, or as a complement to them. For example, blinds will add to the drama if used behind formal curtains, while on their own they can create a businesslike, uncluttered look. They are also useful for dormer windows or roof lights where it is difficult to fit curtains.

Making a Roman blind

1. Measure the narrowest width of the window recess, and deduct 1cm (³⁄₈in). For surface-mounting, measure the window width and add 5cm (2in) plus an extra 9cm (3½in) for turnings.

2. Measure from the top of the window to the sill, and add 12.5cm (5in) for turnings. For surface-mounting, add an extra 5cm (2in).

3. Cut the fabric to these measurements. Cut the lining to the same width minus 12.5cm (5in), and to the same length as the fabric. For the dowel casings, cut some lining fabric 5cm (2in) deep and the width that the finished blind will be.

4. Lay the top fabric on the lining, right sides together, raw edges level. Machine-stitch the sides, then turn the fabric right side out. With the lining uppermost, press the outer edges so that an equal margin of top fabric shows on each side.

5. Turn the fabric and lining under along the bottom edge and press. Turn another 7cm (2¾in) for the casing, and machine-stitch close to the fold.

6. Turn in and press lengthwise along the centre of each lining strip to mark the middle. Turn in the edges and press 1cm (⅜in) along all sides. Use tailor's chalk to mark evenly spaced lines from top to bottom across the back of the blind for dowels. Pin the centre of the lining strips to the marked lines, 1cm (⅜in) in from the blind edges.

7. Machine-stitch each strip in place along the centre line. Fold in half along the centre line and slipstitch close to the folded edges. Slide a dowel into each pocket and a lath into the bottom casing; stitch the ends. Sew two rings to each dowel pocket, 2cm (¾in) from the sides of the blind. Add vertical rows in between, spaced 25–30cm (10–12in) apart.

8. Using staples or nails, fix the top edge of the blind over the wide side of a batten.

9. Fix a screw eye to the underside of the batten above each row of rings. To calculate the length of cord required, double the length of blind, add the distance between the left- and right-hand rows of rings, and multiply by the number of vertical rows. Cut the cord into equal

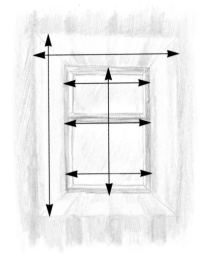

Measure the narrowest width of the window recess, then from the top of the window to the sill. For surface mounting, measure the outer edge of the window.

lengths, tie one to the bottom ring of each vertical row, thread it through the row and through the screw eye above. Thread each cord through the previous screw eyes to the eye at the end, where the pull cord will be. Gather up the cords at the side, trim them to equal length, thread on a wooden ball and knot.

10. Fix the blind on to the window frame using angle irons or by screwing upward through the batten into the reveal.

Making a roller blind

A roller-blind kit will include all the components you need, plus full instructions. If you are using untreated fabric, apply stiffener to it – following the manufacturer's instructions carefully – before making up the blind.

Joining fabric widths

If your fabric is too narrow, add 3 cm (1¼ in) to the width for every join. Make sure that joins are equally spaced from the centre.

1. Machine together fabric and lining, right sides together, raw edges level. Turn right side out so that an equal margin of top fabric shows on each side.

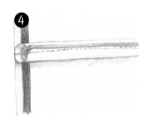

2. Turn the fabric and lining along the bottom edge towards the lining; press. Turn under another 7cm (2¼in) as a casing.

3. Make dowel casing strips with lining fabric; pin strips in evenly spaced lines and stitch in place, one every 20–25cm (8–10in).

4. Machine stitch, fold in half along the centre, then slipstitch close to the folded edge.

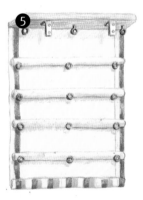

5. Sew two rings to each dowel pocket, 2cm (¾in) from the sides of the blind and one or more vertical runs in between. Fix the screw eye to the underside of the batten above each row of rings.

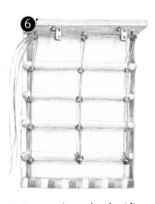

6. Measure the cord and cut it into equal lengths. Tie one to the bottom ring of each vertical row and thread it vertically and through the screw eye at the top, then through the previous screw eyes to the side of the blind.

Cushions, pillows and seating

Cushions provide the finishing touch for a new decorating scheme, or you can simply use them as a cheap way to alter the feeling of a room and to give it a fresh, new look. Cushions are enormously versatile, and can be large enough to put on the floor or tiny to scatter over a small sofa; they can be quite casual or highly tailored in fabrics to co-ordinate with other furnishings, with added piping or tassels. The tailored look is suitable for a room intended for formal entertaining, or for a scheme that reflects a particular historical style; in either case, the cushions should relate to the furniture, be tightly stuffed and finished with care. At the other extreme, you can spread cushions about in a mixture of shapes, sizes and fabrics to go with a more eclectic interior – perhaps reflecting past travels and holidays or simply a love of colour.

Cushions can be neat and square for sitting on, or blowzy and overstuffed for visual effect. They can be secured with simple ties, disciplined zips or old-fashioned or ethnic buttons. Cushions can match your curtains or complement your favourite oriental rug and, because so little fabric is needed for each cover, you could use really exotic and expensive fabrics: small pieces of luxurious watered silk, an Italian-type brocade or a delicate Liberty lawn would all make beautiful cushions. For bedrooms, broderie

anglaise looks very fresh and pretty for both pillowcases and cushion covers, but heavier fabrics such as wool weaves and cotton velvets may go better with wool-covered upholstery. A little piece of antique tapestry weave can also make a charming and individual cushion or bolster cover.

Adding cushions is a very easy way to lend colour or texture to a scheme that needs a little livening up. One small splash of vibrant colour will instantly transform a basically monochrome scheme: a dash of scarlet, for instance, will create a really eye-catching focal point in a mainly grey or black-and-white scheme. Texture is another important quality: if a living room is largely furnished with shiny or hard surfaces, the softness of cushions can be enough to add that all-important feeling of comfort and well-being; while a bed

piled with pretty pillows and cushions in fresh fabrics will make the whole room look inviting.

Best of all, cushion covers are fun and easy to make; pillowcases are even simpler. Once you have acquired the basic skills for cushions, you can go on to make bolsters or boxed cushions, and add frills, lace, ribbons, buttons, beads, piping or even appliqué pictures and patterns to the fabric. When making cushions yourself, it is important to use a good pad or to be generous with the stuffing; fillings can range from the soft and giving (such as feather and down) to the firm (such as polyester). Use heavy-duty feather-proof cambric as the basic case for stuffing. Ready-made, firm seat cushions often consist of fire-retardant foam, which you can cover with cotton or polyester wadding to soften the lines and give a padded look.

Main picture It only needs a few cushions to unite, co-ordinate and enliven a room. Here, a selection of woven wool fabrics amd embroideries in characteristic dusky colours create a homogenous corner. *Above* Different fabrics, all with a particular raspberry red in common, are used on the bolster, sofa seat and small square cushion to give lively interest to this small corner of a room.

Cushions

Whatever style of cushion you decide on, choose fabrics for the covers that will wear well and can be washed or dry-cleaned. Fabrics made from natural fibres such as wool, cotton, linen and silk are usually best. If the fabric is washable, wash it before making it up into a cover to avoid possible shrinkage later.

Different sizes and shapes of cushions can add interest, provided there is some unifying factor; in this case, the similar shades of yellow and green, picking up the green of the sofa cover and of the curtain hanging behind it, and the wallpaper beyond. Interest is then added with tassels and fringes, cord and braid.

Using cushions for colour

Cushions are extremely useful for 'lifting' a room. For instance, if the room's colours seem a little careful or bland when all the decorating is done, cushions in carefully chosen contrasting colours can make all the difference. However, you can also exploit cushion colours in other ways, such as picking up a minor colour in a wallpaper or fabric in a way that brings the paper or fabric to life; you could also choose colours to pick up a main colour in a background wallpaper or fabric, although this will be less subtle.

You could give a simply furnished, basically white room a completely different atmosphere, depending on the colour and style of cushions you use to furnish it. Ideas are almost limitless: for example, one or two shocking-pink cushions will have an enormous impact, whereas a mock leopardskin fabric will give this type of scheme sophistication; wide blue-and-white-striped covers will give the room an eighteenth-century Swedish (or Gustavian) look, particularly if the walls are covered in narrower-striped wallpaper; and large, bright red cotton cushions will add a modern Scandinavian feel. Cushions can also pick up the base colour of a decorative paint technique, more brightly than the finished painted surface while still relating to it and bringing it to life.

Trimmings

Cushions may be perfectly simple with no trimming at all, or embellished with one or more of the great variety of buttons, bows, ribbons, braids, cords, frills and fringes now available. Just as when decorating walls, it is a good idea to create a colour board specifically for fabrics and trimmings so that you can play around with textures and colours at will. A noticeboard fixed to the wall will be ideal, particularly if you want to make a number of cushions.

There are two main categories of trimmings: those designed to be inserted into the seams around the edge of the cushion, and those that are topstitched to the face of the fabric (these are usually added before the cover is made up). The former include piping, gathered strips of fabric to match the cushion cover, a gathered lace trim with a frill of crisp printed cotton, or a length of *broderie anglaise*;

Above A Gothic corner, with unfinished wood and a pointed Gothic screen, is made comfortable with a traditional plaid weave covering of soft cushions. *Below* A bedroom can seem more like a reception room if colourful cushions are piled onto the bed, such as this collection of cushions and bolsters.

the latter comprise a huge choice of woven braids, ribbons, cords, lace and fabrics to contrast with the main fabric. Wavy ric-rac braid – very popular in the 1940s, when it was one of the few trimmings available – is good for cottage-style cushions or for those in children's rooms.

Bought trimmings are available in many styles and colours but, if you cannot find what you want in local stores, it will be well worth looking in specialist furnishing stores which may have a much wider choice; specialist manufacturers may also be able to make a trimming specially to order. Secondhand shops also sometimes have some beautiful antique braids and fringes.

Buttons and beads

You can add decorative buttons, beads and sequins to cushions as well as to clothes, although it is important to use them in the right setting. For example, beads and buttons are not the right decorations for young children's rooms – no matter how pretty they may be – as they could be chewed or swallowed; nor would they look appropriate in a workaday room where the emphasis is on practicality rather than decoration. However, they could look marvellous in a feminine bedroom or in a Rococo-style living room where they are not likely to receive too much wear.

Closures

The cover opening should be the same width as the cushion pad so that the pad can be inserted and removed easily when the cover needs washing or dry-cleaning. You can simply slipstitch this opening closed when the cover is on the cushion, but it is usually more

convenient to provide some form of fastening. Zips look well finished – particularly on formal cushions – and are easy to use. You can set a zip into a seam, but it will be much easier to insert it into a panel of fabric on the back of the cover.

There are plenty of alternative forms of closure that have a charm in their own right. Ties are easy to make, are more decorative than zips and are less inclined to pull delicate fabrics. Rolled-fabric ties (or *rouleaux*) can look very attractive, particularly with cotton fabrics: long, narrow lengths will create floppy bows with tails, whereas short, wide lengths are ideal for making large, handsome bows. You could also use binding tape, cotton weaving and decorative braids instead of making ties of self-fabric; these will save time because all they need is to be cut, hemmed and sewn on.

Buttons give an old-fashioned, country look to cotton cushion covers. The best way to use these is to stitch the cover along three sides and add a lined flap along the opening edge. Bound or machine-stitched buttonholes will both look good.

Directory of cushions and pillows

Scatter cushions in quantity strengthen the warm effect of this scheme by using identical and complementary colours to the fabrics on the sofa and seats.

You can make cushions in any size or shape you like, from *broderie anglaise*-covered confections to floor cushions. They can be round and fat for heaping together, slim with a foam pad for dining chairs, or firm and square or sausage-shaped for benches or sofas. Ready-made seat cushions are made of fire-retardant foam; you can cover this with cotton or polyester wadding to soften the lines, or create an even softer look by wrapping a mini feather quilt around the foam.

Scatter cushions

These are cushions intended to make an impact by their design and colour. They are often used in groups, either casually thrown together or carefully placed. The covering fabric can match, co-ordinate or contrast with other fabrics in the room. A collection of ethnic weaves can look good together, and a group of cushions – some in print and some in a plain colour that picks up the print colour – can be interesting and lively. In contrast, a row of simple, plain-coloured calico or ticking cushions on an antique wooden settee with a matching boxed seat cushion will also look stunning.

No-sew cushions

These are cushions for quick effect, and are useful if you have no time for sewing. You can tie them through eyelets let into the cover material, or wrap and tie them at the ends (for example, miniature bolsters can be covered in this way); or you could cover a small cushion with two decorative tray cloths or napkins joined by tiny French knots.

Frilled cushions

Frills give cushions a softer or sometimes a more exotic look, depending on the fabric used. They look wonderful as part of the soft furnishings in a bedroom or in a really luxurious living room, and suit floral fabrics very well although they can also look equally stylish in plain, checked or striped cottons or silks.

Bordered cushions

These cushions have a flat border rather than a frill and go well with the less voluptuous, more spartan designs of many contemporary interiors. You can use a tuck-in (Oxford-style) opening or a zip for these. A double border gives extra sophistication to this type of cushion cover; a padded border – using a layer of wadding or iron-on fleece to add softness to the front of the cushion and to emphasize the bordered edge – looks extremely stylish.

Children's cushions

Children love great big cushions which can sit on the floor. Make up simple bean bags (filled with polystyrene beads) for extra seating, or large, square blocks for the children to play and sit on. These cushions should always be made in washable fabrics and in bright, primary colours or simple prints.

Bed pillows

Pillowcases usually have a flap to tuck in at one end that will not be uncomfortable if it gets in the way while a person is sleeping. Pillow shams are decorative covers used on cushions

1. Although small, this scatter cushion makes an impact with its unusual shape and the very elegant embroidered velvet cover.

2. A satisfying combination of colours has been used on these three seat cushions which are covered in a strong, good-looking repp.

3. Frills add a soft, pretty quality to cushions that goes well with the tiny motifs of a Provençale print.

4. Small pieces of carpets and rugs can make robust, colourful cushions which go well with a strong scheme.

5. The natural and red buttoned covers seem much at home with the traditional *toile de Jouy* patterned fabric in a prettily co-ordinated combination.

6. An unusual use of stripes and piping on a cushion cover adds an extra touch of style and interest.

7. Midnight blue patterned velvet next to a woollen paisley bedcover gives a highly exotic feel to this bed.

8. Large pieces of appliqué, using cotton checks and spots on calico, make a fun cushion for a child.

9. Towelling and ties make this child's cushion cover easy to remove and wash.

10. A bolster cover with baby-blue ribbons is carefully co-ordinated with the blue and white lace and embroidery on the pillows.

that cover the sleeping pillows during the day; these are very useful in bed-sitting rooms, where they help to conceal the fact that the settee is actually a bed. Pillowcases used for sleeping should be made in comfortable, soft fabrics that are easy to wash, such as fine cotton, linen or a polyester-cotton mix. All cotton or linen covers will need to be ironed.

Oxford pillowcases

These are ordinary pillowcases that have a flat border all around the edge which makes them look more elegant.

Cushion trimmings

Bias binding can be used for enclosing piping cord when binding edges; you can make this yourself from a length of fabric (cut on the bias and joined as necessary), or buy it ready-made in various widths and many colours. Other trimmings include braid, which is a narrow decorative strip with fancy patterning, good for edging cushions; decorative cord, which is made of twisted strands of silk, wool or cotton in varying thicknesses (some cords come with a flange for inserting between seams); fringes made from silk, wool or cotton, which can be long or short, fine or thick, and sometimes have beads; and tapestry strips, which are firm, woven bands imitating hand-woven tapestry, used to decorate the fronts of cushions.

Basic techniques: closures and fastenings

Cushions take very little time to put together, and you may well be able to use small offcuts of other furnishing materials, making them even more economical. Washing or dry-cleaning will be easier if you give your cushions an opening of some sort, such as zips, buttons or ties.

Adding buttons

When using buttons, stitch the cushion cover along three sides and add a lined flap on the opening edge. Work bound or machine-stitched buttonholes in the flap, or stitch button loops along the edge.

Rouleau loops

Rouleau loops are made from long fabric strips. Each loop should be long enough to go over the button's diameter, plus seam allowances to stitch into the opening's edge. Work out each loop's length, including seam allowances, and cut a single strip of fabric the total length required, about 2.5cm (1in) wide. Turn under 6mm (¼in) down each long edge, then fold in half, right side out. Stitch down the middle to enclose the raw edges.

INSERTING A ZIP

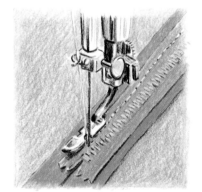

Put a zip into a separate panel of fabric at the back of the cover.

Inserting a zip

You can set the zip along a seamline, but it is much easier to put it into a separate panel of fabric at the back of the cover. When buying a zip, remember that the opening should be as wide as the cushion so that you can insert the pad easily, without pulling on the fabric. If the cushion is rectangular, it will obviously be cheaper to use the short side for the zip.

Machine stitched buttonholes

Buttonholes are best worked through more than one fabric layer, so allow a generous turning on the overlapping edge where you wish to stitch the buttonhole. Measure the button's diameter and mark the position and length of the buttonhole. Use the settings on your machine (some are automatic) to work the outline of the buttonhole. Use fine embroidery scissors to cut the fabric between the stitches, without cutting into them.

Making and attaching ties

Ties are an attractive way of closing a cushion cover, and are straightforward to make.

1. Once you have cut out the front and back pieces for the cushion cover, cut two further pieces of fabric to act as facings: these should be about 5cm (2in) longer than the opening and 12.5cm (5in) wide.

2. Cut two or three pairs of ties: each half of each tie should be at least 25cm (10in) long, or you can make a double length to attach to an edge or to insert in a seam. If you cut the

ROULEAU LOOPS

Turn under long edges, fold strip in half, stitch down middle to enclose raw edges.

Set lops into a faced opening along raw edge. Stitch facing over loops, turn facing to inside.

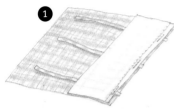

1. Place the ties on the right side of the front panel with the facing on top, right sides together; stitch.

3. Pin the back to the front panel, but open out the front panel facing.

fabric 10cm (4in) wide, the finished tie will be about 4cm (1.5in) wide. With the fabric inside-out, stitch the long ends together, attach a piece of cord to one short raw end and then pull it right through to turn the tie right side out.

3. Position the ties on the right side of the front and back cover panels, along the opening side. Place a facing on top, with right sides together, thus sandwiching the ends of the ties. Stitch along the seam line. Double stitch over each tie. Repeat the process for the back panel.

4. Trim the front panel facing to 6cm (2½in), fold it under in half and stitch the fabric close to the fold.

5. Neaten the raw back edge of the back facing, turn under 1cm (½in) and stitch.

2. Fold the front panel under, stitch close to fold. Turn the raw back edge of the back facing to the wrong side; stitch. Turn the facings to the wrong side.

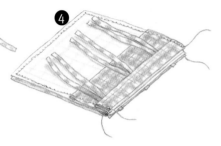

4. Fold the front facing over the back panel. Stitch the side and end seams.

6. Turn the facings to the wrong sides and press.

7. With right sides together, join the front and back panels: pin the back panel to the front panel, but open out the front panel facing, then fold and pin it over the back panel. Stitch the side and end seams. Trim all corners to reduce bulk and then turn the cover right side out. Push out the corners using a point turner or pencil, and press each seam.

Other closures

Hooks and eyes and press studs are also suitable closures for cushion covers, especially for tailored foam or boxed seat cushions. They are sold on lengths of tape by the metre (yard) in several sizes and weights.

Basic techniques: cushions

lower edge of both pieces. Pin the fabrics together along the pressed line and tack for just 4cm (1½in) at each end. Position the zip so that it is central to the tacked seam line. Pin and tack in place, then, from the right side, topstitch the zip in position, across the ends and down both sides. Use a zip or piping foot on your machine to avoid damaging the zip, but do not stitch too close to the zip or the fabric will gape and the zip will be difficult to operate.

If you do not have a great deal of sewing experience, it will be best to start with simple cushions and then to move on to more complicated frills and finishes as you gain in confidence.

Hints on making basic cushions

To fit snugly, the cover should be 2cm (¾in) smaller than the pad. Allow a 2cm (¾in) seam allowance on three sides, and 2.5cm (1in) at the opening edge; attach the closures on this edge before stitching the other three sides. Snip across each corner to reduce the bulk of fabric, neaten the raw edges if necessary and then turn the cover right side out.

The correct way to insert a zip in a cushion is to press 2.5cm (1in) to the wrong side of the fabric along the

MAKING BASIC CUSHIONS

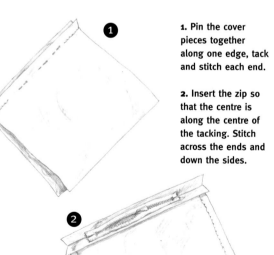

1. Pin the cover pieces together along one edge, tack and stitch each end.

2. Insert the zip so that the centre is along the centre of the tacking. Stitch across the ends and down the sides.

1. Mark a selvedge from one corner to the opposite corner. Mark the strips of the width you want parallel with this line and cut along the marked lines.

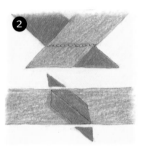

2. Join the strips by positioning them at right angles, right sides together. Stitch together; press open and trim the corners.

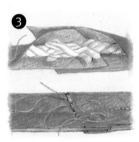

3. To join the ends, trim the fabric ends diagonally and cut the cord leaving a seam allowance at each end. Unravel the cord, twine the loose cords together, turn under the covering and slipstitch.

4. To turn a corner, stitch as far as the corner, snip into the seam allowance at the corner point. For a gentle curve, make several cuts.

Making piping

Measure the amount of piping cord you will need and add 10cm (4in) for joins. Cover the cord with fabric strips cut on the bias: fold a rectangle of fabric diagonally so that the selvedge is parallel to the nearest edge, and cut strips about 5cm (2in) wide along this diagonal; join the strips on the straight grain to make up the required length, and trim.

Lay the piping cord along the centre of the strip on the wrong side, fold the fabric around it and machine-stitch, using the zipper foot. If you need to join two pieces of piping, trim the cord so that the ends butt together before stitching. Turn in one end of the covering fabric and then overlap the other.

Piping a cushion

To add the prepared piping to the cushion cover, begin by pinning and tacking it to the right side of the front cover. Snip into the piping fabric at corners to keep them square. Leaving an opening for the zip, stitch the back cover to the front with right sides together, sandwiching the piping between them.

ATTACHING PIPING

Pin piping to the front, starting at the centre bottom. Line up the piping stitching line and raw edges on the other three sides. Clip into the piping fabric at the corners.

Preparing a frill

Cut out and join fabric strips twice the circumference of the cushion by twice the finished width plus 2cm (¾in) seam allowances. Join the ends to make a continuous loop and press the seams flat. Fold the strip in half lengthways, right side out. Stitch two gathering threads near the raw edge. Fold the frill into four and mark with pins to indicate the position of each corner of the cushion front. Pull up the gathers, distributing them evenly and aligning the four marking pins with the corners. Tack and machine-stitch along the seamline, then remove the tacking.

MAKING AND ATTACHING A FRILL

1. Make a continuous loop at least twice the cushion circumference and press all the seams flat. Fold the strip in half lengthwise right side out. Stitch two gathering threads near to the raw edge.

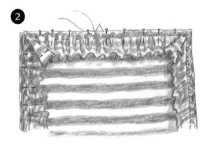

3. Fold the frill into four and mark with a pin where the corners will be. Pull up the gathering and pin evenly to the corner. Stitch close to the piping.

Directory of seating and upholstery

A well upholstered armchair is essential for relaxation. This little chair has been upholstered in pretty, formal striped fabric.

Upholstery, sofa and armchair cushions and covers are expensive to replace. However, it is not difficult to make replacement cushions and covers, particularly if you have already had experience of making loose cushions. Provided that you are careful with your measurements and are prepared to deal with the larger bulk of fabric, there is no reason why you should not succeed in making your furniture as good as new. A few simple patterns will fit most shapes of chair, and can be adapted to particular pieces.

Boxed cushions

These may be square or rectangular, and have squared edges and piping that give them a tailored look. They are useful in all sorts of situations: for example, as chair and sofa seats and backs, as floor cushions or in window seats; they can also provide welcome support in chairs that have no existing cushions, such as wicker chairs, wooden chairs and benches. As boxed cushions are essentially for sitting on it is important that they should be comfortable, so you should make the cover with a gusset, thus turning the cushion into a firm yet soft 'box'.

Any upholstery fabric will be suitable for box cushions, although in most cases the fabric should, of course, be easily washable (or dry-cleanable). Canvas, ticking and floral chintzes all make good washable covers. You can button a boxed cushion very easily, and this will add to its decorative quality as well as preventing the cover from moving about.

Bolsters

Originally, these sausage-shaped pillows were used to provide extra support for bed pillows, and were also used as decorative back and side cushions on early wood-frame sofas. These sofas are currently enjoying a renaissance of popularity, as are bolsters for softening their lines. Bolsters can also be particularly useful in a dual-purpose room in which the bed is required to act as a sofa in the day.

The simplest cover for a bolster can be a long tube knotted at each end. If you would like a Scandinavian look you could create a simple, stitched cover in gingham or another simple woven material (red-and-white or blue-and-white would be especially suitable); or, for an altogether grander look, you could use a luxurious fabric such as velvet, adorned with piping, fringing and tassels.

Drop-in chair seats

Drop-in seats are often used on dining chairs. They take little fabric and are very easy to re-cover because the seat simply lifts out of the chair so that you can take it to a convenient place to work on. If you are going to re-cover a seat like this, it will be worth cleaning up or painting the chair at the same time. For instance, you could give an old-fashioned, ornate chair a completely new lease of life by cleaning and polishing it up, and then covering the seat with velvet; or by painting it white and then dressing it in a sprightly cotton weave.

1. Shabby square foam cushions can be given a completely different look with new cushion covers.
2. A traditional armchair has been given a green and white loose cover which is smart but easy to launder.
3. The choice of a strong, but stylish fabric can give old dining chairs a new lease of life.
4. Bolsters, such as this tasselled one, can give the simplest seating added comfort and style.
5. A winged chair looks both comfortable and dressy upholstered in a firm cotton damask.
6. Leather or mock leather covers look good in a library or home office.
7. A plaid weave can give formality to a small dining room.
8. Individual chairs with drop-in seats can be covered in a fabric to tie in with the rest of the interior environment.
9. Cotton or synthetic velvet is available in many wonderful colours. Although it is expensive, you need very little for each chair seat.

Over-stuffed chair seats

Over-stuffed seats are upholstered and fixed permanently to their chair frames. If you wish to re-cover this type of chair, you may need to add more stuffing and you have to work with the seat in situ; the work may also involve re-fitting the webbing and springs. However, it may be enough simply to add a new slip-on cover with a gathered skirt.

Loose covers

Loose covers are the quick way to give old upholstery – for example, on armchairs and sofas – a new look, and are very useful in that they can be removed for washing or dry-cleaning. They are not difficult to make, although to look good you must measure and fit them carefully. Although described as loose, the covers should actually follow the contours of the furniture accurately or they will look scruffy. The fabric should be of upholstery quality, and most loose covers look best if they are piped.

Slip-on covers

Semi-fitted chair covers have inverted pleats with decorative bows, or button up at the back so they slip over the chair easily. They make good covers for small, uncomplicated armchairs and look their best in informal situations such as bedrooms or as covers for dining chairs – particularly in a conservatory. Any fresh, pretty cotton fabric will be suitable.

Basic techniques: cushion and seat covers

Bolster covers are not difficult to make. Choose fabric to mix and match as in this Scandinavian-style living room.

Some tasks – such as making bolster cushion covers for a sofa, or upholstering seats for occasional chairs – may seem a little daunting if you have not had previous experience, but they are actually not difficult and you will save a lot of money by making them yourself. Care taken in the finishing off process will give the cushions a professional look.

Making a bolster cover

Cut a piece of fabric the length and circumference of the bolster, plus 2cm (¾in) seam allowances. Cut two circles to fit the bolster ends, plus seam allowances. On the wrong side, join the long sides of the bolster tube, and then set a zip into the seam. Add piping around each end, keeping the raw edges of the piping level with the raw edge of the fabric on the right side. With right sides together, join the flat ends, snipping the seam allowances to keep the fabric flat.

MAKING A BOLSTER COVER

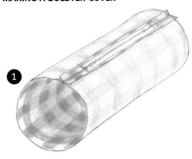

1. Join the long sides of the bolster cover and set the zip into the seam.

2. Pin the piping all round each end of the tube on the right side, with the raw edges together.

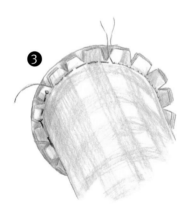

3. Make snips in seam allowances round both ends. Pin round the flat ends, right sides together, making more snips, if necessary. Tack and then stitch.

Re-covering a drop-in chair seat

1. Take out the seat and remove the old cover. Cut out the new cover piece, fold it in half from back to front and use tailor's chalk to mark the foldline. Fold the fabric in half from side to side and mark this fold-line. Mark centre points on the underside of the front, back and two side sections of the frame.

2. Lay the fabric wrong side up on a flat surface and place frame on top,

COVERING A DROP-IN SEAT

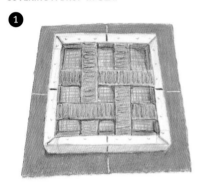

1. Lay the cover fabric right side up. Line up the centre marks on the fabric and frame.

2. Pull the fabric taut and partially hammer a tack at each centre mark. Add more partially inserted tacks at intervals along the edges.

3. Stretch the fabric taut diagonally at the corners and put in temporary tacks. Fold each piece into a pleat.

lining up the centre marks. Pull the fabric taut and hold it in place by partially hammering in a tack at each mark. Check from the top that the fabric is positioned correctly, then add more partially inserted tacks along each edge.

3. Stretch the fabric taut diagonally at each corner and put a temporary tack through the fabric. Pleat each corner piece and trim the excess fabric under it. Tack the pleats. Check the top side again and then hammer all the tacks home.

4. On cut-out corners, pull the fabric taut, as before. Put a temporary tack through the fabric in the centre of the fabric on the back of the seat. Pleat the fabric carefully at the outer corners and tack in place.

5. Finally, cut out the underside fabric, turn under 3cm (¼in) all round. Position right side up and tack firmly in place.

4. For cut-out corners, pull the fabric taut and then temporarily tack in the centre of each cut out on the back of the seat. Pleat the fabric carefully at each corner and tack.

5. Place a robust fabric on the underside right side up to cover all the raw edges of the top fabric. Finally, turn under along all sides and hammer in the tacks.

Basic techniques: covers

Many seemingly shabby little chairs can often be transformed with a cover over the seat and back which can be co-ordinated with other pieces in the same room.

Loose covers can be as simple as a rug thrown over a sofa or as sophisticated as a fully fitted cover, complete with piping, in a robust fabric and sewn to last for years. Fitted loose covers are not difficult to make, but do require patience and large quantities of fabric.

Making a loose cover

1. Measure each section of chair or sofa, following the seamlines on the existing fabric and measuring at the widest point. Add 10cm (4in) to all measurements for adjustments, and at least an extra 15cm (6in) to the inside back and sides as a tuck-in.
2. Cut out pieces of fabric to correspond with the measurements.
3. Pin the pieces, wrong side out, on to the piece of furniture and to one another in order to achieve an accurate fit.
4. Mark the seam positions with tailor's chalk, then remove the pieces and trim them to a 2.5cm (1in) seam allowance.
5. Stitch the sections together, incorporating piping (if using). Leave an opening along one back seam for removing the cover, and finish with Velcro or press studs.
6. Finish the lower edge.

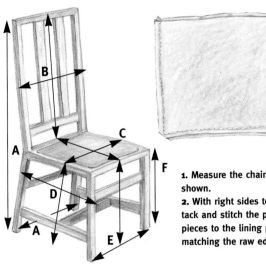

1. Measure the chair, as shown.

2. With right sides together, tack and stitch the panel pieces to the lining pieces, matching the raw edges.

3. Place the chair back and inside back sections on the chair, wrong sides outside. Adjust, pin and then stitch.

4. Replace the back sections on the chair inside out and pin the seat section to the inside chair. Add the side and front skirt pieces. Last of all, centrally position one false pleat over each skirt cover.

Making a slip-on dining-chair cover

The first step is to take all the detailed measurements that you will need.

1. Measure the chair-back width and length from the top edge to the floor (A) for the outside back cover. Also measure from the seat to the floor for the back panel lining.

2. Measure the chair width (including the frame sides), and the length from the top back edge to the seat (B) for the inside back cover.

3. Measure from side to side and from back to front to the frame edge (C) for the seat.

4. Measure from the top of the seat frame to the floor and from the outer edge of the back to the outer edge of the front leg (D) for the side panels.

5. Measure from the top of the seat frame to the floor and from the outer edge to outer edge of each front leg (E) for the front panel.

6. Measure from the seat frame top to the floor (F) for false corner pleats, and cut each 22.5cm (8¾in) wide.

7. Having completed all the measurements, make pattern pieces of each section from paper. Label each piece, pin it on to the fabric and cut out. From lining fabric cut two side panels, one front panel, one short outer back panel and eight false-pleat pieces.

8. Line the skirt pieces and false corner pleats and turn them right side out. Place the back and inside back sections on the chair; pin. Make a small dart in the inside back piece at each of the top back corners to fit the frame; stitch the darts. Stitch the two back sections along the top and sides.

9. Replace the back sections on the chair, inside out. Pin the chair seat section, wrong side up, to the inside chair back along the back edge. Add the side and front skirt pieces, with the lining side out, and pin them to the seat section so that the seam runs along the outer frame edge and the skirt edges meet at the back and front leg corners. Tack all the pinned seams.

10. Position one false pleat section over each skirt corner. Tack through all layers. Stitch. Turn right side out, remove the tacking and fit.

Home style

Seven inspirational design styles

The secret of successful styling in small rooms is to make the most of the available space. In this small, but elegantly-furnished living room, the theme of checks and squares is carried right through to the smallest details, and the walls, floors and furnishings are linked together to create a peaceful, harmonious environment. Pale colours help to make the room appear more spacious and emphasize the available natural light.

Small

When space is limited, you need to work out clever ways to make the most of it. Instead of wishing you had more room, think positively about what you can do with the space you already have. You can use all kinds of visual tricks to give an impression of spaciousness and to adjust awkward dimensions.

With careful planning, there is no reason why you should not include all the features that are enjoyed in larger homes – comfortable seating and eating areas, restful bedrooms and interesting lighting. In fact, larger rooms can often be more difficult to decorate and furnish successfully than smaller ones.

The basic design rules here are to keep colours and details fairly plain, avoid distorting visual lines with complicated shapes and blocks of colour, and choose neat furnishings in simple forms.

Maximizing the space

Whether you are starting from scratch or revamping an existing room, planning plays an important role.

Bathrooms are often squeezed into awkward spaces but there is still a surprising amount that you can do. A bathroom obviously has to accommodate furnishings such as a washbasin, lavatory and bath or shower which immediately limits the available space. If you are thinking of replacing them, consider smaller-scale items that are now being produced as these will be more in proportion. A shorter bath may fit snugly across the end of the room leaving more space elsewhere or you may decide to install a shower unit in its place. A compact lavatory with a slim-line cistern is an excellent

space saver and a washstand fitted with a basin on top provides good storage space.

Scaling down is also an ideal first step when planning a small kitchen. Mini-washing machines, fridges, freezers and dishwashers are all available; some will sit comfortably on a worktop. Small cookers or even a combination microwave/grill/conventional oven also work well. If space is cramped, there is no reason why you should have to keep certain appliances in the kitchen. A freezer could be stored under the stairs or you could fit a washing machine into a bathroom cupboard. If you are installing a fitted kitchen – the best option for a small space – consider the choices carefully before you buy. Space-saving ideas include carousel trays in cupboards to use corner space, drawers with multi-tiered pull-out racks, open-fronted units which avoid the need to dodge

open cupboard doors and overhead units that make the most of the available wall space.

In other rooms, built-in cupboards are a good choice: floor-to-ceiling or even wall-to-wall designs will work well with the space. Alcoves lend themselves perfectly to built-in storage, perhaps fitted on either side of a fireplace, where you could have low-level cupboards with shelving above. This is an ideal solution for storing electrical goods which often take up valuable space and have unsightly trailing wires.

Multi-purpose furniture

In a small house or apartment, rooms often need to be multi-purpose – for instance, the kitchen may need to be used for cooking and eating, whilst the bedroom is a place for sleeping and working – so furnishings need to be hard-working. If you have a bedroom that doubles up as a daytime office, you may like to choose one of the made-to-measure room schemes that are designed to convert quickly from one use to the other, with a bed that folds up into the wall. A stacking bed, where one single bed is stored under another, is another option and a Japanese futon could double up as a sofa. If you have only one bedroom, a sofa bed will be invaluable when

guests come to stay and some chairs are also designed to be converted into single beds.

Buy a blanket box instead of a coffee table. Make sure that the lid is perfectly flat so that mugs and glasses will not topple over and use the box as a storage space for pillows and linen. Fold-away furniture is an excellent investment, especially for chairs that are not always in use. If you do not have a separate dining table, a kitchen counter with stools tucked underneath is a good alternative. A semi-circular occasional table will fit neatly against a wall and could hold a lamp.

Go for low, simple designs in a light wood or finish to maintain the spacious feel. Use wardrobe tops to stack and display attractive luggage or wicker baskets full of out-of-season clothes, and a chest of drawers makes a good display surface.

Choosing a bed

If you are buying a new bed, consider all the options. The area underneath can be a good storage space and boxes fitted with wheels will fit conveniently in this area. Alternatively, box-shaped zip-up bags can hold jumpers and other clothes, whilst keeping the moths away. Use a valance to keep everything neatly out of sight.

Divan beds usually have little or no space underneath but a storage divan is a good alternative although this will be quite a firm bed as it has few springs. If you choose a drawer divan, make sure that you have enough space to open the drawers fully, otherwise look for one with sliding panels.

Wall and ceiling colours

Colour is the key to success in a small room. A limited palette of paler shades will make the walls, ceiling and floor merge comfortably together and enlarge the whole space, especially if the same shade is carried through to different areas. And if you paint structural features, such as beams or columns in the same colour, this will have a receding effect.

Traditionally, cool receding colours such as blues and greens are chosen for smaller rooms. However, if you accentuate the size and intimate character of a small room by painting it in a richer tone, this can actually work well particularly when combined with the right lighting. Pale colours can produce a cold, rather clinical effect in certain rooms. Always assess each room individually and pay particular attention to how much natural light it will receive. Collect tester pots of

paint and fabric swatches, and place these on a sample board in the room. Live with the colours for a few days and study them at different times of day before commiting yourself.

For smaller spaces, plain walls are best as patterns will make a room look smaller. When designs are large and bold, and especially when the ceiling is papered too, the room will visibly shrink. However, a small bathroom decorated with an all-over design – perhaps a neat floral print – can look charming. In other rooms, try vertical stripes or a checkered pattern as their linear quality can maximize the sense of space.

Warmer, bolder shades – yellows, reds, browns and oranges – work best in bedrooms, where the advancing colours will be welcoming; rich ruby reds or deep greens are excellent in dining rooms or studies. When your room has a high ceiling and awkward proportions, try breaking up the colour, perhaps by painting a deeper shade below a dado rail and leave the area above and the ceiling white. Textured paint effects

can be very effective but keep these quite small because you will not be able to move far enough away to see the overall texture, and large strokes can appear messy.

Floor colours

Floor surfaces form a large part of any room, so light colours used here can have great impact and will make the area appear larger, particularly if the colour runs from wall to wall. Pale carpeting is impractical, but it is suitable for bedrooms or bathrooms where it will not receive heavy use. Downstairs, pale hardwood flooring creates an airy Scandinavian feel. Laid diagonally, it will give a further illusion of space. Painting floorboards in a pale colour, sealed with two or three coats of floor varnish, is an excellent option if the boards are badly marked. Avoid rugs – especially in darker colours or heavy patterns – as they break up the floor

and can make it look smaller. Patterned carpets have the same effect. A light base colour used over the whole floor area and one large, pale rug may be the best solution.

Pale tiles are hardwearing for kitchen and bathroom floors, and they are easy to clean. Marble bathroom tiles can be wonderfully luxurious especially if they also run up the side of the bath. Mosaic is expensive but it could be used on a smaller scale and the pieces will be in scale here.

Natural and artificial light

Making the most of natural light is essential. Keep window treatments simple – it is surprising how much larger a room can appear when you remove the curtains. Often Venetian or basic roller blinds work best as just the window is covered and they can be kept out of the way when not in use. If you prefer curtains, use a lightweight fabric that closely matches the wall colour and extend tracks or poles so that whenever the curtains are pulled back, the glass is not hidden away. To

***Above* When space is limited, opt for a bed with built-in drawer space underneath, such as the one shown here. Spare bedding, winter quilts and out-of-season clothes can all be stored neatly out of sight.**
***Below* In small rooms, often one simple ornament or accessory is all that is needed to create an impact. The porcelain bowl is a good example of simple, but effective styling, and its beautiful shape is reflected in the glass table.**

block out the light completely at night, you may want to use shutters which also provide extra security. If a room is short on daylight, use low-voltage halogen lighting to make the area seem much brighter.

Light fittings are on display all the time so unless you want them to be a feature, opt for neat designs. If you can gain access from the room above, you could decide to use some tiny, low-voltage recessed downlighters to bathe the walls with pools of light. Alternatively, you could just go for simple wall lighting which is space-saving and the lights can be painted to match the walls to make them virtually disappear. These uplighters also throw light on to the ceiling which visibly heightens the proportions of the room. In a restricted space, there is not much room for heavy table lamps. However, many modern designs are streamlined and are easily moved around according to your needs. In bedrooms, wall-mounted spotlights with neat fittings avoid the need for bedside cabinets, and lights inside fitted wardrobes are also very effective.

Above Space-saving shelves are slotted into the area over a sink to make the most of this tiny bathroom. The white tiles and mirror help to create a feeling of space. *Right* Careful planning is crucial for small spaces. Here shelving, cupboards, a work surface and double sinks have been accommodated in a small corner with maximum daylight.

Reflective surfaces

Mirrors and other reflective surfaces, such as glass and metal, will bounce back and increase the natural light, giving an illusion of greater space and this can make any room seem brighter and more airy. Keep mirror frames simple in a pale room – Art Deco designs can look especially attractive. In a more richly decorated dining room or study, you could go for a carved giltwood frame, and a circular convex mirror placed here could look wonderful. The fish-eye effect of the curved glass can reflect the entire room back to make it appear much larger. In a window-less bathroom, you could even fix a window frame on to the wall with mirrors to act as false panes. These will reflect part of the room and give the illusion of looking through into another room. The same effect can be achieved by positioning mirrors on to two adjacent walls.

In living rooms, a glass-topped coffee table can be an excellent choice as nothing is obscured and it can almost seem to disappear into the room. The shiny surface will also reflect light. Rows of fitted glass shelving, with spotlights added into the recess above to illuminate accessories on display, are also a good idea in a small space and you can increase the level of light still further by lining the wall directly behind the shelves with sheets of mirror glass. With a little flair and imagination you will soon be able to design an attractive space that works beautifully, whatever size it may be.

There is no unnecessary clutter in this contemporary, Shaker-style kitchen. Plenty of storage space has been included in the design so that the more utilitarian pieces of kitchen equipment can be neatly tucked away. Generally, the impression is one of calm practicality and each item serves a useful purpose, as well as being pleasing to the eye. If you wish to retain the authenticity of the Shaker look, choose display baskets, wooden boards, plain utensils and traditional peg boards to complement the typically simple colours and natural woods.

Shaker

'Beauty rests on utility' is the belief behind Shaker style. The Shakers were a religious community who settled in New York in the 1770s. Harmony and efficiency in all things was one of their main aims and this was reflected in the elegant and simplistic appearance of their homes.

The Shaker approach to decoration is a clean, uncluttered look with deep colours, clever storage solutions and use of natural materials. This same beauty and balance is as appropriate today, particularly in the kitchen where each item is useful and, at the same time, attractive to the eye.

There is something universally appealing about this light and airy look, and the beauty of a traditional Shaker room lies in its unbroken simplicity, which is not difficult to reconstruct. There are no complicated colourways, only a few distinctive features such as peg boards for display and storage, cupboards and racks in wood and wicker, which can be repeated throughout the whole home.

Metal hanging racks are just one of the clever ideas that we have inherited from the Shakers. Today, ready-made racks, complete with fixings, are widely available or, alternatively, you could decide to design your own rack to fit into a particular area of the kitchen. The rack shown here is ideal for the busy cook as the utensils are all within easy reach, as well as being attractively displayed. A set of metal pans has been carefully chosen to tie in with the overall design scheme.

Adapting the Shaker look

Shaker style can be rather plain in appearance but you do not need to follow the look exactly – just take some of the elements that you particularly like and make them work in your own home. The Shakers lived communally and they did not have as many rooms in their dwelling houses as can be found in today's homes. They slept in small dormitories, used bowls and jugs for washing and every minute of their day was filled with either work or prayer, which made living rooms superfluous. However, their basic design principles and fine craftsmanship can still work well in a modern home, where furniture and accessories are grouped together to achieve a warm and versatile ambience.

Authentic materials and colours

The Shakers used only natural materials in their homes and wood played an important role. Shaker houses were built of wood and a lot of woodwork, such as doors, floors, window frames, skirtings, built-in cupboards and peg boards, was featured inside. The natural colouring and grain of the wood was given particular attention and this was often highlighted using a translucent stain or varnish, or painted.

Rooms were characterized by whitewashed walls and there were no architectural details, as they had no function to play. However, deep skirt-

ings and wainscots built to waist height are in keeping with the style and these can help to break up a wide expanse of white wall.

For splashbacks in the kitchen and bathroom, tongue-and-groove panelling, fitted over part or all the way up the walls, is a good option, and its regular pattern fits in with the Shaker sense of order. Varnish or paint the wood to seal it and if you decide to use paint, pick a gloss or water-resistant vinyl. The Shakers did not have ceramic tiles but if you decide to have them in your own rooms, choose plain colours, such as whites, creams or terracottas, to match the woodwork.

Despite their calm approach to design, the Shakers were happy to use bright colours and this was noticeable in a bold range of shades on woodwork, which was often painted using reds, browns, mustard yellows, oranges, and deep blues and greens. Pigments came from local clays and plants and while colours were strong, their natural origins meant that they could be used to achieve a muted softness. Traditional Shaker colours work well on their own or in combination, so don't be afraid to use more than one or two colours together in a room.

Flooring

Shaker floor surfaces were sometimes made of stone and you could choose natural stone or terracotta tiles for a kitchen or one of your other downstairs rooms. However, for true authenticity, polished floorboards are best. Sanding floors is a messy task but it is well worth the effort.

If your floorboards are unsuitable for stripping, then you could cover them up with wood strip flooring. This is reasonably priced and comes in a range of finishes. Lino – a natural material made from a hessian base coated with cork, linseed oil and pigment – will also work well and has the advantage of being warm underfoot.

Right The glasses make an interesting display, offset by the soft lemon shelves.
Below The Shakers lived communally and shared all their possessions, and so it was vital for everything to be carefully stored, easy to clean and readily to hand. This maxim is just as appropriate today. This cupboard has been fitted with wicker baskets which are perfect for storage. The wicker also introduces a warm colour which works well with the cool blues.

Furniture

The Shaker lifestyle meant that they had few material needs and this was reflected in their furniture design. In the kitchen, strong, large tables with trestle legs allowed plenty of room at mealtimes and lightweight chairs had ladder backs so that they could be hung on rails whilst floors were cleaned. If space is limited, you could add a plain wooden counter with stools or a drop-leaf table. Side tables, often incorporating a single drawer, and round pedestal tables, designed to hold candles, were also common.

Authentic handmade Shakerware – often in cherry or maple woods – is expensive, but some manufacturers are now producing good reproductions that exemplify the original principles of practicality and elegance, without fussy patterning or other ornamenta-

tion. Scandinavian furniture, with its simple lines and light, natural woods, is also worth investigating, as are Colonial style pieces.

For some aspects of decorating, it is impossible to be strictly authentic. For instance, the Shakers had no need for upholstered furniture because they had no real leisure time in which to sit and talk or read. However, simply-styled, comfortable sofas and chairs, covered in a fabric with appropriate plain or checked colours, will not look out of place. Similarly, a square white butler's sink fitted in the kitchen is an excellent substitute for one of Shaker stone, and a plain bathroom suite will also blend in with the style.

Storage solutions

The founder of the Shakers, Mother Ann Lee, is reputed to have said: 'Provide places for all your things so that you may know where to find them at any time of day or night'. Indeed, practicality was vital for communal living, where everything was shared and needed to be properly stored and easy to clean.

Built-in cupboards and drawers provided the typical basic storage in a Shaker home. They were usually built from floor to ceiling to fill and maximize the use of an entire wall space, and no dust-collecting surfaces remained. This simple design rule can be applied equally well to the modern home, and many manufacturers now produce good ranges of built-in furniture for kitchens, bathrooms and bed-

rooms. Some furniture styles are designed to fold away and they can even be turned into a daytime office area – an excellent use of space of which the Shakers would surely have approved. Try to adapt any unused areas of space, however small – including alcoves on either side of a chimney breast or under the stairs – for built-in storage.

The peg board was one of the most useful accessories to be found in the Shaker home. This was a hanging system that was recessed into walls at picture-rail height. It appeared in every room and was usually left bare to avoid repainting through constant use. The pegs were used for hanging chairs to keep them out of the way, and to hold small cupboards, cooking utensils, tools, brushes, clothes and hats.

You can achieve instant Shaker style by fitting a peg board around the walls in your own home – a carpenter should be able to make a board to fit your wall space exactly.

A peg board will be especially useful in the kitchen as you probably own far more utensils, pots and pans than the original Shakers; other items should be stacked or arranged neatly on worktops. Fitted kitchen furniture will provide maximum storage space for larger pots and other equipment, and modern appliances can be hidden behind matching doors. Many manufacturers sell units in plain, unadorned styles. Complete Shaker-style kitchens can be expensive, but you could simply choose cheaper units in plain styles or change the door and drawer

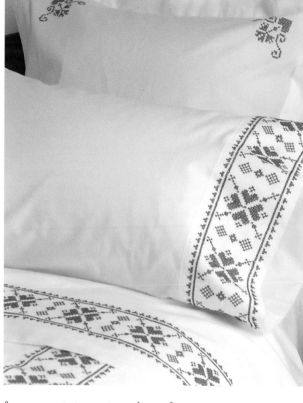

fronts on existing units and transform them with a few coats of paint in one of the classic Shaker shades. Ornate knobs or handles supplied with the units should be easy to remove with a screwdriver; replace these with plain wooden knobs, varnished or painted to match the units. A plain wooden finish for worktops is ideal and wooden shelving and racks can be used to complete the look.

In the bathroom, storage should always, first and foremost, be practical. A marble-topped wooden washstand provides valuable storage space for cleaning materials, while wicker baskets or plain wooden cupboards can conceal bottles and jars. Simple metal or wooden hooks and rails will also help to keep the room tidy.

Plain and patterned fabrics

Shaker fabrics were made from natural fibres – wool, cotton, flax and silk – and these were dyed using local plant materials. They were often plainly

Above Crisp cotton linen with a simple border pattern brings a restrained decorative touch to the bedroom.
Below left This bathroom combines a number of Shaker elements, including wooden panelling and storage furniture, a peg board and simple colour scheme, to create an easy to maintain, bright and tidy washing and dressing room.

woven, although checked fabrics using several colours were common. Fabrics were used for curtains, bedding and table linen, with harmonizing colours mixed and matched in the same way as paint colours. Plain and checked natural fabrics are cheap and widely available as ready-made items or in lengths that can be used to make cushions, seat covers and table linen. Simple woven wool or rag rugs were used in dormitory bedrooms and these can add a homely touch as well as being warm underfoot. Choose earth-like shades such as mustard yellows or terracottas to complement natural wooden flooring.

Shaker houses often had large windows fitted on opposite walls to allow maximum daylight. In keeping with the style, you may like to leave some windows (such as those in kitchens and bathrooms) curtain-free. Wooden shutters, which can be flung open during the day, are another possibility. In other rooms, avoid pelmets or heavy fabrics but opt instead for light cotton curtains with simple loop headings suspended from plain wooden or wrought-iron poles, or you could even use plain roller blinds.

Combining display and purpose

Everything in the Shaker home had a role. Among the everyday items on display were wall sconces and metal or wooden candlesticks, and these were essential as electricity was shunned. Tinware, basketware and brushes were all out on view, and the Shakers also made goods that were for sale, including wreaths, rag dolls and cushions in plain or checked designs. These are widely available today and will work well with the style.

The kitchen is a good place in which to display wicker baskets (ideal for storing table linen, vegetables or cleaning materials), wooden boxes and trays. Keep the equipment and utensils on view as simple as possible – plain wooden, ceramic and metal items all have great visual and textural appeal – and you can disguise clutter in beautifully-crafted boxes. Shaker boxes are oval and made with intricate swallowtail joints, and they are avail-

able in various sizes and colours. Fill them with spices, herbs, pulses and grains in the kitchen; with soaps or bath salts in the bathroom, and pot pourri in the bedroom. Alternatively, simply stack boxes on shelves to make a feature in the living room.

When choosing accessories, remember that often the simplest items are the most pleasing to the eye. The revival of the Shaker look has led to plain wooden, wicker and ceramic accessories being widely available and this means that you will never be short of ways to offset the delightfully restricted hues of the Shaker palette.

A peaceful rustic style has been achieved in this cheerful kitchen. The different pieces of furniture work well together and a traditional Aga cooker completes the old-fashioned look. The navy blue colour scheme complements the natural wooden furniture and flooring. Fabrics in checks, Provençal prints and plain blocks of colour all co-ordinate well with the simple ceramic tiles and collection of jugs on the fitted shelving. Antique recipe books, a jug of fresh flowers from the garden and appealing ornaments all add to the relaxed atmosphere of this kitchen.

Country

Inspired by Nature and rural life, country style is uncontrived, informal and eclectic. Influenced by the demands of rural living rather than the dictates of fashion, it creates a practical, comfortable, timeless environment with a warm, welcoming, lived in ambience.

Interiors full of rustic charm can be created using a blend of floral and checked fabrics, simple colours, unrefined textures and solid wooden furniture. There are no formal rules and furniture from different periods can be mixed and matched as you desire.

Although country interiors give the impression of evolving over many years (and many no doubt have), the look can be recreated in a short amount of time, and cheaply too, with secondhand furniture and accessories. With the right elements, you can bring the true heart of the country into any home.

Low beams are a strongg feature in any cottage-style interior. However, they can obscure the light. Here, maximum use is made of the natural light that streams in from the living room window, by completely drawing back the velvet floor-length curtains during the day. Although the sofas and armchair are all from different periods, they have been unified by complementary fabrics. Low level tables give an illusion of height and a charming collection of primulas on the window sill, together with other accessories, brings the look to life.

Setting the style

There are two variations for country interiors – a homely, almost cluttered look with an eclectic mix of faded floral fabrics, masses of cushions, worn furniture and accessories on every surface, and the more restrained approach of stripped floorboards or stone flags, scrubbed tables and gingham fabrics, where everything on view is designed to be used. The beauty of this style is that you can combine the two ideas.

You could make a small living room cosy with a wealth of soft furnishings, decorative details and rugs, whereas the kitchen and hallway may suit a simpler look. The approach can be varied again upstairs with perhaps a

lavishly styled master bedroom complete with colourful cushions, a comfortable armchair and large wooden bed in contrast to a spare room with a simple wooden chair, dressing table and wardrobe with perhaps a patchwork quilt as the focal point. Generally, the style and age of your home, as well as the room dimensions, determines the character but there are few restrictions for this look.

Many country-style furnishings and fabrics are inexpensive but first of all, consider your existing furnishings and possessions. You may decide to change their appearance using paint, by stripping, staining, bleaching or distressings or even find new ways of putting them together. Raid junk stores and try auction houses for elements to build up the effect. Collect swatches of fabric and samples of paint, and make a sample board of colours and patterns. Always experiment with your own ideas: the joy of the country look is that it is entirely individual.

Architectural features

If you live in a period cottage, your first priority will be to highlight any original features. Left bare, exposed beams give an immediate country feel although you could stain or paint them in a dark colour, perhaps also picking up on the warm tone with old furniture. The bleached, honey colours of sand-blasted timber can help to lighten a dark room. Another option is to paint the beams and ceiling in a paler colour to give height to the space. This more sophisticated effect is reminiscent of rural interiors in Scandinavia and North America. If there are no existing beams, you could add some yourself – try salvage yards for timber or use more regular lengths of new softwood. Beams can also be used to conceal modern spotlights.

Aim to make the most of unusual window shapes, alcoves and original fireplaces. Create a feature out of the fireplace by filling the grate with bunches of dried flowers, hang old horse brasses around it or display a copper coal scuttle and other fire tools. To replace a mantelpiece, add a reclaimed length of timber supported on wrought-iron brackets.

Right Seedheads hung up to dry behind a door are a perfect example of the practical decorative touch typical of country style.
Below A rocking chair is a traditional cottage feature. This one has been given a facelift with a distressed paint effect which co-ordinates with the blues and purples in the Provençal-style cushion fabric.

Using colour and texture

In country interiors the colours and textures are inspired by nature and this means you have a large number of options. Consider the enormous range of green tones that can be found in the country; use pale yellows reminiscent of the first spring primroses or the rich yellow of a rape field in summer, the earthy russet and ochre tones of fallen leaves, and the palest blues as well as the deep indigo of a summer night sky.

In certain rooms the colour scheme may be prompted by an existing item such as the carpet or a piece of furniture but remember too, that your choice of colour can influence the mood. In a cottage with low-level, small windows, opt for plain white walls or perhaps a sunny yellow to bring light into your home. Colour values are important – a pale shade of yellow can appear to be cool whereas a deeper tone creates a warm, sunny feeling. Warmer colours are said to advance while cooler shades recede, so a room painted with a strong emphasis on red will appear smaller than if it is painted in pale blue or green. This treatment works well in large rooms which can be difficult to furnish comfortably. A deep crimson red or leafy green could also look good in a study or dining room.

In some rooms, you could choose a low key look with restful creams, russets and browns. This may be ideal for the kitchen as these shades would complement a display of old-fashioned copper pans and utensils, wooden worktops and bunches of colourful dried flowers beautifully. In a scheme like this, use a range of textures for interest and contrast – a stone-flagged floor, brickwork around a stove, wicker baskets and terracotta jars are all ideal.

Floor surfaces are another area in which to use natural colour and texture. Fitted carpets are not often seen in the country home, but jute or sisal matting, with its wheat-like texture, is a practical and attractive solution. Other floor surfaces could be made up of stone flags, quarry tiles or bricks, or polished floorboards of pine, oak or elm, with the occasional colourful rug.

Problem areas

Use optical illusions to improve the proportions of an awkwardly shaped room. For instance, cooler colours will visually expand a small space and a pale painted ceiling and floor adds height to a room. Pattern also has an influence as large, dominant patterns can seem to advance while small patterns recede. On a large wall, small patterns, such as sprigs of tiny flowers, will appear indistinct and more like an overall texture, and these can be used to great effect as a backdrop. Delicate, naturalistic designs are very much in keeping with country character and if you choose a small repeat pattern, this will make it easier to match paper lengths around beams or nooks and crannies. For larger rooms, a bold design works well. If you add co-ordinating borders at dado height or ceiling level, this is a clever way to add interest to a large and empty-looking room or to disguise an oddly shaped one.

Another awkward area can be windows – perhaps where there is insufficient room for a rail above the window or no space at the sides for curtains to be drawn back. Options here are a ceiling-hung pole or a blind. On a sloping dormer window you may need to fit curtains or a blind into the recess. Alternatively, hang curtains on a rail that is completely free of the window area. In some cases, the windows are so charming that they can be left plain.

Uneven surfaces

In an old cottage, it is unnecessary to straighten crooked walls, flatten bowed ceilings and create symmetry as many wallcoverings, including textured papers, are eminently suitable for use on irregular surfaces. Use wallcoverings that imitate the patina of distressed paintwork or broken paint effects such as sponging, rag-rolling or dragging. These techniques will disguise any imperfections and surfaces can be repainted as necessary, and linked into other decorative or furnishing features. The basic principle is to use colour and pattern to enhance timeworn surfaces, not to compete with or conceal them. If you prefer plain colours, the thick consistency of traditional paints made with natural pigments will be ideal for very bumpy and uneven walls.

Aged furniture

Country furniture is simple and sturdy. You may like to leave it plain and polished, or you could paint items for the kitchen or a child's bedroom in cheerful blues or yellows. Some pieces immediately conjure up the country image – the oak rocking chair by the fireside and the scrubbed pine table and dresser in the kitchen. If you cannot find or afford the originals, try painting a new pine dresser in dark brown or green, then sanding back the paintwork to age it. Alternatively, try a light- or medium-oak brushing wax; this is easy to apply and produces a lovely mellow finish. Unfitted kitchen furniture is more in keeping with the style and you could include pieces normally found in other rooms, such as pine chests of drawers and a mix of wooden chairs, each with its own bright cushion. A gingham cloth will conceal a modern laminated table top.

Above Natural materials are central to the country look. In this living room the exposed ceiling beams are enhanced by a collection of wicker baskets. One wall has simply been whitewashed, leaving the texture of the stonework to contrast with the smooth outer wall and ceiling. *Left* A clean white bath, matching tiles and old-fashioned chrome taps epitomize the freshness of the country look. Cow parsley gathered from the fields is the perfect finishing touch.

lightweight fabrics that work well with the wall colour and hang them onto wooden poles. Frilled blinds are ideal for kitchen windows where curtains would get in the way and roller blinds could look too utilitarian. Elsewhere in the kitchen, gingham always looks cheerful: make table linen, seat covers, basket linings and frills to trim dresser shelves. Upstairs, anything homemade, from a patchwork quilt to simple cushions, will make the beds look very inviting.

Accessories

The kitchen is the main room in the home where country-style accessories come into their own. You can include anything from bunches of dried flowers to baskets of dried herbs; from classic blue-and-white china on the dresser to a gently ticking country clock. Items here should also be practical because today's kitchen needs to be multi-purpose in the same way as the original farmhouse ones. Earthenware and old glass storage jars, traditional scales and measures, wooden utensils and copper-bottomed pans are all ideal for display. In other rooms, use handcrafted objects such as local pottery and wicker baskets for storage. A single collection of one kind of object – china jugs, for instance – can look very effective and these could be displayed on a shelf running around the walls.

Plants and flowers are natural additions throughout the home. They will add accents of colour and delicious fragrance. Alternatively, a large bowl of scented pot pourri placed in a guest bedroom, the bathroom or on a landing window sill is a delightful finishing touch to complete the country look.

This delightful bedroom is full of country charm. The sloping roof sets the snug, olde world character of the room. This is complemented by the floral wallpaper offset by crisp, white linens. The white woodwork echos the linens and acts as a foil to the darker wooden furniture.

Comfortable padded sofas and armchairs are often sold cheaply at auctions. Their covers can be removed for cleaning or you could change the look by re-covering. If your budget will not stretch this far, cheap cotton throws can disguise worn areas while providing extra colour and character. For new sofas and chairs, choose plain colours that can be easily lived with and you can lift these neutral tones with colourful accents elsewhere.

Country fabrics

Fabrics are a key element of country style. Complementary colours and designs – including flowers, checks and stripes – on natural cottons, linens and chintzes will all co-ordinate beautifully and have a timeless quality. Keep it simple: rich damasks or velvets will look out of place here.

Purchase curtains from secondhand stores. These can often be cut down to fit cottage windows and use offcuts to make cushions and to cover lampshades. Fade new fabrics using bleaching agents (always test a small sample first). For curtains, choose

In global style the very best of the decorative designs from around the world are captured and then put together to achieve an eclectic touch of grandeur. The combination of sharp, bold colours, dramatic furniture, rich patterning and detail in this bedroom creates a distinctive look that is truly exotic. Timeless, informal, yet opulent, the overall feel is dignified and stately, and the owners have clearly enjoyed choosing the different elements. The finished result is an imaginative setting which is also relaxing and warm.

Global

Inspiration from around the world is the force behind global style, which is possibly the most free-ranging approach to decorating. Draw on these influences to decorate your own home with a unique reflection of the world outside.

The idea of bringing back souvenirs from travels abroad has always had a strong appeal. Travellers throughout the ages have returned with ideas and souvenirs, aiming to recreate in their homes a flavour of far-off lands.

Today the world is accessible to everyone. Your starting point for a scheme could begin with a place you have visited or even a single object, such as a Mediterranean plate. You could stick to one identity, create individual styles in different rooms or even mix decorative influences within the same room. When you have such a wonderful wealth of bold colours, dramatic furniture and rich patterning and detail to play with, you will never be short of ideas.

Style sources

Unlike some decorative treatments which rely on specific colours and other detailing, global style has no formal rules. However, the style of home in which you live may guide you towards certain choices. For instance, an old cottage with rough walls and free-standing furniture will lend itself beautifully to rustic wall finishes, whereas a modern city apartment could be ideal for a neutral colour scheme that combines smooth textures and natural materials such as wood, bamboo and paper to achieve a serene Oriental-style environment.

If you are not sure where to begin, visit museums and galleries with ethnic and cultural collections, and keep a folder of eye-catching images from magazines as well as your own collections of photographs taken abroad. Study the materials and textures that have been typically used for decorating homes in your favourite countries or regions of the world, remembering that texture can play just as important a role in creating an effect as the colour you decide to paint on to your walls. A global-style room may appear at first glance to be an eclectic, almost random mix of colours and objects, but it will take careful planning to create a successfully integrated scheme. Once you have built up the look, you can continue to add details, but you do need to have a good idea of what you wish to achieve at the very start.

Your chosen style must suit your taste and fit in with the demands of your lifestyle so when assessing any room, consider all the practicalities. The kitchen – one of the hardest-working rooms in any home – is a good example. Will you require much storage space here? Does the kitchen also need to double up in use as a room for

entertaining guests? Once you have considered your initial requirements, you can then design a scheme to complement all your needs.

When planning the look, think about your favourite decorative influences. You may like the intense, colourwashed appearance of Mediterranean houses, with their vivid tiles and cool stone floors; or perhaps the clean lines of Scandinavia, where pale woods, rush matting and wickerwork are often used, are far more to your liking.

Choosing colours and paint effects

You can capture the essence of a culture with just a few predominant shades of colour. Turquoise, cobalt blue, aqua and fresh white suggest the Caribbean or Mediterranean countries whereas warm terracottas, russets and beige conjure up images of hotter climates such as Africa and the East. Bold primaries evoke exuberant South American style. Whatever palette you

A collection of hand-painted china makes a strong display against a citrus-coloured wall. For the global look, rich patterns and colour can all be confidently mixed together, so experiment with your favourite accessories. The hand-crafted feel of the pieces adds charm to the overall effect. Alternatively, you may choose to follow one particular design scheme.

Right Simplicity of form is often the key to successful displays of hand-crafted ethnic objects. The cooking utensils laid out on a wooden table all originate from different countries, but they blend well together.
Below Folk art chests are perfect for displaying collections of global art. Here, a wheeled horse from India, a decoy duck from America and decorated eggs from around the world sit comfortably with a wooden candlestick and bowl from a local antique shop. The picture on the wall behind adds extra height and pulls the arrangement together.

choose, the colours should be bold and vibrant to make a strong statement.

A lively style, such as Mexican or Mediterranean, will give you an opportunity to indulge in a wide range of bright colours. Another advantage of these styles is that any uneven plasterwork will be reminiscent of roughly-plastered walls from the original source. If the exact shade of paint is not available, then go to a DIY store and have it specially mixed.

Should you decide to mix your own colours, you will find that surprisingly little concentrated colour is necessary in order to tint a whole tin of white paint. Old-fashioned whitewash and limewash can be mixed up with powder pigments and they have a wonderful powdery finish.

In addition to solid, flat colours, you could consider a decorative finish. Folk art painting is a style that is quite easy to recreate as it has a naive simplicity. Alternatively, you could consider copying the rich patterning used in Mexican interiors or geometric styles from the Middle East. Indian designs too would also work well as borders, details in rooms and on furniture. Visit galleries and museums, and study sourcebooks for ideas and inspiration.

Carry paint effects through to furniture to add interest and link them in with the scheme. Pick up cheap pieces from junk stores then apply sponging, ragging, stencil work or colourwashing. You can also sand paintwork back to give a distressed appearance. Apply this treatment to whatever surface you choose, from kitchen cupboards to bathroom cabinets, stools and plant pots. You could even apply a stencilled border to a stripped or painted floor.

Additional wall and floor treatments

Texture is so important in a global scheme and this particular effect can be exploited by using tiles, mosaics and panelling to create a range of different effects on your walls and floors.

Specialist stores stock an increasingly wide range of tiles, from shiny plain ceramic squares to terracotta tiles, and from exotic interlinking designs to heavy, hand-painted floor squares. For an Oriental-style interior, ceramic tiles – especially in pale, plain colours – are ideal, whereas hardwearing floor tiles made of unglazed, natural materials would be wonderful for a rural scheme. Some imported tiles (Morocco is an excellent source) have beautiful designs and although these are quite expensive, they will transform hallways, kitchens or conservatories. With any type of tile, it is often possible to buy seconds at greatly reduced prices, often with minor faults such as uneven glazing or small chips.

Mosaicwork can be an excellent choice for bathroom walls and/or floor surfaces. Iridescent aquas, blues and sea-greens can be used to evoke a watery paradise; you could even install a sunken bath by building up the sides of an ordinary bath using mosaic boards and adding steps, rather than sinking it into the floor. Alternatively, if the bath has a broad surround, start the tiling here, taking it down the sides and across the floor.

Tongue-and-groove panelling is easy to install and can enhance any room. Choose a rich tone for a more homely look or a light wood to give an airy

Scandinavian feel. Stripped and varnished floorboards would complement the style perfectly, or you could white-wash the floorboards. Natural sisal or jute matting is another excellent floor treatment. If you plan to use panelling in kitchens or bathrooms, you will need to varnish it for protection.

Soft furnishing fabrics

Once you have established your basic scheme, it is time to add in all the elements that will bring it to life. Many contemporary designers have been influenced by fabrics from around the world and these ideas have been worked into their own collections. When upholstering sofas and arm-chairs, it is best to choose modern fabrics in preference to genuine ethnic ones as they will be more hardwearing. Reserve traditional fabrics for curtains, blinds and cushions, which will receive less wear. Printed cottons are widely available and inexpensive, as are colourful Turkish kilims or Indian dhurries for floor surfaces. Many fabrics are coloured with natural dyes and

Left An exciting mixture of rich pattern and colour is combined in these fabrics to achieve a vibrant effect. Birds, animals, flowers, plants and other strong motifs are used as the basis of ethnic designs. You may even decide to echo the themes throughout the design of your home.
Below left Global style is a mixture of many different countries. Here, a distinctly European style basin arrangement is given a Moroccan feel with the use of brass accessories and rich earthy-red walls.

these will work well together even though they may have originated from different parts of the world. A more expensive but rather exotic touch for a Middle Eastern or Venetian-style room scheme would be a rich sari silk traced with gold.

For a design that is reminiscent of hot climates, use simple treatments at the windows. Blinds in light fabrics or wooden slats are perfect as these are basic and functional. Draped muslin is also a good option, and shutters can provide extra privacy and darkness at night time.

Furniture and accessories

If you decide to go for a rural ethnic look, choose wooden furniture, kitchen utensils, tools and decorative objects (perhaps painted or carved), as well as polished stone, cotton matting, ceramics and cotton or wool rugs coloured with natural dyes. For a Mediterranean style, choose carved or sun-bleached wood. If you prefer a Moroccan or Middle Eastern feel, perforated screens or door panels can be used to imitate fretwork detailing (imported furniture is available or you could use decorative pre-cut hardboard), and mirrors and pictures framed in gold or silver will enhance the walls. Oriental ambience can be achieved with bamboo furniture and lacquerwork combined with glass, metal and plain fittings. Remember

that cultures often overlap – for instance, decorative elements from Egypt, Morocco, Spain and Turkey can all sit together quite comfortably.

The charm of global objects often lies in their tactile quality, as well as their simplicity of form. Try using everyday or even ceremonial items from other cultures in unusual ways – make a pair of colourful curtains or a pile of cushions from a cotton bedspread; throw a native American blanket over a sofa or table; adapt a Chinese ginger jar to make a lampbase, or use an African drum as a side table. Pots and dishes made of old metals such as brass and copper can be functional as well as decorative and these can be used in bathrooms as soap dishes or toothbrush holders. Carry the natural feeling through with unbleached flannels, sea sponges, wooden-handled loofahs and natural-coloured soaps. Alternatively, if you decide to go for a Mediterranean scheme, display bright transparent soaps in blues and greens. Use candles and incense in the bathroom for ultimate relaxation, display a collection of smooth wooden bowls to add texture in a plain living room, and place fresh vegetables in a tiered bamboo plant holder. The joy of global style is that the possibilities are quite endless.

This living room represents the ultimate in city style: a sophisticated blend of old and new. By grouping the furniture in various parts of the room, the space becomes more adaptable and so it can be used for a variety of different purposes. The raised platform gives the impression that this particular area is a totally different room and adds to the feeling of space. Cream-coloured walls provide a plain backdrop to enhance the elegant rug and interesting pieces of furniture belonging to the owner.

City

When you live in the city it is important to create a cool and contemporary yet comfortable living space in which to unwind after a busy day at work. This particular style has an informal, uncluttered feel with an emphasis on clever use of furnishings and materials as opposed to fussy or complicated wall, floor, window and ceiling decorations.

For this look, fresh white or pale coloured walls maximize reflective light to give an airy atmosphere and a clean backdrop for displaying carefully chosen pieces of furniture and accessories. Chrome and glass often feature and bright splashes of colour can be introduced through paintings and posters, rugs and soft furnishings to create a dramatic contrast. Stylish storage solutions keep the area free and complete a low-maintenance style that is ideal for fast, modern living.

Think too, about characteristics that you could reinstate. Many city apartments have been converted from larger houses and their features have been removed in favour of modern fittings, but you can easily replace these with the originals or even clever reproductions. If the doors have been replaced with flat modern substitutes, look for panelled ones in antique or junk stores or try architectural salvage yards. Another solution is to add simple wooden mouldings to flat doors to make panels which, when painted up, can look remarkably effective.

Space in the city home is generally at a premium so it is essential that it should be multi-purpose to reflect your changing needs. One area may be used as both a living and dining room. In this case, you could decide to place your dining furniture in a window alcove or try adding a folding screen to divide the space. The living room itself may need to be used for several different purposes – for entertaining friends, as an office space or simply for relaxing – so flexibility is paramount here.

Decorating walls

City style is not immediately colourful. Colour generally works as a contrast and shades must be chosen and placed with care. Your best option is to keep the basic shell of the scheme – the walls, ceilings and doors – fresh and sharp in cool white to maximize light. This will also provide the ideal canvas on which to add colour and texture through furnishings and accessories. If you find pure white a little

In this city kitchen the space is relatively small but through the clever use of pale colours on the walls, floor and units, keeping the work units to the bottom of the room and leaving the windows curtain-free, the room appears to be larger than it really is. The cool, uncluttered feeling is further enhanced by the use of white laminate and stainless steel fittings and accessories.

Space considerations

The first priority when designing any room is to look at its basic shape and proportions. Are there any unique features that you can accentuate or incorporate into the overall look, such as a high ceiling or an arched window? Consider the condition of the floorboards – could they be stripped and varnished to restore them to their original condition? Have any interesting elements, such as an antique fireplace, been disguised or completely covered up? If you are lucky enough to have a warehouse apartment, then traditional brickwork, stylish metal pillars or expansive floor to ceiling windows can all be played up. Even exposed pipework will contribute to the dramatic effect in this setting.

stark, a white paint with a hint of colour can be used to soften the look without detracting from the effect.

In an open-plan apartment, you could pick out one wall in a solid bold shade such as blue or orange to define and accentuate the space. This also gives a dramatic background for your accessories. You could decide to paint bright primary-coloured borders around the walls to give the impression of panels, or why not run a colour around the room as a mock dado or picture rail? Take the basic wall colour over the doors to make the most of the space, perhaps painting their panels or mouldings in a contrasting tone. Alternatively, if you have stripped and varnished the floors, then you could also treat the doors in the same way.

Although paint effects, such as sponging and stippling, are perfect for certain styles, they are less suitable for

Right City spaces often have to double up as work areas. The computer, the carefully chosen desk light and stylish leather chair all work well together and contrast effectively with the Gothic window. *Below left* Lime green apples in a marbled grey bowl enliven a stark corner in a slate-grey city kitchen.

the slick city look, where a smooth, even paint finish works best. Non-reflective matt paint will disguise uneven walls and you may not need to paper them first. If you want to introduce pattern into your scheme, keep it subtle or it may detract from the crisp image which is your basic aim. Pale pin-striped papers on all the walls would look good: viewed from close up, the walls will appear to be finely detailed, whereas from a distance you will see a pleasant glow of colour.

Tiling is a good solution for bathrooms and kitchens. Whether you prefer glazed, marbled or mosaic tiles, stick to plain, pale colours. You could use one line of tiles in a bold primary shade to break up the space and pick out colours with carefully chosen accessories. Marble tiles can look stunning in a bathroom but they are quite expensive. However, you could use them in one of the smaller areas such as around a built-in mirror unit.

Floor treatments

City apartments are not so heavily used as country cottages, but the flooring still needs to be hardwearing and easy to clean. If the floorboards are in a good condition, they can be stripped and varnished. Alternatively, lay new wooden flooring – narrow strips of a pale wood such as beech look effective here. A pale floor colour can be carried up through the walls and across the ceiling to give a feeling of space and light, and the room then appears to be much taller.

Ceramic tiles are practical for kitchen and bathroom floors. Again, one sweep of colour in a white or pale shade can be used to enlarge the room. Choose a dark colour for the grouting as this can quickly become dirty – dark

blue or green could be used to echo the colour of your kitchen pans or cupboard doors. The classic combination of black and white is perfect for city style and this can be easily imitated with cheaper floor coverings.

Sisal or jute matting makes an elegant and hardwearing floor material and it has a pleasingly textural finish. It is available in natural shades and woven designs. If you prefer fitted carpets – possibly in the bedroom – choose light, plain colours with a short pile and add a rug or two for extra colour and texture.

Window treatments and lighting

Natural light will enhance the simple lines of the city look. Keep window treatments to a minimum to make the most of the effect otherwise the space will visibly shrink, particularly in kitchens and bathrooms. Where this solution is impractical, add compact roller blinds in plain colours to provide privacy and these can be lowered on sunny days. Venetian blinds or louvred shutters are also good options here.

Gauzy fabrics can be used to diffuse daylight to give a wonderfully cooling effect, as well as softening shadows and hard surfaces in a room. Muslin is available very cheaply in a

wide range of delicate designs and colours. For the simplest of all window treatments, wrap fabric around a wooden or scrolled iron pole, or hang it from matching fabric loops. Roller blinds are available in different weights, from light, translucent muslin to a heavier density that is more suitable for bedrooms. Alternatively, use frosted glass to filter the light and to hide less attractive views.

Discreet track lighting is a flexible choice for living rooms and kitchens. Position wide-angled spotlights for general lighting and individual spotlights along the track to highlight pictures or work areas. Plain table or angle-poise lamps create softer effects and provide task lighting.

In the bathroom, keep light fittings neat and unobtrusive – go for recessed lights with simple metal surrounds. Strip lighting positioned below window sills and shelving adds extra light while accentuating interesting features. Mirror units too are available with built-in light fixtures.

Fixtures and fittings

When you have plain walls and floors, the emphasis is placed on details so fixtures and fittings are important considerations. Industrial light fittings are perfect for city style and there is an amazing variety on the market. Check out specialist stores and suppliers, or visit architectural salvage yards. Traditional door fittings will work perfectly well but these should be kept plain. In the bathroom, chrome (first used in the 1920s), is the ideal material for taps, towel rails, bath racks and light fittings for a modern, streamlined look. Chrome taps, rails and racks are often useful features in contemporary kitchens where the clean, minimalist style makes a pleasant working space.

Furnishings and accessories

If you follow the principle of Bauhaus – the great modernist German design house – that 'form follows function', you will not go far wrong. Furnish living rooms with slim-legged chairs in plain colours and simple lines; metal chairs and glass-topped metal-framed tables will lend the necessary horizontals and balance expanses of walls, particularly where ceilings are high.

Storage is an important consideration as untidiness will quickly destroy the effect. Today, this is one of the fastest-growing design areas and there is a wealth of choice available. In kitchens, stick to utilitarian materials such as stainless steel for equipment and shelving, add laminate or granite worktops and units, pale walls and light wooden flooring. Introduce splashes of colour with ceramics and glass. Chrome has also come into its own with a revival of 1950s items such as toasters, mixers and fans. In studies, many pieces of modern office equipment will fit in perfectly, so do not hide them away. Choose designs in striking colours and finishes.

Continue the effect with simple furniture, including fitted wardrobes, to allow plenty of bedroom storage space while glass is ideal for bathrooms. However, avoid partition walls here as they will break up the space and create shadowy areas. Instead, if you need to partition off a shower area, try glass bricks. You will find that the thick glass distorts the light as it passes through to create a cooling effect. If you position a mirror beside or opposite a window, this will bounce

back the light and make the room appear much larger.

When accessorizing, a combination of antique and modern elements works well here but again, keep it simple. Bold colours and rich textures will look wonderful when set against the plain backdrop. You can introduce interest without jeopardizing the feeling by concentrating detail in one area. Try using a set of bright bedlinen on a free-standing bed to achieve an island of lively colour or you could decide to highlight one large, glossy-leaved plant

for added effect. Go for groupings of dramatically shaped cacti planted in terracotta or brightly painted pots. Alternatively, an arrangement of twisted willow twigs in a tall glass vase also looks elegant for an oriental feel. Fresh flowers are always a focal point and are ideal for enlivening areas such as small hallways with bright spots of colour, and also for making your city space appear even more welcoming.

A single wall of strong colour becomes a striking backdrop for the still life arrangement in this stunning hall. The cool clarity of the setting with its careful selection of objects, patterns, textures and colours is characteristic of city style.

Ornate and generous in detail, traditional-style bathrooms work beautifully in period homes where a more streamlined modern approach would be highly inappropriate. This style of bathroom is inspired by the romanticism of the late nineteenth century lifestyle and the practicality of the twentieth century. Rich drapes hang at the tall sash window and the strong colour is echoed in the rug on the floor and the cushions on the mahogany chair. Blue and white china makes a splendid display against the powder blue walls and the claw-legged white porcelain bath has been given pride of place.

Traditional

The traditional look is always a popular choice for home design. This style conjures up images of rich colours and an abundance of pattern, detail and texture, and it provides a wonderful opportunity to experiment with printed wallpapers, velvety, matt paint effects and luxurious soft furnishings.

Complete with ornate furniture and other accessories such as prints and light fittings, traditional style has a strong family emphasis and it can be used to create a warm and relaxing atmosphere.

If you live in a period building, the basic elements such as cast-iron baths, cornicing, bow or sash windows that allow plenty of light, and dados or picture rails are likely to exist already and the traditional treatment will complement these features perfectly. However, inexpensive reproduction cornices, ceiling roses and wooden mouldings for skirtings, dados and picture rails are all available today to give any home that period feel.

Although traditional in style, this bedroom has been given a lighter touch than the more formal rooms downstairs. A gentle colour scheme of fresh pinks and creams, combined with delicate patterns, makes this room into a peaceful and pretty retreat with an air of spacious luxury. The bed has been given a canopy treatment to make it the focal point. A soft ottoman positioned at the base of the bed has been covered in the same fabric.

Getting started

Traditional style usually evokes an image of period artefacts and a wealth of patterns and fabrics, and these can all be a source of endless ideas. However, your home may be better suited to a plainer look with a lighter touch for a more contemporary approach. You may even prefer to consider a colour palette of sage greens, amethysts and sky blues as opposed to dark, rich tones that can make a room appear heavy and imposing. Another option is to decorate your reception rooms more formally and to use lighter treatments for the rooms upstairs.

Whatever your choice, remember that the main aim of decoration in the past – creating an elegant, yet comfortable atmosphere – still applies.

With today's busy lifestyle, it is important to combine these aspects with practicalities. For instance, side tables dotted with intricate ornaments will be unsuitable for those who have young children and/or little time for dusting, but you could compromise and include these details in your bedroom or place them on high-level shelving. Consider each room and how it will be used so that the traditional look can work for you.

Practicalities were just as important in the nineteenth-century city household: patterned, dark wallpapers and fabrics for example were used to disguise the dirt from gas lamps and pollution. Today, they not only have decorative appeal; they may also be used to conceal imperfections in walls or to improve the proportions of an awkwardly shaped room. You could even use *trompe l'oeil* wallpaper with a design of flower-filled alcoves to give interest to a flat space.

Inspiration and initial planning

Visits to museums and historical houses will give you a real sense of traditional style; interiors magazines are also full of inspiration. Collect samples of wallcoverings, paints and fabrics so that you can test them out at home; they will change when used with different lighting and on small or large areas. Be adventurous in your combinations as linking different patterns, colours and textures is the essence of traditional style. Mix-and-match collections of wallcoverings, borders and fabrics can also be an excellent starting point.

Before you buy any materials, think carefully about room proportions and how each of your rooms will be used. Contemporary kitchens, for instance, are often the most lived-in rooms in the home and they need to be a comfortable yet practical area for cooking, relaxing and entertaining. Maximize the feeling of space in smaller rooms by using lighter colours to make the walls appear to recede, and a pale-coloured ceiling to give the impression of height.

Floor treatments need to be practical and hardwearing. In the living room this surface will receive a great deal of wear and tear, whereas bedrooms can be the place to indulge in soft carpets in paler colours and delicate rugs. Lino is a traditional choice for the kitchen and bathroom, and vinyl will also work well.

Left These grand shutters are painted in traditional Scandinavian style, using restrained tones with simple decorative motifs. *Below* This elegant table arrangement is inspired by the idea of themed collections. Leatherbound books, a wicker basket and a miniature painting all suggest the nineteenth century grand tour.

Traditional wallcoverings

Fashion has always dicatated styles of wallcoverings. In contrast to the plainer walls of the eighteenth century, dense patterns with quite complex repeats were popular in the nineteenth century and favourite motifs included tropical birds, fruit, ivy-leaf trellises and flowering vines. You may not wish to cover a whole room with a 'busy' design, but it can be extremely effective in certain areas such as inside wooden panel mouldings or alcoves. This is also a good way to make the most of a more expensive paper. In the past, walls were often divided into three parts using a darker, textured paper such as Anaglypta beneath a dado rail to imitate otherwise costly plaster relief work; a lighter paint colour was then added above the dado rail, with a plaster frieze or cornice at ceiling height. Woodwork was typically treated with a dark varnish or painted in an off-white or cream colour.

Wallcoverings were block-printed by hand at first. However, the introduction of machine printing meant that production could be greatly increased. By the 1920s machines were capable of printing up to twenty colours and the same technique was used to print fabrics in linked designs and colourways. The huge range of co-ordinated wallpapers, borders and fabrics available today means that you can effortlessly create a whole room scheme and many of these designs are based on original archive material. Most of the historic papers now available are produced by screen-printing methods but if your budget allows, you could use 'document' papers that have been block-printed using the same colourways as examples from the eighteenth and nineteenth centuries.

Paint effects and colours

In the 1980s there was a revival of interest in paint effects such as rag-rolling, sponging and marbling. This had happened before – in the late eighteenth century – when it became fashionable to decorate Georgian townhouse interiors with distemper which was then distressed and scumbled using oil paints to simulate marbling or grained to imitate wood.

Paint effects can be an excellent choice for traditional interiors and they are cheaper than papering. Some techniques, such as sponging, are very easy and they can conceal imperfections but others, notably marbling, require smooth surfaces and plenty of practice first. Simple designs such as hand-painted stripes are also effective and can be scaled to suit your room. You could also combine paint effects and papers – above and below a dado rail, for instance.

Plain colours can also play an important role. Some manufacturers produce ranges based on period colours to complement particular styles and these have a velvety, matt

Left Faux stonework has been skilfully painted on the walls to add grandeur to this hallway and create a fitting backdrop to a fine oil painting. *Below* The clawed feet of this Victorian-style bath have been painted gold to make them stand out from the rich burgundy of the side of the bath, and they also match the brass fittings.

finish. There are bold ranges of colours and paints that reflect the introduction of chemical pigments and these are even more vibrant. The most authentic paints are the ones made with natural pigments. They have a milky quality and their thick consistency makes them ideal for covering rough walls; they are also an ideal base for colourwashes. Whitewash can be a good choice for a more traditional home as pastel shades were not introduced until the 1930s.

Soft-furnishing fabrics

Fabrics are the central focus of any traditional room scheme. Nineteenth-century designers used them in great profusion, mixing prints and plain, but richly textured, fabrics such as velvets together with different weaves and textures, from damask to lace. The idea of co-ordinating these elements had not yet been introduced although overall harmony was achieved by building up a range of contrasting and complementary fabrics. The secret of co-ordinating different patterns is to choose fabrics with similar colours. Pinks and blues were easy shades of dye to produce. These were often used on period fabrics and with a restricted palette such as this, it is really quite hard to go wrong.

Attractive groupings of accessories typify the traditional look. Here, a pretty set of blue and white china makes a lovely, fresh display on a window sill. The pieces do not have to match – often different designs in the same colourway can be very effective. Scented pot pourri is a delicious finishing touch here.

'Document' fabrics based on traditional designs are available and although expensive, they will add to the authenticity of your scheme. Bring samples home first so that you can see how they will look in situ before you invest in large amounts of fabric. Alternatively, raid secondhand stores for offcuts that can be used to cover cushions and as trimmings; old curtains too can be cut down to fit your own windows. In the nineteenth century, window treatments in reception rooms were lavish and opulent, often using several layers of different fabrics, and they were decorated with swags and tails, braiding and tassels. Bedrooms were more restrained and plain, pale-coloured curtains with just a hint of trimming were a popular choice. Curtains were usually hung from ornate brass poles and many originals or good reproductions can still be found today.

Buying and adapting furniture

To accessorize your room, you could opt for original or good quality reproduction pieces of furniture, bearing in mind your existing furniture and budget. Choose button-back chairs, armchairs and sofas with generous curves for the living room, while a brass or iron bedstead could be the focal point in the bedroom. You could even use drapes to create a half-tester bed. For kitchens, an early style of fitted furniture with plain cupboards, wide worktops and a dresser is ideal.

Existing furniture that is inappropriate for your new look could be re-upholstered in rich velvets, brocades, damasks or tapestry styles of fabric. Alternatively, add throws and cushions in rich, dark shades. Drop-in seats on dining chairs can easily be re-covered by tacking new fabric over the top. Découpage is another form of decorative treatment. Use fine scissors to cut out motifs such as flower garlands from traditional wallpaper or wrapping papers, glue these to wooden furniture then seal with a few coats of matt varnish. Table tops, chair seats and

backs, stools and boxes were all once decorated in this way. To give a piece of furniture an aged effect, apply crackle glaze (available from craft stores) over paint and this will produce an antique look.

Fittings and accessories

A few carefully chosen fittings and accessories can really add to the period feel. China jugs and washbowls dating back to the nineteenth century can still be found in antique shops, along with claw-foot baths. Electric lighting was not widely available until the late nineteenth century and so gas lamps were used on walls as well as candlesticks and sconces. Once electricity was introduced, along came chandeliers, table and wall lamps. Many original examples of all these items can still be purchased today, along with some clever imitations.

Plumbing was another innovation. Bathroom and kitchen fittings, including cast-iron baths with brass taps, marble washstands, mahogany fittings and butler's sinks, can often be found in junk stores. Original iron radiators are also available from architectural salvage yards.

Your choice of accessories depends on the purpose of the room. The current vogue for all things traditional has meant that excellent reproduction accessories (especially for the kitchen) are widely available including classic pots and pans, clothes-drying racks and wrought-iron rails to hold utensils. Collections of original blue and white china, old-fashioned scales, jelly moulds and copper pans can all look very effective in a traditional home.

Unusual cobra-shaped bedside lamps are a stunning feature in this Colonial-style bedroom. An intricate, carved headboard and a row of framed Indian silk miniatures complement the look of understated luxury. Fresh Madras checked bedlinen and exotic blooms on either side of the bed make this bedroom into a true fantasy retreat. The beauty of this form of decorating is that you can choose as little or as much of the style as you like and if you want to adapt the design of an existing room, you can limit yourself to just a few key items.

British Colonial

Colonial is a unique decorative style that is full of nostalgia. It immediately brings to mind romantic images of afternoon tea on verandahs and cocktail parties held in the cool of the evening; tented mosquito nets and slow-moving fans.

British Colonial style has its roots in the colonies of India and the resulting hybrid decorative look is a marriage of the tastes of two entirely different lands. Colonial-style furnishings are distinguished by their rather beautiful, highly patterned fabrics in jewel colours and dark, often carved, wooden furniture and decorative accessories, tempered by a more sober European influence and a touch of imperial grandeur.

A sunfilled room leading out onto a shady verandah, with views across glorious countryside epitomises the image of British Colonial style. You are unlikely to have such a setting, but a little of that distant magic can be brought into your home with a touch of ingenuity. Accessories such as this floor rug or a hand printed bed cover coupled with some carved wooden furniture against the plain walls and the look will begin to take shape.

Creating Colonial atmosphere

Colonial style is quite simple to put together: it is more concerned with what goes into the rooms as opposed to the colour on the walls, and this makes it an excellent choice for all kinds of homes. Even if you have a small house, much can be achieved with careful use of furniture and textiles. Modern houses also work well because the decorations were characteristically left plain to lend an air of refreshing coolness, while the real colour and flavour was primarily from fabrics and accessories. If you have an older house, however, architectural details such as cornicing and ceiling roses will blend in well with wooden, carved accessories.

Colonial interiors mean an unstructured, relaxed form of styling, with free-standing furniture, central light fittings and table lamps, so expensive alterations are unlikely to be necessary. You can opt for as little or as much of the style as you like. For instance, if you want to add some of the flavour to a bedroom without having to re-decorate and re-furnish, limit yourself to just a few accessories – perhaps a hand-printed cover draped across the bed, some cushions or a collection of polished wooden boxes.

Walls, doorways and windows

The light, airy atmosphere of Colonial interiors is best achieved with white-washed walls and ceilings. For contrast in smaller rooms such as studies, bedrooms, hallways or landings, you could go for a bold, jewel-toned colour on part of the walls, perhaps between a dado and picture rail. This would provide a striking backdrop for a collection of pictures. Unless the room has a particularly high ceiling, keep ceilings in pale colours to avoid a rather stifled atmosphere.

To imitate the earthy plaster mix used in the original homes, choose chalky matt paints rather than silk emulsions. Traditional paint ranges made with buttermilk are ideal. If you are re-plastering, press decorative shapes into the still-damp plaster to embellish the area around doorways or windows. This is a good way of imitating the low-relief decorations that were used for emphasis and it can look particularly effective in an otherwise plain area such as a hallway. Original wooden printing blocks with hand-carved floral, bird, animal or paisley designs are widely available today. As an alternative, you could try modern wooden or rubber stamps.

On previously plastered and painted walls, use blocks to print your own designs, picking up colours or patterns in the soft furnishings. (Wipe the block every few prints with a soft cloth to keep the edges of the prints clean and smudge-free.)

In addition to low-relief and printing, small ceramic tiles and chips of mirror tiles were sometimes added around doorways. The most important doorways in the home were hung with an intricately embroidered frame of fabric called a toran, which often had shisha (mirror) pieces worked into the stitching to keep the evil eye at bay, and these can still be purchased today.

Colonial woodwork, including window frames, doors and skirtings, would have been left plain, perhaps stained or waxed to match the dark furniture. If your woodwork is in good condition, consider stripping away the paint. Otherwise, leave it white to tie in with the walls.

Wooden furniture

Dark, polished furniture forms an essential part of this look. If you have contemporary pieces in lighter woods, stain and varnish them, or use a tinted brushing wax to produce a mellow gleam. Another solution is to cover a table or chair with brightly patterned fabric. Replace modern handles on chests and cupboards with intricate brass fittings or plain wooden handles.

This sort of furniture was traditionally combined with Indian pieces and these generally featured elaborate carving, particularly on chair and table legs, bedheads and wardrobes. Local craftsmen often built furniture in teak and other exotic woods, then added their own embellishments and carved detailing. This type of furniture has recently become very collectible and is now widely available. Low, small

Top right This elegant, rattan-style chair has been restored to its former glory. With its softly-padded Indian cotton cushions, it is evocative of the leisurely Colonial lifestyle, with unhurried days rounded off with slow drinks in the early evening. *Below right* A brass bowl holds scented rose petals and, when combined with silver-topped glass fragrance bottles and a jug of orange blossom, it makes a delightful tabletop decoration.

tables with carved legs and wrought-iron detailing, for instance, are made in numerous sizes and these are fairly inexpensive. Tables with decorative perforations – known as jali work – and cupboards with perforated door panels also typify Colonial style.

Another possibility with a cupboard or wardrobe is to replace solid panels with hardboard. This is available pre-cut in a range of intricate designs from DIY stores. You could also use pan-elling to create a folding screen or to conceal modern radiators, where it will also provide a ledge for displaying colourful accessories. Another option for disguising radiators is to choose custom-made brass screens but these can be quite expensive.

Whatever furniture you have, resist the temptation to clutter a room with too many pieces. Even the most sump-tuous homes were sparsely furnished to retain the spacious, yet unstruc-tured feel.

Flooring, carpets and rugs

As with walls and ceilings, the best policy for floor decoration is to keep it as a neutral base on which to display sumptuous carpets and rugs. In Kashmir, where India's best carpets are created, techniques and styles were introduced from Persia even before the Moguls invaded in the six-teenth century, and the art flourished under their influence. As a result, Colonial-style carpets had a strong Persian design influence.

A polished wooden floor, jute or sisal matting and perhaps plain fitted carpets for upstairs rooms, are ideal surfaces for displaying colourful rugs. (Use non-slip underlay to prevent accidents on wooden or tiled floors.) If

you are decorating floor surfaces throughout the whole home, continue your chosen treatment over the same levels to give continuity.

Rugs and carpets are exported to the West in huge numbers, so you will have an endless choice. If your budget does not run to wool or silk, cotton dhurries are an excellent solution. These flat, woven rugs are hardwear-ing and often highly colourful, with geometric and other interesting pat-terns. Small dhurries in traditional colours make ideal bedside rugs or they can even be used as bath mats.

Fabrics and soft furnishings

It is here that Colonial style really comes into its own, as it draws heavily on Eastern inspiration. Textiles pro-duced in India are often superb and these include embroidery, madras checks, appliqué work (shapes are cut out and stitched on to a background) and shisha (mirror) work with sparkling metallic threads. Source the

Above This mantle-piece creates a focal point for the room and displays a fine array of artefacts from brass candle-sticks to miniature paintings. *Below* This travelling trunk makes an interesting living room feature, and is also an excel-lent form of storage. The mixture of wood and rattan used on this trunk is particu-larly appealing.

These magnificent tigers, hand painted onto plaster, create a wonderfully exotic fireplace which fits perfectly into an old country kitchen. A simple border outlines the surround, and another motif carries the style around the room.

look and get a feeling for the sumptuous, glowing colours and rich fabrics of the East by visiting museums with textile collections, as well as studying design and interiors books.

Fabrics should be primarily cottons and silks and, although you do not have to use the genuine article, imported fabrics are widely available and often very cheap. Patterns range from block printing to tie-dye and paisley. Bear in mind that the cheap price is often a reflection of the way in which the fabrics were produced so they may fade in the sun and dyes could run when they are washed. Another option would be to buy plain cotton fabrics and to block-print them with wooden or rubber prints. This will be especially effective if you have decorated the doorway and windows

of the room in the same way.

If you already have sofas and chairs upholstered in plain fabric, liven them up with heavily patterned and textured throws, and cushions in rich jewel-like colours and fabrics such as velvets, silks or satins. Add cushions with hand-embroidered covers or run them up yourself from fabric offcuts.

Window treatments can be kept simple. Filtered light gives an exotic look and this is easy to achieve by draping sheer fabrics, such as chiffons or muslins, over simple wooden or wrought-iron poles to billow in the breeze. You could even use silk or chiffon sari lengths, which are sold in an incredible range of designs and colours. For greater privacy, pinoleum blinds (made from narrow slats of wood), roller blinds in a lightweight fabric or wicker blinds are ideal.

You could also suspend sheer fabrics above a bed for a touch of elegance. Why not try a mosquito net

gathered on a traditional round or square frame to instantly evoke the right atmosphere?

Other, more decorative uses for fabrics include tablecloths, lampshades, wallhangings, bedspreads and trimmings, and these can add accents of colour around the room.

Fittings and accessories

Many shops sell reproduction Colonial-style fittings as well as originals. You may also source modern, handcrafted alternatives such as simple beaten brass or nickel lampbases.

The ultimate authenticity of the scheme will rest with your accessories. This is a style that demands items of interest, from miniatures and engravings to rattan boxes and sculptural potted plants. While exotically coloured soft furnishings will go a long way towards evoking the atmosphere, it is attention to detail that will complete the look. Accessories can also help to link more difficult rooms such as kitchens. However, suitable kitchen accessories are widely available. Look for old-fashioned fans, wicker baskets, pots of spices, a pestle and mortar, brass cooking pots and unglazed terracotta to add to the atmosphere.

Curiosities from abroad, especially those originating from the East, are an important feature of Colonial style. Copper and brass items, such as candle holders, trays and bowls, were popular and you may even be lucky enough to find brass boxes inlaid with exquisite red, green and blue enamel. You could also display delicate or antique pieces of embroidery to complete the whole effect.

CLAUDE MONET

HERBS

Reference

Measurements

Both imperial and metric measurements have been given throughout this book. When following instructions, you should choose to work in either metric or imperial, never mix the two. Below is a quick reference conversion chart for use when buying and working with fabrics, while to the right, conversion rulers provide an easy checking aid.

Fabric lengths

$\frac{1}{8}$yd	=	10cm	$3\frac{3}{4}$yd	=	3.5m
$\frac{1}{4}$yd	=	20cm	4yd	=	3.7m
$\frac{3}{8}$yd	=	40cm	$4\frac{3}{8}$yd	=	4m
$\frac{1}{2}$yd	=	45cm	$4\frac{1}{2}$yd	=	4.2m
$\frac{5}{8}$yd	=	60cm	$5\frac{7}{8}$yd	=	4.5m
$\frac{3}{4}$yd	=	70cm	5yd	=	4.6m
$\frac{7}{8}$yd	=	80cm	$5\frac{1}{2}$yd	=	5m
1yd	=	1m	10yd	=	9.2m
$1\frac{1}{2}$yd	=	1.4m	$10\frac{7}{8}$yd	=	10m
2yd	=	1.9m	20yd	=	18.5m
$2\frac{1}{4}$yd	=	2m	$21\frac{1}{3}$yd	=	20m
$2\frac{1}{2}$yd	=	2.3m			

Fabric widths

$2\frac{3}{4}$yd	=	2.5m	
3yd	=	2.7m	36in = 90cm
$3\frac{1}{4}$yd	=	3m	44/45in = 115cm
$3\frac{1}{2}$yd	=	3.2m	48in = 120cm
			60in = 150cm

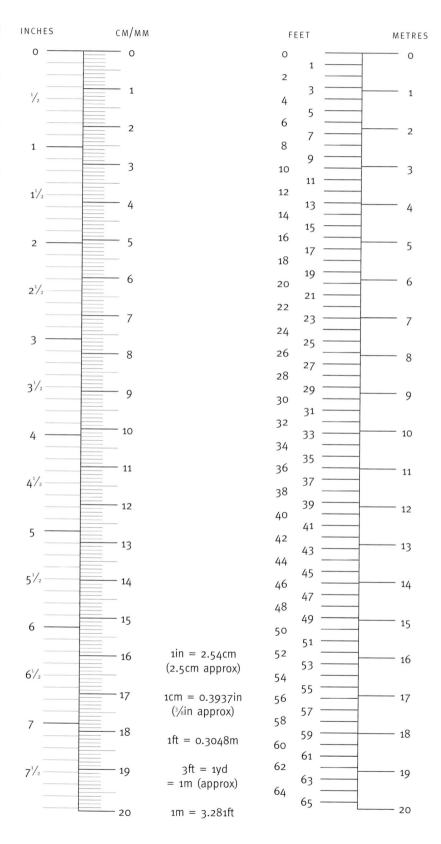

1in = 2.54cm
(2.5cm approx)

1cm = 0.3937in
($\frac{3}{8}$in approx)

1ft = 0.3048m

3ft = 1yd
= 1m (approx)

1m = 3.281ft

Glossary

Abrasive paper Paper coated with abrasive particles for smoothing wood. Graded by grit size and spacing.

Art Deco Name given to the fashions which dominated the decorative arts in the years between the First and Second World Wars. Often used angular lines and geometric shapes with colours described as 'jazzy' based on the yellows, browns and purples of Diaghilev's Ballet Russe'.

Art Nouveau Style popular in the early 1900s which used sinuous, elongated lines. Tendrils and other floral motifs, flowing hair and peacock feathers were all popular.

Baffle A device attached to a light fitting or fixed in front of it that helps to prevent the light from glaring into the eyes.

Batten Strip of wood that can be fixed to a wall to provide supports for fixing panelling or fabric. Finer battens are used to fit into casings when making Roman blinds.

Bi-folding door A door made of two narrow vertical pieces, hinged in the middle, which takes up less room when opened than a standard door.

Bradawl Small tool used to make starting holes for screws and nails and for piercing leather.

Casein or buttermilk paint Traditional paint made by mixing earth-coloured pigments into buttermilk or skimmed milk and a little lime which dries to a smooth, flat finish with a slight sheen. They were much used in painting early American houses.

Casement window Opens inwards or outwards on vertical hinges.

Casing A channel in a piece of fabric made by folding over the top and making two lines of stitching: used to make drawstring bags, curtain headings, Roman blinds etc.

Chinoiserie Furniture, fabric, wallpaper or other decoration inspired by Chinese design.

Colour board A piece of hardboard, cardboard or other board onto which you can pin pieces of fabric and other materials and paint samples until you get a combination that is correct for a particular interior.

Colour washing Application of thin glaze or water-based wash over a ground coat of paint to create subtle veils of colour.

Colour wheel The colour wheel shows colours as they appear in their natural sequence, including primary, secondary and tertiary colours with the cool colours grouped on one side and the warm colours on the other.

Condensation Small droplets of water collect on window panes and other cold surfaces causing damp problems and discomfort. The only cure is to have constant low level heating, good ventilation and warm surfaces.

Cork Soft, warm material made from the bark of a tree. Good for floors (if sealed); also used on walls. Provides good insulation.

Cornice Decorative moulding strip, usually made of wood or plaster, that runs round the wall of a room, just below the ceiling.

Coving Horizontal plaster or expanded polystyrene moulding used to cover the join between walls and ceiling.

Dado rail A wooden rail fixed horizontally to the wall, usually about two-thirds of the way down. The area below is often panelled or painted a different colour to the area above it.

Document wallpapers Papers reproduced from originals using the same materials and techniques as the originals. Some are hand block printed which gives them a greater body and 'depth' than many modern papers.

Dusting brush Decorating brush with soft, medium-length bristles in a wooden handle.

Eyeball spots Semi-recessed lights which are set into the ceiling and can be adjusted to shine in a limited number of directions.

Fanlight A window, often semicircular with radiating glazing bards (in the shape of an open fan), often found above doors.

Filament lighting Light produced by heating a small filament within the bulb (the common light bulb is a filament lamp).

Finials Decorative knobs, loops and twirls supplied to fit to the end of curtain tracks or poles.

Flock wallpaper Wallpaper with a raised pattern created by tiny particles of fibre on the surface. They are often in designs similar to woven silks.

Fluorescent light A tube with a gas fitted inside which lights up when it is heated. This gives a brighter and a whiter light than filament lighting while not casting shadows. It can be rather bleak unless fitted with a baffle to soften the light but many modern fittings include baffles anyway.

Frieze A decorated band along the top of a room wall. Wallpaper friezes are often available to match specific wallpaper designs.

Gilding The application of gold leaf or gold paint or cream to a piece of furniture or a picture or mirror frame. Gilt cream or gilt wax are often used for touching up old gilding or adding metallic highlights.

Glazed chintz Floral cotton fabric with a glazed finish.

Gothic Style This is a style which takes its inspiration from the cathedral and church architecture of the Middle Ages with their pointed arches, rich fabrics, stained glass windows and wrought metal hinges.

Graining Paint technique used to imitate wood grain.

Grout Mortar used to fill gaps between ceramic tiles. Grout is usually white but can be coloured to match the tiles.

Gusset A narrow panel, sometimes shaped or gathered to give fullness; for example the side panels of a box-shaped cushion.

Hardboard Fibre building board generally used for covering framework. There are many different types. Can be useful as the basis for a colour board.

Heading tape: A specially manufactured tape which is stitched across the top of a curtain; it has an arrangement of cords so that the curtain can be gathered and curtain hooks slotted through the tape. Different heading tapes will produce different gathering effects.

High tech A style that uses products originally designed for factories, hospitals and so on, in domestic interiors. This may include industrial shelving, flooring, kitchen equipment and furniture.

Highlighting Lighting used to emphasise a particular feature of a room or a picture or sculpture in it. Spotlamps are often used for this, but specialised lighting using small strip bulbs is useful for pictures.

Hold-backs Metal or wooden knobs or hooks, fitted at the sides of windows, so that you can loop curtains clear of the window.

Hot air stripper Electric device for softening paint ready for stripping.

Jig saw Power saw for making curved cuts in timber and man-made boards.

Kilim A flat woven (i.e. not tufted) rug usually originating from the Caucasus or the Middle East.

Laminate Layers of various substances that are pressed and glued to create a tough surface material. Used for kitchen and work surfaces and sometimes as wall panelling.

Limewash Finish used on wood with a definite grain such as oak and ash in which limewash is diluted and applied to furniture, panelling or floorboards to bring out the grain.

Lining Layer of fabric added to give improved wear, a more satisfactory hang and better insulation. Curtain lining fabric is usually a satin weave cotton fabric. Sometimes a second, sheer curtain may be hung behind an unlined curtain instead of lining the curtain itself.

Linoleum Form of flooring made of cork and linseed oil, similar to vinyl but warmer to the touch.

Low voltage lighting (low voltage tungsten-halogen or LVTH) These are tiny little bulbs fitted with built-in reflectors. They are more efficient than ordinary filament bulbs and last longer. The 12v supply has to have a transformer and should be fitted by a professional electrician.

Masking tape Low tack tape used to mask off areas when applying a finish, such as paint, to selected areas only, for creating straight lines on decorative work and for sticking things temporarily onto surfaces.

Minimalist Style which uses the minimum amount of furniture and decoration, relying on simple shapes and white as a background.

Monochromatic scheme A colour scheme that uses only one colour (plus white) in varying tones.

Motif Abstract or figurative outline or pattern on printed or woven fabric or wallpaper, or pattern for embroidery or appliqué and so on.

Mural A picture painted on a wall, sometimes covering the whole wall. Popular in children's rooms or can take the form of trompe l'oeil. Can be covered in acrylic varnish to make it more permanent.

Nail punch Pointed steel shaft used with hammer for driving nail heads just below the surface of wood without damaging it.

Natural flooring Matting made of woven natural fibres such as coir and seagrass.

Paint kettle Small plastic bucket or drum in which to decant paint before you start painting. This prevents contamination of paint in the paint pot and is good for mixing colours.

Pasting table Folding table used for laying wallpaper on to paste it.

Picture rail A wooden rail fixed horizontally to the wall usually about 75cm (29½in) from the ceiling. In very tall rooms, the area between a picture rail and the ceiling can be painted a different colour to the main wall.

Pin hammer Lightweight hammer for driving small pins or tacks.

Plumb bob A tool consisting of a vertical cord with a weight hung at the bottom, used to check that a vertical line is true.

Ragging Paint technique producing a three-dimensional effect when a crushed rag is pressed over wet paint.

Rouleau A fine tube of fabric used to make button loops.

Sanding block Shape for holding abrasive paper during sanding.

Sash window A window's with a frame that slides up and down to open and close with a sash cord to hold it in place.

Scraper Tool designed for removing unwanted finishes or coverings on wood or walls. Narrow-bladed scrapers are for paint, wide-bladed ones for wallpaper. A shave hook is a scraper shaped for removing old paint from mouldings. The tool head can be triangular, pear-shaped or a combination of the two.

Seam allowance The allowance for making a seam around the edge of a panel of fabric. Add a seam allowance to the finished dimensions before cutting out.

Shiplap Wooden boarding in which the edge of one board overlaps the edge of the next board. A less sophisticated form of tongue-and-groove boarding.

Skirting Decorative wooden moulding or plain wooden plank running horizontally to conceal the join between wall and floor.

Spacers Small chips of wood or plastic pieces placed between tiles during laying, to leave enough room for the grout.

Spattering Spraying paints in different colours onto a painted surface to create a multi-coloured look.

Spirit level Vial containing liquid and an air bubble fitted into a rectangular holder for checking levels. When the bubble is lined up in the middle, the line is true.

Sponging Paint technique in which a sponge is used to apply or remove paint to a surface in order to achieve a three-dimensional effect.

Stencilling Paint technique in which paint is applied through holes in a template to create a frieze or other repeat pattern. Used on walls, floors, furniture and fabrics.

Stippling Paint technique producing a grainy texture when using dry brushes or a dry roller on wet paint.

Swag Elaborate draping of fabric, usually across the top of a window.

Tie-backs Bands of fabric or lengths of cord used to hold curtains clear of a window.

Tongue-and-groove Wooden boarding with grooves so that the pieces slot together to make an economic form of panelling. Often used below dado level in a room. It is sometimes called matchboarding.

Trompe l'oeil A painted scene intended to deceive the eye. For example a painted window on a wall with a painted view beyond or a painted carpet on the floor.

Try-square Parallel-sided metal blade set at a right angle in a stock for accurate marking and checking of 90 degree angles.

Tungsten-halogen Lighting In which a fllament and gas heat up inside the bulb to create light.

Varnish Clear protective coating for timber. Those made with polyurethane give a waterproof, heat-and-scratch-resistant finish.

Vinyl Hard wearing all-purpose material used for sheet flooring and tiles. Available in a multitude of designs and colours.

Wallplugs Plastic or fibre tubes, either straight or tapered, that are fitted into holes drilled in walls to secure screws.

Wire brush Handbrush with steel wire bristles for removing paint and rust particles from metal.

Index

Acknowledgements

Author's acknowledgement

I would like to thank all the many people who have helped with the various aspects of this book and who have been so generous with their help and information. Above all, thanks to my editors on the project, Katie Cowan, Kate Yeates, Jane Royston and Jane Donovan who have all made this book a pleasure to work on.

Acknowledgements for props

Thanks is also due to those indivuduals and companies who generously loaned materials and props for studio photography:

Nu-line Builders Merchants, 305-307 Westbourne Park Road, London W11 1EF, tel. 0171 727 7748; *Dulux*, for nationwide stockists, tel. 01753 550555; *Farrow and Ball*, 249 Fulham Road, London SW3, tel. 0171 351 0273; *Fired Earth*, Twyford Mill, Oxford Road, Adderbury, Oxon, OX17 3HP, tel. 01295 812088; *Leylands Paints SDM*, 361-365 Kensington High Street, London W14, tel. 0171 602 4099; *Laura Ashley*, for nationwide stockists, tel. 0171 880 5100; *Cath Kidston*, 8 Clarendon Cross, London W11 4AP, tel. 0171 221 4000; *Osborne & Little*, 304 Kings Road, London SW3 5UH, tel. 0171 352 1456; *Ian Mankin*, 109 Regents Park Road, London NW1 8UR, tel. 0171 722 0997; *Elna Sewing Machines* 41-45 Southwark Bridge Road, London SE1, tel. 0171 403 3011.

Finally special thanks to furniture decorator Cathy Fillion Richie for doing the paint effect techniques.

The Publishers would like to thank the following sources for their permission to reproduce the photographs in this book:

Abode: 40 Top Centre Left, 48 Top, 79 Centre, 86 Top, 107 Top Left, 107 Top Right, 141 Centre Right, 145 Top Centre Right, 145 Bottom Right, 149 Top, 151 Top Left, 151 Top Right, 151 Bottom Left, 155 Top Right, 197 left; **The Alternative Flooring Company,** tel. 01264 335111: The Coir Panama Collection 139 Top Right; **Anaglypta Original Wallpapers**, tel. 01254 704951: pattern no. RD865 77 Centre Right, pattern no. RD916 77 Bottom Centre Left; **Arcaid**: *Earl Carter/Belle* 79 Bottom Centre Right, 155 Bottom Centre Right; *Simon Kenny/Belle* 39 Top Centre Left, 135 Bottom Centre Right; *Alan Weintraub* 173 Top Centre Left; **Artisan**, designers of classic and contemporary curtain rails, tel. 0171-498-3979: 151 Top Centre Right; **Axminster Carpets Ltd**, tel. 01297 33533: Royal Seaton Victorian Posy 238/87541 139 Bottom Right; **Bhs**: Frontcover Centre Right, 39 Bottom Right, 39 Bottom Left; **Byron and Byron Ltd**, tel. 0171-700-0404: 150 Top; **Crowson Fabrics**, tel. 01825 761055: The Surabaya Collection 77 Bottom Right, 140 Centre Left, 143 Bottom, 143 Right; **där lighting limited**, tel. 01295 259391: *Chris Coggins* 39 Bottom Centre Left; **Decorwool**: Nouwens Bogaers, tel. 01943 603888 139 Bottom Centre; The Simply Natural Collection, tel. 01297 32244 139 Top Left; Crown Damask from Ryalux 139 Top Centre Right; Ryasilk Collection by Ryalux, tel. 01706 716000 137 Bottom; **DIY Photo Library**: 139 Centre Left;

Elizabeth Whiting & Associates: *Nick Carter* 68 Top Left; *Michael Crockett* 72 Top, 141 Top Centre Right, 164 Top; *Michael Dunne* 145 Bottom Centre Right; *Brian Harrison* 66 Top Left; *Steve Hawkins* 84 Top; *Rodney Hyett* 37 Top Centre Right, 104 Top, 112 Bottom Centre Right, 121 Top Right, 123 Bottom Centre Right, 123 Bottom Right, 136 Top; *Ian Knaggs* 140 Top Left, 149 Bottom; *Tom Leighton* 40 Top Right, 69 Bottom Right, 112 Bottom Right, 115 Top; *Neil Lorimer* 195 Top Right, 218 Top Left; *Ian Parry* 129 Bottom Centre Right; *Spike Powell* 92 Bottom Left, 108 Top; *Dennis Stone* 80 Top, 82 Top, 155 Top Centre Left, 221 Top; *Simon Upton* 213 Top; *Andreas Von Einsiedel* 31 Top Left, 38 Top, 76 Top, 79 Bottom Centre Left, 113 Centre Right, 120 Top, 121 Centre Left, 141 Top Right, 154 Top, 173 Centre Right; *Peter Wolosynski* 107 Centre Left, 129 Centre Left; 5 Bottom, 5 Top, 21 Top, 26 Top, 41 Centre Left, 41 Top Right, 44 Bottom Left, 61 Bottom Centre Left, 69 Top Left, 73 Top, 112 Centre Left, 113 Bottom, 113 Top Right, 115 Bottom, 117 Top Right, 122 Top, 123 Centre Left, 124 Top, 133 Right, 135 Top Left, 135 Top Right, 141 Centre Left, 148 Top, 152 Top; **Fired Earth**, tel. 01295 814300: 61 Top Right, 92 Top Left, 92 Centre Left, 128 Centre Left, 129 Centre Right, 129 Top, 130 Top, 131 Bottom, 135 Top Centre Left, 137 Top, 139 Centre Left, 145 Top Left, 145 Centre Left; **GP & J Baker**: 173 Top Left; **Robert Harding Syndication**: *Country Homes and Interiors/Simon Brown* 140 Bottom Right, 144 Top, /*Andrew Cameron* Front Endpaper, Back Endpaper, 145 Top Centre Left, /*John Miller* 61 Bottom Centre Right, /*Lucinda Symons* 68-69 Centre, /*Nadia Mackenzie* 92-93 Centre, /*Schulenburg* 47 Top; *Joanne Cowie* 17 left; *Homes and Gardens* 30 Bottom Right, 32 left, 41 Bottom Centre Right, 43 Bottom, 151 Bottom Right, /*Michael Brockway* 2-3, 4 Top, 128 Top Right, 132 Top, /*Kiloran Howard* 173 Bottom Left, /*Gavin Kingcome* 151 Centre Left, /*Tom Leighton* 97 Right, /*James Merrell* 77 Top Left, /*Bill Reavell* 61 Bottom Right, /*Trevor Richards* 40 Top Left, 73 Bottom, /*Graham Seager* 135 Bottom Left, /*Debi Treloar* 151 Centre Right, 155 Top Centre Right, /*Polly Wreford* 94 Top; *Homes and Ideas/Polly Wreford* 165 Bottom Right; *Ideal Home* 10 Bottom Right, 19 left, 39 Top Centre Right, 71 Top, /*Graham Rae* 40 Bottom Right, 52 Top, 222-223, /*Malcome Robetson* 61 Top Left; *Brad Simmons* 31 Bottom, 33 left, 78 Top, 100 Top; *Wedding and Home/Tom Leighton* 107 Top Centre Right; *Woman's Journal/Chris Drake* 135 Bottom Centre Left, /*James Merrell* 21 Bottom Left, 25 Bottom Right, 110 Top; **Harlequin Fabrics and Wallcoverings** Ltd, tel. 01509 813112: 140 Bottom Left, 158 Top, 160 Top; **ICI Paints/Dulux**, 1997: 21 Centre Right, 24 Top; **The Interior Archive Ltd**: *Tim Beddow* 101 Bottom Right, 101 Centre Left, 121 Top Centre Right, 129 Bottom Left, 138 Top, 166 Top, 214 Top Right; *Simon Brown, designer R. Banks* 168 Top; *Tim Goffe* 101 Top Right, 135 Bottom Right, 165 Top Left; *James Mortimer* 79 Top Centre Left; *Schulenburg* 20 Bottom Right, 27 Bottom, designers *Mimmi O'Connell and Peter Farlow* 28 Top, 77 Top Centre Right, 121 Bottom Left, 139 Centre Right, 145 Top Right; *Henry Wilson* 1, designer *Celia Lyttleton* 6 left, 7 Top Left, 31 Top Right, 36 Top, 37 Centre Right, 39 Centre Right, 49 Top, 54 Top, 56 Top, 62 Top, 64 Top, 77 Bottom Left, 77 Centre Left, 77 Top Right, 77 Top Centre Left, 77 Bottom Centre Right, 79 Bottom, 79 Top Left, 79 Top Right, 88 Top, 90 Top, 93 Top, 95 Top Left, 97 left, 102 Top, 106 Top, 107 Bottom, 112 Top, 114 Top, 129 Bottom Right, 135 Centre Right; **Lelievre (UK) Ltd**, tel. 0171-636-3461: 172 Top; **Paint Magic Ltd**, tel. 0171-354-9696: Impasto and Midnight Blue Woodwash 61 Top Centre Right; **Simon McBride**: 4 Bottom, 96 Top, 112 Centre Right, 113 Top Left, 116 Top, 123 Centre Right, 128 Bottom Right, 134 Top, 140 Top Right, 142 Top, 155 Top Left; **Reed Consumer**

Books Ltd: *Tim Beddow* 145 Centre Right; *Bryant* 167 Top Centre Right; *Peter Dudgeon* 145 Bottom Left; *Rupert Horrox* 21 Bottom Right, 27 Top, 61 Top Centre Left, 155 Bottom Right, 170 Top, 173 Bottom Right; *Di Lewis* 176 Top; *Peter Myers* Frontcover Centre Left, 216-217 Centre; *David Parmitter* 41 Bottom Left, 43 Top, 146 Top Left, 146-147 Centre, 155 Bottom Left, 167 Bottom Left, 167 Centre Right, 173 Bottom Centre Left; *Paul Ryan* 155 Bottom Centre Left, 141 Top Left, 162; *Debi Treloar* 167 Bottom Centre Right; *Peter Myers/Adler* 30 Top Right, 34 left, 167 Bottom Centre Left, /*Andraos Hampson* 11 Centre, 14 left, 23 Bottom, 107 Bottom Centre Left, 123 Top Right, 167 Top Left, 204-205, 207 Top Right, /*Kay* 30 Bottom Left, 31 Centre Left, 33 Right, 37 Top Right, 128 Top Left, 133 left, 208 Bottom Right, /*McCloud* 214 Bottom Left, /*Penny Morrison* 167 Bottom Right, 173 Centre Left, 210-211 Centre, 212 Top, 215 Top, /*Orefelt* 40 Bottom Left, 58 Top, 209 Top, /*Patterson* Frontcover Bottom Centre, 173 Bottom Centre Right, /*Portobello Hotel* 101 Centre Right, /*Pounds* 30 Centre Left, 30 Top Left, 35 Top, 37 Top Left, 37 Top 39 Top Right, 39 Bottom Right, 40 Centre Left, 47 Bottom, 121 Top Left, 135 Top Centre Right, /*Raven* 126 Top, 190 Bottom Left, /*Raven/Hayloft Woodwork* 40 Bottom Centre Left, 46 Top, /*Ronald* 5 Centre, 8-9, 20 Top, 41 Bottom Right, 42 Top, 60 Top Left, 141 Bottom, 163 Top, 167 Top Right, 225 Top, /*Stevens* 41 Centre Right, 71 Bottom Right, 206 Top Left, 213 Bottom, /*Wainwright* 30 Top Centre Left, 37 Bottom Centre Right, 41 Top Left, 44-45 Centre, 219 Top, 220 Bottom, 220 Top Right, /*Williams* Backcover Top Right, 10 Top Right, 17 Right, 31 Centre, 35 Bottom, 37 Bottom Right, 37 Bottom Left, 101 Bottom Centre Right, 155 Centre Right, 173 Top Right, 208 Top; *Polly Wreford/Adler* 202 Top Right, /*Annabel Bryant* Frontcover Bottom Left, 39 Top Left, 121 Centre Right, 121 Bottom Right, 178-179, /*Nadia Bryant* Frontcover Top Right, Backcover Bottom, 10 Centre Left, 10 Top Centre Left, 11 Bottom Left, 13 Right, 15 left, 16 Top, 61 Bottom Left, 121 Top Centre Left, 123 Top Centre Left, 139 Top Centre Left, 139 Bottom Left, 151 Bottom Centre Right, 167 Centre Left, 184 Top Right, 192-193 Centre, 194 Top Left, 196 Top Right, 196 Bottom Left, 201 Bottom Left, /*Emma Caderny* 95 Bottom Right, 151 Bottom Centre Left, /*Peter Checkitt* 11 Top Left, 11 Top Right, 13 left, 18 left, 31 Centre Left, 37 Bottom Centre Left, 123 Bottom Left, 183 Top Right, 185 Bottom Right, /*Graham Dixon* Backcover Centre Left, 10 Bottom Left, 19 Right, 121 Bottom Centre Left, 180-181 Centre, 182 Top Left, 183 Bottom Left, 184 Bottom Left, 185 Top Left, 207 Bottom Left, /*Greer/Halliday* 101 Bottom Centre Left, 123 Top Left, 145 Bottom Centre Left, /*Marion Lichtig* Backcover Top Left, 10 Top Left, 12 left, 45 Top, 117 Bottom Left, 112 Bottom Left, 155 Centre Left, /*Andrew Macinosh* Frontcover Bottom Left, 186-187 Centre, 188 Top Left, 189 Right, 189 Bottom, 191 Top Left, /*Reece* 20 Bottom Left, 22 left, 101 Top Left, 101 Bottom Left, 195 Bottom Left, 200 Top, /*Riddell* 11 Bottom Right, 15 Right, 101 Top Centre Left, 135 Centre Left, /*Travers* 20 Centre Right, 23 Top, 37 Centre Left, 198-199 Centre, 202 Bottom Left, 203 Top Left, /*Debi Treloar* 167 Top Centre Left, /*Wainwright* 7 Bottom Right, 201 Top Right, 219 Bottom Right; **Salamander Picture Library**: 151 Top Centre Left; **Sanderson**: 70 Top, 128 Bottom Left, 131 Top, 174 Top; **Shaker**, tel. 0171-352-3918: 190 Top Right; **David Sherwin**: 29 Top, 29 Bottom, 51 Top Right, 51 Top Centre Right, 75 Centre Right, 98 Bottom Centre Right, 119 Bottom Centre; **Dominic Vorillon**: 107 Centre Right; **Shona Wood**: 50 Top, 51, 53, 63, 64 Top Right, 65 Bottom, 65, 67, 74 Top, 75, 98, 99, 118 Top, 119, 156 Top, 157.